Hesperides

Hesperides

Robert Herrick

Edited by M.K. Pace

CRESCENT MOON

CRESCENT MOON PUBLISHING
P.O. Box 1312, Maidstone
Kent, ME14 5XU
Great Britain
www.crmoon.com

First published 1885. This edition 2017.
Introduction © M.K. Pace, 1996, 2008, 2017.

Printed and bound in the U.S.A.
Set in Book Antiqua Book 11 on 16pt.
Designed by Radiance Graphics.

British Library Cataloguing in Publication data available

ISBN-13 9781861715869

Contents

A Note On the Text   6

Hesperides   11

A Note On Robert Herrick   554
Notes   561
Bibliography   562

A NOTE ON THE TEXT

This edition is taken from the 1885 edition (2nd ed.), edited by Henry Morley, and published by Routledge and Sons, London.

I have modernized some of the spellings in Robert Herrick's poems, but have kept his capitalizations and use of italics. These are part of the flavour of Herrick's verse, and do not detract, I think, from the power or nuance of his poetry.

Unfortunately, as *Hesperides* is such a large collection of poetry, it hasn't been possible to print every poem on a page on its own (it would be over 850 pages long). To keep the book at a manageable length, sometimes two or more poems have been printed on the same page.

Robert Herrick

Title pages of Hesperides by Robert Herrick
(this page and over)

HESPERIDES:

OR,

THE WORKS

BOTH

HUMANE & DIVINE

OF

ROBERT HERRICK *Esq.*

OVID.

Effugient avidos Carmina noftra Rogos.

LONDON,

Printed for *John Williams*, and *Francis Eglesfield*,
and are to be fold by *Tho: Hunt*, Book-feller
in *Exon*. 1648.

John William Waterhouse, Gather Ye Rosebuds While Ye May,
1909, private collection

HESPERIDES

Hesperides and His Noble Numbers

HESPERIDES:
OR,
THE WORKS
BOTH
HUMANE & DIVINE
OF
Robert Herrick Esq.

Ovid.
Effugient avidos Carmina nostra Rogos.

TO THE MOST
ILLVSTRIOVS,
AND
Most Hopefull Prince,
CHARLES,
Prince of Wales.

Well may my Book come forth like Publique Day
When such a Light as You are leads the way:
Who are my Works Creator, and alone
The Flame of it, and the Expansion.
And look how all those heavenly Lamps acquire
Light from the Sun, that inexhausted Fire:
So all my Morne, and Evening Stars from You
Have their Existence, and their Influence too.
Full is my Book of Glories; but all These
By You become Immortall Substances.

For these Transgressions which thou here dost see,
Condemne the Printer, Reader, and not me;
Who gave him forth good Grain, though he mistook
The Seed; so sow'd these Tares throughout my Book.

The Argument of his Book.

I sing of Brooks, of Blossomes, Birds, and Bowers:
Of April, May, of June, and July-Flowers.
I sing of May-poles, Hock-carts, Wassails, Wakes,
Of Bride-grooms, Brides, and of their Bridall-cakes.
I write of Youth, of Love, and have Accesse
By these, to sing of cleanly-Wantonnesse.
I sing of Dewes, of Raines, and piece by piece
Of Balme, of Oyle, of Spice, and Amber-Greece.
I sing of Times trans-shifting; and I write
How Roses first came Red, and Lillies White.
I write of Groves, of Twilights, and I sing
The Court of Mab, and of the Fairie-King.
I write of Hell; I sing (and ever shall)
Of Heaven, and hope to have it after all.

To his Muse.

Whither, Mad maiden wilt thou roame?
Farre safer 'twere to stay at home:
Where thou mayst sit, and piping please
The poore and private Cottages.
Since Coats, and Hamlets, best agree
With this thy meaner Minstralsie.
There with the Reed, thou mayst expresse
The Shepherds Fleecie happinesse:
And with thy Eclogues intermixe
Some smooth, and harmlesse Beucolicks.
There on a Hillock thou mayst sing
Unto a handsome Shephardling;
Or to a Girle (that keeps the Neat)
With breath more sweet then Violet.
There, there, (perhaps) such Lines as These
May take the simple Villages.
But for the Court, the Country wit
Is despicable unto it.
Stay then at home, and doe not goe
Or flie abroad to seeke for woe.
Contempts in Courts and Cities dwell;
No Critick haunts the Poore mans Cell:
Where thou mayst hear thine own Lines read
By no one tongue, there, censured.
That man's unwise will search for Ill,
And may prevent it, sitting still.

To his Booke.

While thou didst keep thy Candor undefil'd,
Deerely I lov'd thee; as my first-borne child:
But when I saw thee wantonly to roame
From house to house, and never stay at home;
I brake my bonds of Love, and bad thee goe,
Regardlesse whether well thou sped'st, or no.
On with thy fortunes then, what e're they be;
If good I'll smile, if bad I'll sigh for Thee.

Another

To read my Booke the Virgin shie
May blush, (while Brutus standeth by:)
But when He's gone, read through what's writ,
And never staine a cheeke for it.

Another.

Who with thy leaves shall wipe (at need)
The place, where swelling Piles do breed:
May every Ill, that bites, or smarts,
Perplex him in his hinder-parts.

To the soure Reader.

If thou dislik'st the Piece thou light'st on first;
Thinke that of All, that I have writ, the worst:
But if thou read'st my Booke unto the end,
And still do'st this, and that verse, reprehend:
O Perverse man! If All disgustfull be,
The Extreame Scabbe take thee, and thine, for me.

When he would have his verses read.

In sober mornings, doe not thou reherse
The holy incantation of a verse;
But when that men have both well drunke, and fed,
Let my Enchantments then be sung, or read.
When Laurell spirts 'ith fire, and when the Hearth
Smiles to it selfe, and guilds the roofe with mirth;
When up the Thyrse is rais'd, and when the sound
Of sacred Orgies flyes, A round, A round.
When the Rose raignes, and locks with ointments shine,
Let rigid Cato read these Lines of mine.

Upon Julia's Recovery.

Droop, droop no more, or hang the head
Ye Roses almost withered;
Now strength, and newer Purple get,
Each here declining Violet.
O Primroses! let this day be
A Resurrection unto ye;
And to all flowers ally'd in blood,
Or sworn to that sweet Sister-hood:
For Health on Julia's cheek hath shed
Clarret, and Creame commingled.
And those her lips doe now appeare
As beames of Corrall, but more cleare.

To Silvia to wed.

Let us (though late) at last (my Silvia) wed;
And loving lie in one devoted bed.
Thy Watch may stand, my minutes fly poste haste;
No sound calls back the yeere that once is past.
Then sweetest Silvia, let's no longer stay;
True love, we know, precipitates delay.
Away with doubts, all scruples hence remove;
No man at one time, can be wise, and love.

The Parliament of Roses to Julia.

I dreamt the Roses one time went
To meet and sit in Parliament:
The place for these, and for the rest
Of flowers, was thy spotlesse breast:
Over the which a State was drawne
Of Tiffanie, or Cob-web Lawne;
Then in that Parly, all those powers
Voted the Rose; the Queen of flowers.
But so, as that her self should be
The maide of Honour unto thee.

To his Booke.

Come thou not neere those men, who are like Bread
O're-leven'd; or like Cheese o're-renetted.

No bashfulnesse in begging.

To get thine ends, lay bashfulnesse aside;
Who feares to aske, doth teach to be deny'd.

Treason.

The seeds of Treason choake up as they spring,
He Acts the Crime, that gives it Cherishing.

Two Things Odious.

Two of a thousand things, are disallow'd,
A lying Rich man, and a Poore man proud.

The Frozen Heart.

I freeze, I freeze, and nothing dwels
In me but Snow, and ysicles.
For pitties sake give your advice,
To melt this snow, and thaw this ice;
I'll drink down Flames, but if so be
Nothing but love can supple me;
I'll rather keepe this frost, and snow,
Then to be thaw'd, or heated so.

To Perilla.

Ah my Perilla! do'st thou grieve to see
Me, day by day, to steale away from thee?
Age cals me hence, and my gray haires bid come,
And haste away to mine eternal home;
'Twill not be long (Perilla) after this,
That I must give thee the supremest kisse;
Dead when I am, first cast in salt, and bring
Part of the creame from that Religious Spring;
With which (Perilla) wash my hands and feet;
That done, then wind me in that very sheet
Which wrapt thy smooth limbs (when thou didst implore
The Gods protection, but the night before)
Follow me weeping to my Turfe, and there
Let fall a Primrose, and with it a teare:
Then lastly, let some weekly-strewings be
Devoted to the memory of me:
Then shall my Ghost not walk about, but keep
Still in the coole, and silent shades of sleep.

A Song to the Maskers.

Come down, and dance ye in the toyle
    Of pleasures, to a Heate;
But if to moisture, Let the oyle
    Of Roses be your sweat.

Not only to your selves assume
    These sweets, but let them fly;
From this, to that, and so Perfume
    E'ne all the standers by.

As Goddesse Isis (when she went,
    Or glided through the street)
Made all that touch't her with her scent,
    And whom she touch't, turne sweet.

To Perenna.

When I thy Parts runne o're, I can't espie
In any one, the least indecencie:
But every Line, and Limb diffused thence,
A faire, and unfamiliar excellence:
So, that the more I look, the more I prove,
Ther's still more cause, why I the more should love.

To his Mistresses.

Helpe me! helpe me! now I call
To my pretty Witchcrafts all:
Old I am, and cannot do
That, I was accustom'd to.
Bring your Magicks, Spels, and Charmes,
To enflesh my thighs, and armes:
Is there no way to beget
In my limbs their former heat?
AEson had (as Poets faine)
Baths that made him young againe:
Find that Medicine (if you can)
For your drie-decrepid man:
Who would faine his strength renew,
Were it but to pleasure you.

The Wounded Heart.

Come bring your sampler, and with Art,
      Draw in't a wounded Heart:
      And dropping here, and there:
Not that I thinke, that any Dart,
      Can make your's bleed a teare:
      Or peirce it any where;
Yet doe it to this end: that I,
        May by
        This secret see,
    Though you can make
That Heart to bleed, your's ne'r will ake
        For me.

No Loathsomnesse in love.

What I fancy, I approve,
No Dislike there is in love:
Be my Mistresse short or tall,
And distorted there-withall:
Be she likewise one of those,
That an Acre hath of Nose:
Be her forehead, and her eyes
Full of incongruities:
Be her cheeks so shallow too,
As to shew her Tongue wag through:
Be her lips ill hung, or set,
And her grinders black as jet;
Ha's she thinne haire, hath she none,
She's to me a Paragon.

To Anthea.

If deare Anthea, my hard fate it be
To live some few-sad-howers after thee:
Thy sacred Corse with Odours I will burne;
And with my Lawrell crown thy Golden Urne.
Then holding up (there) such religious Things,
As were (time past) thy holy Filitings:
Nere to thy Reverend Pitcher I will fall
Down dead for grief, and end my woes withall:
So three in one small plat of ground shall ly,
Anthea, Herrick, and his Poetry.

The Weeping Cherry.

I saw a Cherry weep, and why?
    Why wept it? but for shame,
Because my Julia's lip was by,
    And did out-red the same.
But pretty Fondling, let not fall
    A teare at all for that:
Which Rubies, Corralls, Scarlets, all
For tincture, wonder at.

Soft Musick.

The mellow touch of musick most doth wound
The soule, when it doth rather sigh, then sound.

The Difference Betwixt Kings and Subjects.

Twixt Kings and Subjects ther's this mighty odds,
Subjects are taught by Men; Kings by the Gods.

His Answer to a Question.

Some would know
    Why I so
Long still doe tarry,
    And ask why
    Here that I
Live, and not marry?
    Thus I those
    Doe oppose;
What man would be here,
    Slave to Thrall,
    If at all
He could live free here?

Upon Julia's Fall.

Julia was carelesse, and withall,
She rather took, then got a fall:
The wanton Ambler chanc'd to see
Part of her leggs sinceritie:
And ravish'd thus, It came to passe,
The Nagge (like to the Prophets Asse)
Began to speak, and would have been
A telling what rare sights h'ad seen:
And had told all; but did refraine,
Because his Tongue was ty'd againe.

Expences Exhaust.

Live with a thrifty, not a needy Fate;
Small shots paid often, waste a vast estate.

Love what it is.

Love is a circle that doth restlesse move
In the same sweet eternity of love.

Presence and Absence.

When what is lov'd, is Present, love doth spring;
But being absent, Love lies languishing.

No Spouse but a Sister.

A bachelour I will
Live as I have liv'd still,
And never take a wife
To crucifie my life:
But this I'll tell ye too,
What now I meane to doe;
A Sister (in the stead
Of Wife) about I'll lead;
Which I will keep embrac'd,
And kisse, but yet be chaste.

The Pomander Bracelet.

To me my Julia lately sent
A Bracelet richly Redolent:
The Beads I kist, but most lov'd her
That did perfume the Pomander.

The shooe tying.

Anthea bade me tye her shooe;
I did; and kist the Instep too:
And would have kist unto her knee,
Had not her Blush rebuked me.

The Carkanet.

Instead of Orient Pearls of Jet,
I sent my Love a Karkanet:
About her spotlesse neck she knit
The lace, to honour me, or it:
Then think how wrapt was I to see
My Jet t'enthrall such Ivorie.

His sailing from Julia.

When that day comes, whose evening sayes I'm gone
Unto that watrie Desolation:
Devoutly to thy Closet-gods then pray,
That my wing'd ship may meet no Remora.
Those Deities which circum-walk the Seas,
And look upon our dreadfull passages,
Will from all dangers, re-deliver me,
For one drink-offering, poured out by thee.
Mercie and Truth live with thee! and forbeare
(In my short absence) to unsluce a teare:
But yet for Loves-sake, let thy lips doe this,
Give my dead picture one engendring kisse:
Work that to life, and let me ever dwell
In thy remembrance (Julia.) So farewell.

How the Wall-flower came first, and why so called.

Why this Flower is now call'd so,
List' sweet maids, and you shal know.
Understand, this First-ling was
Once a brisk and bonny Lasse,
Kept as close as Danae was:
Who a sprightly Springall lov'd,
And to have it fully prov'd,
Up she got upon a wall,
Tempting down to slide withall:
But the silken twist unty'd,
So she fell, and bruis'd, she dy'd.
Love, in pity of the deed,
And her loving-lucklesse speed,
Turn'd her to this Plant, we call
Now, *The Flower of the Wall.*

Why Flowers change colour.

These fresh beauties (we can prove)
Once were Virgins sick of love,
Turn'd to Flowers. Still in some
Colours goe, and colours come.

To his Mistresse objecting to him neither Toying or Talking.

You say I love not, 'cause I doe not play
Still with your curles, and kisse the time away.
You blame me too, because I cann't devise
Some sport, to please those Babies in your eyes:
By Loves Religion, I must here confesse it,
The most I love, when I the least expresse it.
Small griefs find tongues: Full Casques are ever found
To give (if any, yet) but little sound.
Deep waters noyse-lesse are; And this we know,
That chiding streams betray small depth below.
So when Love speechlesse is, she doth expresse
A depth in love, and that depth, bottomlesse.
Now since my love is tongue-lesse, know me such,
Who speak but little, 'cause I love so much.

Upon the losse of his Mistresses.

I have lost, and lately, these
Many dainty Mistresses:
Stately Julia, prime of all;
Sappho next, a principall:
Smooth Anthea, for a skin
White, and Heaven-like Chrystalline:
Sweet Electra, and the choice
Myrha, for the Lute, and Voice.
Next, Corinna, for her wit,
And for the graceful use of it:
With Perilla: All are gone;
Onely Herrick's left alone,
For to number sorrow by
Their departures hence, and die.

The Dream.

Me thought, (last night) love in an anger came,
And brought a rod, so whipt me with the same:
Mirtle the twigs were, meerly to imply;
Love strikes, but 'tis with gentle crueltie.
Patient I was: Love pitifull grew then,
And stroak'd the stripes, and I was whole agen.
Thus like a Bee, Love-gentle stil doth bring
Hony to salve, where he before did sting.

The Vine.

I dream'd this mortal part of mine
Was Metamorphoz'd to a Vine;
Which crawling one and every way,
Enthrall'd my dainty Lucia.
Me thought, her long small legs & thighs
I with my Tendrils did surprize;
Her Belly, Buttocks, and her Waste
By my soft Nerv'lits were embrac'd:
About her head I writhing hung,
And with rich clusters (hid among
The leaves) her temples I behung:
So that my Lucia seem'd to me
Young Bacchus ravisht by his tree.
My curles about her neck did craule,
And armes and hands they did enthrall:
So that she could not freely stir,
(All parts there made one prisoner.)
But when I crept with leaves to hide
Those parts, which maids keep unespy'd,
Such fleeting pleasures there I took,
That with the fancie I awook;
And found (Ah me!) this flesh of mine
More like a Stock, then like a Vine.

To Love.

I'm free from thee; and thou no more shalt heare
My puling Pipe to beat against thine eare:
Farewell my shackles, (though of pearle they be)
Such precious thraldome ne'r shall fetter me.
He loves his bonds, who when the first are broke,
Submits his neck unto a second yoke.

On himselfe.

Young I was, but now am old,
But I am not yet grown cold;
I can play, and I can twine
'Bout a Virgin like a Vine:
In her lap too I can lye
Melting, and in fancie die:
And return to life, if she
Claps my cheek, or kisseth me;
Thus, and thus it now appears
That our love out-lasts our yeeres.

Love's play at Push-pin.

Love and my selfe (beleeve me) on a day
At childish Push-pin (for our sport) did play:
I put, he pusht, and heedless of my skin,
Love prickt my finger with a golden pin:
Since which, it festers so, that I can prove
'Twas but a trick to poyson me with love:
Little the wound was; greater was the smart;
The finger bled, but burnt was all my heart.

The Rosarie.

One ask'd me where the Roses grew?
    I bade him not goe seek;
But forthwith bade my Julia shew
    A bud in either cheek.

Upon Cupid.

Old wives have often told, how they
Saw Cupid bitten by a flea:
And thereupon, in tears half drown'd,
He cry'd aloud, Help, help the wound:
He wept, he sobb'd, he call'd to some
To bring him Lint, and Balsamum,
To make a Tent, and put it in,
Where the Steletto pierc'd the skin:
Which being done, the fretfull paine
Asswag'd, and he was well again.

The Parce, or, Three dainty Destinies. The Armelet.

Three lovely Sisters working were
    (As they were closely set)
Of soft and dainty Maiden-haire,
    A curious Armelet.
I smiling, ask'd them what they did?
    (Faire Destinies all three)
Who told me, they had drawn a thred
    Of Life, and 'twas for me.
They shew'd me then, how fine 'twas spun;
    And I reply'd thereto,
I care not now how soone 'tis done,
    Or cut, if cut by you.

Cherry-pit.

Julia and I did lately sit
Playing for sport, at Cherry-pit:
She threw; I cast; and having thrown,
I got the Pit, and she the Stone.

To Robin Red-brest.

Laid out for dead, let thy last kindnesse be
With leaves and mosse-work for to cover me:
And while the Wood-nimphs my cold corps inter,
Sing thou my Dirge, sweet-warbling Chorister!
For Epitaph, in Foliage, next write this,
Here, here the Tomb of Robin Herrick is.

Discontents in Devon.

More discontents I never had
Since I was born, then here;
Where I have been, and still am sad,
In this dull Devon-shire:
Yet justly too I must confesse;
I ne'r invented such
Ennobled numbers for the Presse,
Then where I loath'd so much.

To his Paternall Countrey.

O Earth! Earth! Earth heare thou my voice, and be
Loving, and gentle for to cover me:
Banish'd from thee I live; ne'r to return,
Unlesse thou giv'st my small Remains an Urne.

Cherrie-ripe.

Cherrie-Ripe, Ripe, Ripe, I cry,
Full and faire ones; come and buy:
If so be, you ask me where
They doe grow? I answer, There,
Where my Julia's lips doe smile;
There's the Land, or Cherry-Ile:
Whose Plantations fully show
All the yeere, where Cherries grow.

To his Mistresses.

Put on your silks; and piece by piece
Give them the scent of Amber-Greece:
And for your breaths too, let them smell
Ambrosia-like, or Nectarell:
While other Gums their sweets perspire,
By your owne jewels set on fire.

To Anthea.

Now is the time, when all the lights wax dim;
And thou (Anthea) must withdraw from him
Who was thy servant. Dearest, bury me
Under that Holy-oke, or Gospel-tree:
Where (though thou see'st not) thou may'st think upon
Me, when thou yeerly go'st Procession:
Or for mine honour, lay me in that Tombe
In which thy sacred Reliques shall have roome:
For my Embalming (Sweetest) there will be
No Spices wanting, when I'm laid by thee.

The Vision to Electra.

I dream'd we both were in a bed
Of Roses, almost smothered:
The warmth and sweetnes had me there
Made lovingly familiar:
But that I heard thy sweet breath say,
Faults done by night, will blush by day:
I kist thee (panting,) and I call
Night to the Record! that was all.
But ah! if empty dreames so please,
Love give me more such nights as these.

Dreames.

Here we are all, by day; By night w'are hurl'd
By dreames, each one, into a sev'rall world.

Ambition.

In Man, Ambition is the common'st thing;
Each one, by nature, loves to be a King.

Sorrowes succeed.

When one is past, another care we hav
Thus woe succeeds a woe; as wave a wave.

Money gets the masterie.

Fight thou with shafts of silver, and o'rcome,
When no force else can get the masterdome.

His request to Julia.

Julia, if I chance to die
Ere I print my Poetry;
I most humbly thee desire
To commit it to the fire:
Better 'twere my Book were dead,
Then to live not perfected.

The Scar-fire.

Water, water I desire,
Here's a house of flesh on fire:
Ope' the fountains and the springs,
And come all to Buckittings:
What ye cannot quench, pull downe;
Spoile a house, to save a towne:
Better tis that one shu'd fall,
Then by one, to hazard all.

Upon Silvia, a Mistresse.

When some shall say, Faire once my Silvia was;
Thou wilt complaine, False now's thy Looking-glasse
Which renders that quite tarnisht, wch was green;
And Priceless now, what Peerless once had been:
Upon thy Forme more wrinkles yet will fall,
And comming downe, shall make no noise at all.

Cheerfulnesse in Charitie:
or, The sweet sacrifice.

'Tis not a thousand Bullocks thies
Can please those Heav'nly Deities,
If the Vower don't express
In his Offering, Cheerfulness.

Once poore, still penurious.

Goes the world now, it will with thee goe hard:
The fattest Hogs we grease the more with Lard.
To him that has, there shall be added more;
Who is penurious, he shall still be poore.

Sweetnesse in Sacrifice.

'Tis not greatness they require,
To be offer'd up by fire:
But 'tis sweetness that doth please
Those *Eternall Essences*.

Steame in Sacrifice.

If meat the Gods give, I the steame
High-towring wil devote to them:
Whose easie natures like it well,
If we the roste have, they the smell.

Upon Julia's Voice.

So smooth, so sweet, so silv'ry is thy voice,
As, could they hear, the Damn'd would make no noise,
But listen to thee, (walking in thy chamber)
Melting melodious words, to Lutes of Amber.

Againe.

When I thy singing next shall heare,
I'll wish I might turne all to eare,
To drink in Notes, and Numbers; such
As blessed soules cann't heare too much:
Then melted down, there let me lye
Entranc'd, and lost confusedly:
And by thy Musique strucken mute,
Die, and be turn'd into a Lute.

All things decay and die.

All things decay with Time: The Forrest sees
The growth, and down-fall of her aged trees:
That Timber tall, which three-score lusters stood
The proud Dictator of the State-like wood:
I meane (the Soveraigne of all Plants) the Oke
Droops, dies, and falls without the cleavers stroke.

The succession of the foure sweet months.

First, April, she with mellow showrs
Opens the way for early flowers;
Then after her comes smiling May
In a more rich and sweet aray:
Next enters June, and brings us more
Jems, then those two, that went before:
Then (lastly) July comes, and she
More wealth brings in, then all those three.

No Shipwrack of Vertue.
To a friend.

Thou sail'st with others, in this Argus here;
Nor wrack, or Bulging thou hast cause to feare:
But trust to this, my noble passenger;
Who swims with Vertue, he shall still be sure
(Ulysses-like) all tempests to endure;
And 'midst a thousand gulfs to be secure.

Upon his Sister-in-Law, Mistresse Elizab: Herrick.

First, for Effusions due unto the dead,
My solemne Vowes have here accomplished:
Next, how I love thee, that my griefe must tell,
Wherein thou liv'st for ever. Deare farewell.

Of Love.
A Sonnet.

How Love came in, I do not know,
Whether by th'eye, or eare, or no:
Or whether with the soule it came
(At first) infused with the same:
Whether in part 'tis here or there,
Or, like the soule, whole every where:
This troubles me: but I as well
As any other, this can tell;
That when from hence she does depart,
The out-let then is from the heart.

To Anthea.

Ah my Anthea! Must my heart still break?
(Love makes me write, what shame forbids to speak.)
Give me a kisse, and to that kisse a score;
Then to that twenty, adde an hundred more:
A thousand to that hundred: so kisse on,
To make that thousand up a million.
Treble that million, and when that is done,
Let's kisse afresh, as when we first begun.
But yet, though Love likes well such Scenes as these,
There is an Act that will more fully please:
Kissing and glancing, soothing, all make way
But to the acting of this private Play:
Name it I would; but being blushing red,
The rest I'll speak, when we meet both in bed.

The Rock of Rubies: and The quarrie of Pearls.

Some ask'd me where the Rubies grew?
      And nothing I did say:
But with my finger pointed to
      The lips of Julia.
Some ask'd how Pearls did grow, and where?
      Then spoke I to my Girle,
To part her lips, and shew'd them there
      The Quarelets of Pearl.

Conformitie.

Conformity was ever knowne
A foe to Dissolution:
Nor can we that a ruine call,
Whose crack gives crushing unto all.

To the King
Upon his comming with his Army into the West.

Welcome, most welcome to our Vowes and us,
Most great, and universall Genius!
The Drooping West, which hitherto has stood
As one, in long-lamented-widow-hood;
Looks like a Bride now, or a bed of flowers,
Newly refresh't, both by the Sun, and showers.
War, which before was horrid, now appears
Lovely in you, brave Prince of Cavaliers!
A deale of courage in each bosome springs
By your accesse; (O you the best of Kings!)
Ride on with all white Omens; so, that where
Your Standard's up, we fix a Conquest there.

Upon Roses.

Under a Lawne, then skyes more cleare,
Some ruffled Roses nestling were:
And snugging there, they seem'd to lye
As in a flowrie Nunnery:
They blush'd, and look'd more fresh then flowers
Quickned of late by Pearly showers;
And all, because they were possest
But of the heat of Julia's breast:
Which as a warme, and moistned spring,
Gave them their ever flourishing.

To the King and Queene, upon their unhappy distances.

Woe, woe to them, who (by a ball of strife)
Doe, and have parted here a Man and Wife:
Charls the best Husband, while Maria strives
To be, and is, the very best of Wives:
Like Streams, you are divorc'd; but 't will come, when
These eyes of mine shall see you mix agen.
Thus speaks the Oke, here; C. and M. shall meet,
Treading on Amber, with their silver-feet:
Nor wil't be long, ere this accomplish'd be;
The words found true, C. M. remember me.

The Cheat of Cupid:
or, The ungentle guest.

One silent night of late,
    When every creature rested,
Came one unto my gate,
    And knocking, me molested.

"Who's that" (said I) "beats there,
    And troubles thus the Sleepie?"
"Cast off" (said he) "all feare,
    And let not Locks thus keep ye.

"For I a Boy am, who
    By Moonlesse nights have swerved;
And all with showrs wet through,
    And e'en with cold half starved."

    I pittifull arose,
And soon a Taper lighted;
And did my selfe disclose
    Unto the lad benighted.

I saw he had a Bow,
    And Wings too, which did shiver;
And looking down below,
    I spy'd he had a Quiver.

I to my Chimney's shine
    Brought him, (as Love professes)
And chaf'd his hands with mine,
    And dry'd his dropping Tresses:

But when he felt him warm'd,
    "Let's try this bow of ours,
And string if they be harm'd,"
    Said he, with these late showrs.

Forthwith his bow he bent,
    And wedded string and arrow,
And struck me that it went
    Quite through my heart and marrow.

Then laughing loud, he flew
    Away, and thus said flying,
"Adieu, mine Host, Adieu,
    I'll leave thy heart a dying."

To the reverend shade of his religious Father.

That for seven Lusters I did never come
To doe the Rites to thy Religious Tombe:
That neither haire was cut, or true teares shed
By me, o'r thee, (as justments to the dead)
Forgive, forgive me; since I did not know
Whether thy bones had here their Rest, or no.
But now 'tis known, Behold; behold, I bring
Unto thy Ghost, th'Effused Offering:
And look, what Smallage, Night-shade, Cypresse, Yew,
Unto the shades have been, or now are due,
Here I devote; And something more then so;
I come to pay a Debt of Birth I owe.
Thou gav'st me life, (but Mortall;) For that one
Favour, I'll make full satisfaction;
For my life mortall, Rise from out thy Herse,
And take a life immortall from my Verse.

Delight in Disorder.

A sweet disorder in the dresse
Kindles in cloathes a wantonnesse:
A Lawne about the shoulders thrown
Into a fine distraction:
An erring Lace, which here and there
Enthralls the Crimson Stomacher:
A Cuffe neglectfull, and thereby
Ribbands to flow confusedly:
A winning wave (deserving Note)
In the tempestuous petticote:
A carelesse shooe-string, in whose tye
I see a wilde civility:
Doe more bewitch me, then when Art
Is too precise in every part.

To his Muse.

Were I to give thee Baptime, I wo'd chuse
To Christen thee, the Bride, the Bashfull Muse,
Or Muse of Roses: since that name does fit
Best with those Virgin-Verses thou hast writ:
Which are so cleane, so chast, as none may feare
Cato the Censor, sho'd he scan each here.

Upon Love.

Love scorch'd my finger, but did spare
    The burning of my heart:
To signifie, in Love my share
    Sho'd be a little part.

Little I love; but if that he
    Wo'd but that heat recall:
That joynt to ashes sho'd be burnt,
    Ere I wo'd love at all.

Dean-bourn, a rude River in Devon, by which sometimes he
lived.

Dean-bourn, farewell; I never look to see
Deane, or thy warty incivility.
Thy rockie bottome, that doth teare thy streams
And makes them frantick, ev'n to all extreames;
To my content, I never sho'd behold,
Were thy streames silver, or thy rocks all gold.
Rockie thou art; and rockie we discover
Thy men; and rockie are thy wayes all over.
O men, O manners; Now, and ever knowne
To be A Rockie Generation!
A people currish; churlish as the seas;
And rude (almost) as rudest Salvages.
With whom I did, and may re-sojourne when
Rockes turn to Rivers, Rivers turn to Men.

Kissing Usurie.

Biancha, Let
Me pay the debt
I owe thee for a kisse
Thou lend'st to me;
And I to thee
Will render ten for this:

If thou wilt say,
Ten will not pay
For that so rich a one;
I'll cleare the summe,
If it will come
Unto a Million.

By this I guesse,
Of happinesse
Who has a little measure:
He must of right,
To th'utmost mite,
Make payment for his pleasure.

To Julia.

How rich and pleasing thou my Julia art
In each thy dainty, and peculiar part!
First, for thy Queen-ship on thy head is set
Of flowers a sweet commingled Coronet:
About thy neck a Carkanet is bound,
Made of the Rubie, Pearle and Diamond:
A golden ring, that shines upon thy thumb:
About thy wrist, the rich Dardanium.
Between thy Breasts (then Doune of Swans more white)
There playes the Saphire with the Chrysolite.
No part besides must of thy selfe be known,
But by the Topaz, Opal, Calcedon.

To Laurels.

A funerall stone,
Or Verse I covet none;
But onely crave
Of you, that I may have
A sacred Laurel springing from my grave:
Which being seen,
Blest with perpetuall greene,
May grow to be
Not so much call'd a tree,
As the eternall monument of me.

His Cavalier.

Give me that man, that dares bestride
The active Sea-horse, & with pride,
Through that huge field of waters ride:
Who, with his looks too, can appease
The ruffling winds and raging Seas,
In mid'st of all their outrages.
This, this a virtuous man can doe,
Saile against Rocks, and split them too;
I! and a world of Pikes passe through.

The Bag of the Bee.

About the sweet bag of a Bee,
    Two Cupids fell at odds;
And whose the pretty prize shu'd be,
    They vow'd to ask the Gods.

Which Venus hearing; thither came,
    And for their boldness stript them:
And taking thence from each his flame;
    With rods of Mirtle whipt them.

Which done, to still their wanton cries,
    When quiet grown sh'ad seen them,
She kist, and wip'd thir dove-like eyes;
    And gave the Bag between them.

Love kill'd by Lack.

Let me be warme; let me be fully fed:
Luxurious Love by Wealth is nourished.
Let me be leane, and cold, and once grown poore,
I shall dislike, what once I lov'd before.

To his Mistresse.

Choose me your Valentine;
    Next, let us marry:
Love to the death will pine,
    If we long tarry.

Promise, and keep your vowes,
    Or vow ye never:
Loves doctrine disallowes
    Troth-breakers ever.

You have broke promise twice
    (Deare) to undoe me;
If you prove faithlesse thrice,
    None then will wooe you.

To the generous Reader.

See, and not see; and if thou chance t'espie
Some Aberrations in my Poetry;
Wink at small faults, the greater, ne'rthelesse
Hide, and with them, their Fathers nakedness.
Let's doe our best, our Watch and Ward to keep
Homer himself, in a long work, may sleep.

To Criticks.

I'll write, because I'll give
You Criticks means to live:
For sho'd I not supply
The Cause, th'effect wo'd die.

Duty to Tyrants.

Good princes must be pray'd for: for the bad
They must be borne with, and in rev'rence had.
Doe they first pill thee, next, pluck off thy skin?
Good children kisse the rods, that punish sin.
Touch not the Tyrant; Let the Gods alone
To strike him dead, that but usurps a Throne.

Being once blind, his request to Biancha.

When age or Chance has made me blind,
So that the path I cannot find:
And when my falls and stumblings are
More then the stones i'th' street by farre:
Goe thou afore; and I shall well
Follow thy Perfumes by the smell:
Or be my guide; and I shall be
Led by some light that flows from thee.
Thus held, or led by thee, I shall
In wayes confus'd, nor slip or fall.

Upon Blanch.

Blanch swears her Husband's lovely; when a scald
Has blear'd his eyes: Besides, his head is bald.
Next, his wilde eares, like Lethern wings full spread,
Flutter to flie, and beare away his head.

No want where there's little.

To Bread and Water none is poore;
And having these, what need of more?
Though much from out the Cess be spent,
Nature with little is content.

Barly-Break:
or, Last in Hell.

We two are last in Hell: what may we feare
To be tormented, or kept Pris'ners here?
Alas! If kissing be of plagues the worst,
We'll wish, in Hell we had been Last and First.

Zeal required in Love.

I'll doe my best to win, when'ere I wooe:
That man loves not, who is not zealous too.

Dangers wait on Kings.

As oft as Night is banish'd by the Morne,
So oft, we'll think, we see a King new born.

The Definition of Beauty.

Beauty, no other thing is, then a Beame
Flasht out between the Middle and Extreame.

To Dianeme.

Deare, though to part it be a Hell,
Yet Dianeme now farewell:
Thy frown (last night) did bid me goe;
But whither, onely Grief do's know.
I doe beseech thee, ere we part,
(If mercifull, as faire thou art;
Or else desir'st that Maids sho'd tell
Thy pitty by Loves-Chronicle)
O Dianeme, rather kill
Me, then to make me languish stil!
'Tis cruelty in thee to'th'height,
Thus, thus to wound, not kill out-right:
Yet there's a way found (if thou please)
By sudden death to give me ease:
And thus devis'd, doe thou but this,
Bequeath to me one parting kisse:
So sup'rabundant joy shall be
The Executioner of me.

To Anthea lying in bed.

So looks Anthea, when in bed she lyes,
Orecome, or halfe betray'd by Tiffanies:
Like to a Twi-light, or that simpring Dawn,
That Roses shew, when misted o're with Lawn.
Twilight is yet, till that her Lawnes give way;
Which done, that Dawne, turnes then to perfect day.

To Electra.

More white then whitest Lillies far,
Or Snow, or whitest Swans you are:
More white then are the whitest Creames,
Or Moone-light tinselling the streames:
More white then Pearls, or Juno's thigh;
Or Pelops Arme of Yvorie.
True, I confesse; such Whites as these
May me delight, not fully please:
Till, like Ixion's Cloud you be
White, warme, and soft to lye with me.

A Country life:
To his Brother, M. Tho: Herrick.

Thrice, and above, blest (my soules halfe) art thou,
    In thy both Last, and Better Vow:
Could'st leave the City, for exchange, to see
    The Countries sweet simplicity:
And it to know, and practice; with intent
    To grow the sooner innocent:
By studying to know vertue; and to aime
    More at her nature, then her name:
The last is but the least; the first doth tell
    Wayes lesse to live, then to live well:
And both are knowne to thee, who now can'st live
    Led by thy conscience; to give
Justice to soone-pleas'd nature; and to show,
    Wisdome and she together goe,
And keep one Centre: This with that conspires,
    To teach Man to confine desires:
And know, that Riches have their proper stint,
    In the contented mind, not mint.
And can'st instruct, that those who have the itch
    Of craving more, are never rich.
These things thou know'st to'th'height, and dost prevent
    That plague; because thou art content
With that Heav'n gave thee with a warie hand,
    (More blessed in thy Brasse, then Land)
To keep cheap Nature even, and upright;
    To coole, not cocker Appetite.
Thus thou can'st tearcely live to satisfie
    The belly chiefly; not the eye:
Keeping the barking stomach wisely quiet,
    Lesse with a neat, then needfull diet.
But that which most makes sweet thy country life,
    Is, the fruition of a wife:
Whom (Stars consenting with thy Fate) thou hast
    Got, not so beautifull, as chast:
By whose warme side thou dost securely sleep
    (While Love the Centinell doth keep)

With those deeds done by day, which n'er affright
    Thy silken slumbers in the night.
Nor has the darknesse power to usher in
    Feare to those sheets, that know no sin.
But still thy wife, by chast intentions led,
    Gives thee each night a Maidenhead.
The Damaskt medowes, and the peebly streames
    Sweeten, and make soft your dreames:
The Purling springs, groves, birds, and well-weav'd Bowrs,
    With fields enameled with flowers,
Present their shapes; while fantasie discloses
    Millions of Lillies mixt with Roses.
Then dream, ye heare the Lamb by many a bleat
    Woo'd to come suck the milkie Teat:
While Faunus in the Vision comes to keep,
    From rav'ning wolves, the fleecie sheep.
With thousand such enchanting dreams, that meet
    To make sleep not so sound, as sweet:
Nor can these figures so thy rest endeare,
    As not to rise when Chanticlere
Warnes the last Watch; but with the Dawne dost rise
To work, but first to sacrifice;
    Making thy peace with heav'n, for some late fault,
With Holy-meale, and spirting-salt.
    Which done, thy painfull Thumb this sentence tells us,
Jove for our labour all things sells us.
    Nor are thy daily and devout affaires
Attended with those desp'rate cares,
    Th'industrious Merchant has; who for to find
Gold, runneth to the Western Inde,
    And back again, (tortur'd with fears) doth fly,
Untaught, to suffer Poverty.
    But thou at home, blest with securest ease,
Sitt'st, and beleev'st that there be seas,
    And watrie dangers; while thy whiter hap,
But sees these things within thy Map.
    And viewing them with a more safe survey,
Mak'st easie Feare unto thee say,
    A heart thrice wall'd with Oke, and Brasse, that man
Had, first, durst plow the Ocean.

But thou at home without or tyde or gale,
Canst in thy Map securely saile:
    Seeing those painted Countries; and so guesse
By those fine Shades, their Substances:
    And from thy Compasse taking small advice,
Buy'st Travell at the lowest price.

    Nor are thine eares so deafe, but thou canst heare
(Far more with wonder, then with feare)
    Fame tell of States, of Countries, Courts, and Kings;
And beleeve there be such things:
    When of these truths, thy happyer knowledge lyes,
More in thine eares, then in thine eyes.

    And when thou hear'st by that too-true-Report,
Vice rules the Most, or All at Court:
    Thy pious wishes are, (though thou not there)
Vertue had, and mov'd her Sphere.

    But thou liv'st fearlesse; and thy face ne'r shewes
Fortune when she comes, or goes.
    But with thy equall thoughts, prepar'd dost stand,
To take her by the either hand:
    Nor car'st which comes the first, the foule or faire;
A wise man ev'ry way lies square.

    And like a surly Oke with storms perplext;
Growes still the stronger, strongly vext.

    Be so, bold spirit; Stand Center-like, unmov'd;
And be not onely thought, but prov'd
    To be what I report thee; and inure
Thy selfe, if want comes to endure:
    And so thou dost: for thy desires are
Confin'd to live with private Larr:
    Not curious whether Appetite be fed,
Or with the first, or second bread.

    Who keep'st no proud mouth for delicious cates:
Hunger makes coorse meats, delicates.
    Can'st, and unurg'd, forsake that Larded fare,
Which Art, not Nature, makes so rare;
    To taste boyl'd Nettles, Colworts, Beets, and eate
These, and sowre herbs, as dainty meat?
    While soft Opinion makes thy Genius say,
Content makes all Ambrosia.

Nor is it, that thou keep'st this stricter size
So much for want, as exercise:
    To numb the sence of Dearth, which sho'd sinne haste it,
Thou might'st but onely see't, not taste it.
    Yet can thy humble roofe maintaine a Quire
Of singing Crickits by thy fire:
    And the brisk Mouse may feast her selfe with crums,
Till that the green-ey'd Kitling comes.
    Then to her Cabbin, blest she can escape
The sudden danger of a Rape.
    And thus thy little-well-kept-stock doth prove,
Wealth cannot make a life, but Love.
    Nor art thou so close-handed, but can'st spend
(Counsell concurring with the end)
    As well as spare: still conning o'r this Theame,
To shun the first, and last extreame
    Ordaining that thy small stock find no breach,
Or to exceed thy Tether's reach:
    But to live round, and close, and wisely true
To thine owne selfe; and knowne to few.
    Thus let thy Rurall Sanctuary be
Elizium to thy wife and thee;
    There to disport your selves with golden measure:
For seldome use commends the pleasure.
    Live, and live blest; thrice happy Paire; Let Breath,
But lost to one, be th'others death.
    And as there is one Love, one Faith, one Troth,
Be so one Death, one Grave to both.
    Till when, in such assurance live, ye may
Nor feare, or wish your dying day

.

Divination by a Daffadill.

When a Daffadill I see,
Hanging down his head t'wards me;
Guesse I may, what I must be:
First, I shall decline my head;
Secondly, I shall be dead;
Lastly, safely buryed.

To the Painter, to draw him a Picture.

Come, skilfull Lupo, now, and take
Thy Bice, thy Umber, Pink, and Lake;
And let it be thy Pensils strife,
To paint a Bridgeman to the life:
Draw him as like too, as you can,
An old, poore, lying, flatt'ring man:
His cheeks be-pimpled, red and blue;
His nose and lips of mulbrie hiew.
Then for an easie fansie; place
A Burling iron for his face:
Next, make his cheeks with breath to swell,
And for to speak, if possible:
But do not so; for feare, lest he
Sho'd by his breathing, poyson thee.

Upon Cuffe.
Epigram.

Cuffe comes to Church much; but he keeps his bed
Those Sundayes onely, when as Briefs are read.
This makes Cuffe dull; and troubles him the most,
Because he cannot sleep i'th' Church, free-cost.

Upon Fone a School-master.
Epigram.

Fone sayes, those mighty whiskers he do's weare,
Are twigs of Birch, and willow, growing there:
If so, we'll think too, (when he do's condemne
Boyes to the lash) that he do's whip with them.

A Lyrick to Mirth.

While the milder Fates consent,
Let's enjoy our merryment:
Drink, and dance, and pipe, and play;
Kisse our Dollies night and day:
Crown'd with clusters of the Vine;
Let us sit, and quaffe our wine.
Call on Bacchus; chaunt his praise;
Shake the Thyrse, and bite the Bayes:
Rouze Anacreon from the dead;
And return him drunk to bed:
Sing o're Horace; for ere long
Death will come and mar the song:
Then shall Wilson and Gotiere
Never sing, or play more here.

To the Earle of Westmerland.

When my date's done, and my gray age must die;
Nurse up, great Lord, this my posterity:
Weak though it be; long may it grow, and stand,
Shor'd up by you, (Brave Earle of Westmerland.)

Against Love.

When ere my heart, Love's warmth, but entertaines,
O Frost! O Snow! O Haile forbid the Banes.
One drop now deads a spark; but if the same
Once gets a force, Floods cannot quench the flame.
Rather then love, let me be ever lost;
Or let me 'gender with eternall frost.

Upon Julia's Riband.

As shews the Aire, when with a Rain-bow grac'd;
So smiles that Riband 'bout my Julia's waste:
Or like---Nay 'tis that Zonulet of love,
Wherein all pleasures of the world are wove.

The frozen Zone:
or, Julia disdainfull.

Whither? Say, whither shall I fly,
To slack these flames wherein I frie?
To the Treasures, shall I goe,
Of the Raine, Frost, Haile, and Snow?
Shall I search the under-ground,
Where all Damps, and Mists are found?
Shall I seek (for speedy ease)
All the floods, and frozen seas?
Or descend into the deep,
Where eternall cold does keep?
These may coole; but there's a Zone
Colder yet then any one:
That's my Julia's breast; where dwels
Such destructive Ysicles;
As that the Congelation will
Me sooner starve, then those can kill.

An Epitaph upon a sober Matron.

With blamelesse carriage, I liv'd here,
To' th'(almost) sev'n and fortieth yeare.
Stout sons I had, and those twice three;
One onely daughter lent to me:
The which was made a happy Bride,
But thrice three Moones before she dy'd.
My modest wedlock, that was known
Contented with the bed of one.

To the Patron of Poets, M. End: Porter.

Let there be Patrons; Patrons like to thee,
Brave Porter! Poets ne'r will wanting be:
Fabius, and Cotta, Lentulus, all live
In thee, thou Man of Men! who here do'st give
Not onely subject-matter for our wit,
But likewise Oyle of Maintenance to it:
For which, before thy Threshold, we'll lay downe
Our Thyrse, for Scepter; and our Baies for Crown.
For to say truth, all Garlands are thy due;
The Laurell, Mirtle, Oke, and Ivie too.

The sadnesse of things for Sappho's sicknesse.

Lillies will languish; Violets look ill;
Sickly the Prim-rose: Pale the Daffadill:
That gallant Tulip will hang down his head,
Like to a Virgin newly ravished.
Pansies will weep; and Marygolds will wither;
And keep a Fast, and Funerall together,
If Sappho droop; Daisies will open never,
But bid Good-night, and close their lids for ever.

Leanders Obsequies.

When as Leander young was drown'd,
No heart by love receiv'd a wound;
But on a Rock himselfe sate by,
There weeping sup'rabundantly.
Sighs numberlesse he cast about,
And all his Tapers thus put out:
His head upon his hand he laid;
And sobbing deeply, thus he said,
Ah cruell Sea! and looking on't,
Wept as he'd drowne the Hellespont,
And sure his tongue had more exprest,
But that his teares forbad the rest.

Foure things make us happy here.

Health is the first good lent to men;
A gentle disposition then:
Next, to be rich by no by-wayes;
Lastly, with friends t'enjoy our dayes.

His parting from Mrs Dorothy Keneday.

When I did goe from thee, I felt that smart,
Which Bodies do, when Souls from them depart.
Thou did'st not mind it; though thou then might'st see
Me turn'd to tears; yet did'st not weep for me.
'Tis true, I kist thee; but I co'd not heare
Thee spend a sigh, t'accompany my teare.
Me thought 'twas strange, that thou so hard sho'dst prove,
Whose heart, whose hand, whose ev'ry part spake love.
Prethee (lest Maids sho'd censure thee) but say
Thou shed'st one teare, when as I went away;
And that will please me somewhat: though I know,
And Love will swear't, my Dearest did not so.

The Teare sent to her from Stanes.

Glide, gentle streams, and beare
Along with you my teare
    To that coy Girle;
    Who smiles, yet slayes
    Me with delayes;
And strings my tears as Pearle.

See! see she's yonder set,
Making a Carkanet
    Of Maiden-flowers!
    There, there present
    This Orient,
And Pendant Pearle of ours.

Then say, I've sent one more
Jem to enrich her store;
    And that is all
    Which I can send,
    Or vainly spend,
For tears no more will fall.

Nor will I seek supply
Of them, the spring's once drie;
    But I'll devise,
    (Among the rest)
    A way that's best
How I may save mine eyes.

Yet say; sho'd she condemne
Me to surrender them;
    Then say; my part
    Must be to weep
    Out them, to keep
A poore, yet loving heart.

Say too, She wo'd have this;
She shall: Then my hope is,
    That when I'm poore,
    And nothing have
    To send, or save;
I'm sure she'll ask no more.

Upon one Lillie, who marryed with a maid call'd Rose.

What times of sweetnesse this faire day fore-shows,
When as the Lilly marries with the Rose!
What next is lookt for? but we all sho'd see
To spring from these a sweet Posterity.

An Epitaph upon a child.

Virgins promis'd when I dy'd,
That they wo'd each Primrose-tide,
Duely, Morne and Ev'ning, come,
And with flowers dresse my Tomb.
Having promis'd, pay your debts,
Maids, and here strew Violets.

Upon Scobble.
Epigram.

Scobble for Whoredome whips his wife; and cryes,
He'll slit her nose; But blubb'ring, she replyes,
Good Sir, make no more cuts i'th' outward skin,
One slit's enough to let Adultry in.

The Houre-glasse.

That Houre-glasse, which there ye see
With Water fill'd, (Sirs, credit me)
The humour was, (as I have read)
But Lovers tears inchristalled,
Which, as they drop by drop doe passe
From th'upper to the under-glasse,
Do in a trickling manner tell,
(By many a watrie syllable)
That Lovers tears in life-time shed,
Do restless run when they are dead.

His fare-well to Sack.

Farewell thou Thing, time-past so knowne, so deare
To me, as blood to life and spirit: Neare,
Nay, thou more neare then kindred, friend, man, wife,
Male to the female, soule to body: Life
To quick action, or the warme soft side
Of the resigning, yet resisting Bride.
The kisse of Virgins; First-fruits of the bed;
Soft speech, smooth touch, the lips, the Maiden-head:
These, and a thousand sweets, co'd never be
So neare, or deare, as thou wast once to me.
O thou the drink of Gods, and Angels! Wine
That scatter'st Spirit and Lust; whose purest shine,
More radiant then the Summers Sun-beams shows;
Each way illustrious, brave; and like to those
Comets we see by night; whose shagg'd portents
Fore-tell the comming of some dire events:
Or some full flame, which with a pride aspires,
Throwing about his wild, and active fires.
'Tis thou, above Nectar, O Divinest soule!
(Eternall in thy self) that canst controule
That, which subverts whole nature, grief and care;
Vexation of the mind, and damn'd Despaire.
'Tis thou, alone, who with thy Mistick Fan,
Work'st more then Wisdome, Art, or Nature can,
To rouze the sacred madnesse; and awake
The frost-bound-blood, and spirits; and to make
Them frantick with thy raptures, flashing through
The soule, like lightning, and as active too.
'Tis not Apollo can, or those thrice three
Castalian sisters, sing, if wanting thee.
Horace, Anacreon both had lost their fame,
Hadst thou not fill'd them with thy fire and flame.
Phoebean splendour! and thou Thespian spring!
Of which, sweet Swans must drink, before they sing
Their true-pac'd-Numbers, and their Holy-Layes,
Which makes them worthy Cedar, and the Bayes.
But why? why longer doe I gaze upon

Thee with the eye of admiration?
Since I must leave thee; and enforc'd, must say
To all thy witching beauties, Goe, Away.
But if thy whimpring looks doe ask me why?
Then know, that Nature bids thee goe, not I.
'Tis her erroneous self has made a braine
Uncapable of such a Soveraigne,
As is thy powerful selfe. Prethee not smile;
Or smile more inly; lest thy looks beguile
My vowes denounc'd in zeale, which thus much show thee,
That I have sworn, but by thy looks to know thee.
Let others drink thee freely; and desire
Thee and their lips espous'd; while I admire,
And love thee; but not taste thee. Let my Muse
Faile of thy former helps; and onely use
Her inadult'rate strength: what's done by me
Hereafter, shall smell of the Lamp, not thee.

Upon Glasco.
Epigram.

Glasco had none, but now some teeth has got;
Which though they furre, will neither ake, or rot.
Six teeth he has, whereof twice two are known
Made of a Haft, that was a Mutton-bone.
Which not for use, but meerly for the sight,
He weares all day, and drawes those teeth at night.

Upon Mrs. Eliz: Wheeler, under the name of Amarillis.

Sweet Amarillis, by a Spring's
Soft and soule-melting murmurings,
Slept; and thus sleeping, thither flew
A Robin-Red-brest; who at view,
Not seeing her at all to stir,
Brought leaves and mosse to cover her:
But while he, perking, there did prie
About the Arch of either eye;
The lid began to let out day;
At which poore Robin flew away:
And seeing her not dead, but all disleav'd;
He chirpt for joy, to see himself disceav'd.

The Custard.

For second course, last night, a Custard came
To th'board, so hot, as none co'd touch the same:
Furze, three or foure times with his cheeks did blow
Upon the Custard, and thus cooled so:
It seem'd by this time to admit the touch;
But none co'd eate it, 'cause it stunk so much.

To Myrrha hard-hearted.

Fold now thine armes; and hang the head,
Like to a Lillie withered:
Next, look thou like a sickly Moone;
Or like Jocasta in a swoone.
Then weep, and sigh, and softly goe,
Like to a widdow drown'd in woe:
Or like a Virgin full of ruth,
For the lost sweet-heart of her youth:
And all because, Faire Maid, thou art
Insensible of all my smart;
And of those evill dayes that be
Now posting on to punish thee.
The Gods are easie, and condemne
All such as are not soft like them.

The Eye.

Make me a heaven; and make me there
Many a lesse and greater spheare.
Make me the straight, and oblique lines;
The Motions, Lations, and the Signes.
Make me a Chariot, and a Sun;
And let them through a Zodiac run:
Next, place me Zones, and Tropicks there;
With all the Seasons of the Yeare.
Make me a Sun-set; and a Night:
And then present the Mornings-light
Cloath'd in her Chamlets of Delight.
To these, make Clouds to poure downe raine;
With weather foule, then faire againe.
And when, wise Artist, that thou hast,
With all that can be, this heaven grac't;
Ah! what is then this curious skie,
But onely my Corinna's eye?

Upon the much lamented, Mr. J. Warr.

What Wisdome, Learning, Wit, or Worth,
Youth, or sweet Nature, co'd bring forth,
Rests here with him; who was the Fame,
The Volumne of himselfe, and Name.
If, Reader, then thou wilt draw neere,
And doe an honour to thy teare;
Weep then for him, for whom laments
Not one, but many Monuments.

Upon Gryll.

Gryll eates, but ne're sayes Grace; To speak the troth,
Gryll either keeps his breath to coole his broth;
Or else because Grill's roste do's burn his Spit,
Gryll will not therefore say a Grace for it.

Upon Strut.

Strut, once a Fore-man of a Shop we knew;
But turn'd a Ladies Usher now, ('tis true:)
Tell me, has Strut got ere a title more?
No; he's but Fore-man, as he was before.

The suspition upon his over-much familiarity with a
Gentlewoman.

And must we part, because some say,
Loud is our love, and loose our play,
And more then well becomes the day?
Alas for pitty! and for us
Most innocent, and injur'd thus.
Had we kept close, or play'd within,
Suspition now had been the sinne,
And shame had follow'd long ere this,
T'ave plagu'd, what now unpunisht is.
But we as fearlesse of the Sunne,
As faultlesse; will not wish undone,
What now is done: since where no sin
Unbolts the doore, no shame comes in.
Then comely and most fragrant Maid,
Be you more warie, then afraid
Of these Reports; because you see
The fairest most suspected be.
The common formes have no one eye,
Or eare of burning jealousie
To follow them: but chiefly, where
Love makes the cheek, and chin a sphere
To dance and play in: (Trust me) there
Suspicion questions every haire.
Come, you are faire; and sho'd be seen
While you are in your sprightfull green:
And what though you had been embrac't
By me, were you for that unchast?
No, no, no more then is yond' Moone,
Which shining in her perfect Noone;
In all that great and glorious light,
Continues cold, as is the night.
Then, beauteous Maid, you may retire;
And as for me, my chast desire
Shall move t'wards you; although I see
Your face no more: So live you free
From Fames black lips, as you from me.

Hope heartens.

None goes to warfare, but with this intent;
The gaines must dead the feare of detriment.

Single life most secure.

Suspicion, Discontent, and Strife,
Come in for Dowrie with a Wife.

Some comfort in calamity.

To conquer'd men, some comfort 'tis to fall
By th'hand of him who is the Generall.

Upon Jollies wife.

First, Jollies wife is lame; then next, loose-hipt:
Squint-ey'd, hook-nos'd; and lastly, Kidney-lipt.

The Curse.
A Song.

Goe, perjur'd man; and if thou ere return
To see the small remainders in mine Urne:
When thou shalt laugh at my Religious dust;
And ask, Where's now the colour, forme and trust
Of Womans beauty? and with hand more rude
Rifle the Flowers which the Virgins strew'd:
Know, I have pray'd to Furie, that some wind
May blow my ashes up, and strike thee blind.

The wounded Cupid.
Song.

Cupid as he lay among
Roses, by a Bee was stung.
Whereupon in anger flying
To his Mother, said thus crying;
Help! O help! your Boy's a dying.
And why, my pretty Lad, said she?
Then blubbering, replyed he,
A winged Snake has bitten me,
Which Country people call a Bee.
At which she smil'd; then with her hairs
And kisses drying up his tears:
Alas! said she, my Wag! if this
Such a pernicious torment is:
Come tel me then, how great's the smart
Of those, thou woundest with thy Dart!

To Dewes.
A Song.

I burn, I burn; and beg of you
To quench, or coole me with your Dew.
I frie in fire, and so consume,
Although the Pile be all perfume.
Alas! the heat and death's the same;
Whether by choice, or common flame:
To be in Oyle of Roses drown'd,
Or water; where's the comfort found?
Both bring one death; and I die here,
Unlesse you coole me with a Teare:
Alas! I call; but ah! I see
Ye coole, and comfort all, but me.

The Vision.

Sitting alone (as one forsook)
Close by a Silver-shedding Brook;
With hands held up to Love, I wept;
And after sorrowes spent, I slept:
Then in a Vision I did see
A glorious forme appeare to me:
A Virgins face she had; her dresse
Was like a sprightly Spartanesse.
A silver bow with green silk strung,
Down from her comely shoulders hung:
And as she stood, the wanton Aire
Dandled the ringlets of her haire.
Her legs were such Diana shows,
When tuckt up she a hunting goes;
With Buskins shortned to descrie
The happy dawning of her thigh:
Which when I saw, I made accesse
To kisse that tempting nakednesse:
But she forbad me, with a wand
Of Mirtle she had in her hand:
And chiding me, said, Hence, Remove,
Herrick, thou art too coorse to love.

Love me little, love me long.

You say, to me-wards your affection's strong;
Pray love me little, so you love me long.
Slowly goes farre: The meane is best: Desire
Grown violent, do's either die, or tire.

Upon a Virgin kissing a Rose.

'Twas but a single Rose,
    Till you on it did breathe;
But since (me thinks) it shows
    Not so much Rose, as Wreathe.

Upon a Wife that dyed mad with Jealousie.

In this little Vault she lyes,
Here, with all her jealousies:
Quiet yet; but if ye make
Any noise, they both will wake,
And such spirits raise, 'twill then
Trouble Death to lay agen.

Upon the Bishop of Lincolne's Imprisonment.

Never was Day so over-sick with showres,
But that it had some intermitting houres.
Never was Night so tedious, but it knew
The Last Watch out, and saw the Dawning too.
Never was Dungeon so obscurely deep,
Wherein or Light, or Day, did never peep.
Never did Moone so ebbe, or seas so wane,
But they left Hope-seed to fill up againe.
So you, my Lord, though you have now your stay,
Your Night, your Prison, and your Ebbe; you may
Spring up afresh; when all these mists are spent,
And Star-like, once more, guild or Firmament.
Let but That Mighty Cesar speak, and then,
All bolts, all barres, all gates shall cleave; as when
That Earth-quake shook the house, and gave the stout
Apostles, way (unshackled) to goe out.
This, as I wish for, so I hope to see;
Though you (my Lord) have been unkind to me:
To wound my heart, and never to apply,
(When you had power) the meanest remedy:
Well; though my griefe by you was gall'd, the more;
Yet I bring Balme and Oile to heal your sore.

Disswasions from Idlenesse.

Cynthius pluck ye by the eare,
That ye may good doctrine heare.
Play not with the maiden-haire;
For each Ringlet there's a snare.
Cheek, and eye, and lip, and chin;
These are traps to take fooles in.
Armes, and hands, and all parts else,
Are but Toiles, or Manicles
Set on purpose to enthrall
Men, but Slothfulls most of all.
Live employ'd, and so live free
From these fetters; like to me
Who have found, and still can prove,
The lazie man the most doth love.

An Epithalamie to Sir Thomas Southwell and his Ladie.

Now, now's the time; so oft by truth
Promis'd sho'd come to crown your youth.
    Then Faire ones, doe not wrong
    Your joyes, by staying long:
    Or let Love's fire goe out,
    By lingring thus in doubt:
    But learn, that Time once lost,
    Is ne'r redeem'd by cost.
Then away; come, Hymen guide
To the bed, the bashfull Bride.

Is it (sweet maid) your fault these holy
Bridall-Rites goe on so slowly?
    Deare, is it this you dread,
    The losse of Maiden-head?
    Beleeve me; you will most
    Esteeme it when 'tis lost:
    Then it no longer keep,
    Lest Issue lye asleep.
Then away; come, Hymen guide
To the bed, the bashfull Bride.

These Precious-Pearly-Purling teares,
But spring from ceremonious feares.
    And 'tis but Native shame,
    That hides the loving flame:
    And may a while controule
    The soft and am'rous soule;
    But yet, Loves fire will wast
    Such bashfulnesse at last.
Then away; come, Hymen guide
To the bed, the bashfull Bride.

Night now hath watch'd her self half blind;
Yet not a Maiden-head resign'd!
    'Tis strange, ye will not flie
    To Love's sweet mysterie.

Might yon Full-Moon the sweets
Have, promis'd to your sheets;
    She soon wo'd leave her spheare,
    To be admitted there.
Then away; come, Hymen guide
To the bed, the bashfull Bride.

On, on devoutly, make no stay;
While Domiduca leads the way:
    And Genius who attends
    The bed for luckie ends:
    With Juno goes the houres,
    And Graces strewing flowers.
    And the boyes with sweet tunes sing,
    Hymen, O Hymen bring
Home the Turtles; Hymen guide
To the bed, the bashfull Bride.

Behold! how Hymens Taper-light
Shews you how much is spent of night.
    See, see the Bride-grooms Torch
    Halfe wasted in the porch.
    And now those Tapers five,
    That shew the womb shall thrive:
    Their silv'rie flames advance,
    To tell all prosp'rous chance
Still shall crown the happy life
Of the good man and the wife.

Move forward then your Rosie feet,
And make, what ere they touch, turn sweet.
    May all, like flowrie Meads
    Smell, where your soft foot treads;
    And every thing assume
    To it, the like perfume:
    As Zephirus when he 'spires
    Through Woodbine, and Sweet-bryers.
Then away; come Hymen, guide
To the bed the bashfull Bride.

And now the yellow Vaile, at last,
Over her fragrant cheek is cast.
 Now seems she to expresse
 A bashfull willingnesse:
 Shewing a heart consenting;
 As with a will repenting.
 Then gently lead her on
 With wise suspicion:
For that, Matrons say, a measure
Of that Passion sweetens Pleasure.

You, you that be of her neerest kin,
Now o're the threshold force her in.
 But to avert the worst;
 Let her, her fillets first
 Knit to the posts: this point
 Remembring, to anoint
 The sides: for 'tis a charme
 Strong against future harme:
And the evil deads, the which
There was hidden by the Witch.

O Venus! thou, to whom is known
The best way how to loose the Zone
 Of Virgins! Tell the Maid,
 She need not be afraid:
 And bid the Youth apply
 Close kisses, if she cry:
 And charge, he not forbears
 Her, though she wooe with teares.
Tel them, now they must adventer,
Since that Love and Night bid enter.

No Fatal Owle the Bedsted keeps,
With direful notes to fright your sleeps:
 No Furies, here about,
 To put the Tapers out,
 Watch, or did make the bed:
 'Tis Omen full of dread:
 But all faire signs appeare

Within the Chamber here.
Juno here, far off, doth stand
Cooling sleep with charming wand.

Virgins, weep not; 'twill come, when,
As she, so you'l be ripe for men.
      Then grieve her not, with saying
      She must no more a Maying:
      Or by Rose-buds devine,
      Who'l be her Valentine.
      Nor name those wanton reaks
      Y'ave had at Barly-breaks.
But now kisse her, and thus say,
Take time Lady while ye may.

Now barre the doors, the Bride-groom puts
The eager Boyes to gather Nuts.
      And now, both Love and Time
      To their full height doe clime:
      O! give them active heat
      And moisture, both compleat:
      Fit Organs for encrease,
      To keep, and to release
That, which may the honour'd Stem
Circle with a Diadem.

And now, Behold! the Bed or Couch
That ne'r knew Brides, or Bride-grooms touch,
      Feels in it selfe a fire;
      And tickled with Desire,
      Pants with a Downie brest,
      As with a heart possest:
      Shrugging as it did move,
      Ev'n with the soule of love.
And (oh!) had it but a tongue,
Doves, 'two'd say, yee bill too long.

O enter then! but see ye shun
A sleep, untill the act be done.
        Let kisses, in their close,
        Breathe as the Damask Rose:
        Or sweet, as is that gumme
        Doth from Panchaia come.
        Teach Nature now to know,
        Lips can make Cherries grow
Sooner, then she, ever yet,
In her wisdome co'd beget.

On your minutes, hours, dayes, months, years,
Drop the fat blessing of the sphears.
        That good, which Heav'n can give
        To make you bravely live;
        Fall, like a spangling dew,
        By day, and night on you.
        May Fortunes Lilly-hand
        Open at your command;
With all luckie Birds to side
With the Bride-groom, and the Bride.

Let bounteous Fate your spindles full
Fill, and winde up with whitest wooll.
        Let them not cut the thred
        Of life, untill ye bid.
        May Death yet come at last;
        And not with desp'rate hast:
        But when ye both can say,
        Come, Let us now away.
Be ye to the Barn then born,
Two, like two ripe shocks of corn.

Teares are Tongues.

When Julia chid, I stood as mute the while,
As is the fish, or tonguelesse Crocadile.
Aire coyn'd to words, my Julia co'd not heare;
But she co'd see each eye to stamp a teare:
By which, mine angry Mistresse might descry,
Teares are the noble language of the eye.
And when true love of words is destitute,
The Eyes by tears speak, while the Tongue is mute.

Upon a young mother of many children.

Let all chaste Matrons, when they chance to see
My num'rous issue: Praise, and pitty me.
Praise me, for having such a fruitfull wombe;
Pity me too, who found so soone a Tomb.

To Electra.

I'll come to thee in all those shapes
As Jove did, when he made his rapes:
Onely, I'll not appeare to thee,
As he did once to Semele.
Thunder and Lightning I'll lay by,
To talk with thee familiarly.
Which done, then quickly we'll undresse
To one and th'others nakednesse.
And ravisht, plunge into the bed,
(Bodies and souls commingled)
And kissing, so as none may heare,
We'll weary all the Fables there.

His wish.

It is sufficient if we pray
To Jove, who gives, and takes away:
Let him the Land and Living finde;
Let me alone to fit the mind.

His Protestation to Perilla.

Noone-day and Midnight shall at once be seene:
Trees, at one time, shall be both sere and greene:
Fire and water shall together lye
In one-self-sweet-conspiring sympathie:
Summer and Winter shall at one time show
Ripe eares of corne, and up to th'eares in snow:
Seas shall be sandlesse; Fields devoid of grasse;
Shapelesse the world (as when all Chaos was)
Before, my deare Perilla, I will be
False to my vow, or fall away from thee.

Love perfumes all parts.

If I kisse Anthea's brest,
There I smell the Phenix nest:
If her lip, the most sincere
Altar of Incense, I smell there.
Hands, and thighs, and legs, are all
Richly Aromaticall.
Goddesse Isis cann't transfer
Musks and Ambers more from her:
Nor can Juno sweeter be,
When she lyes with Jove, then she.

To Julia.

Permit me, Julia, now to goe away;
Or by thy love, decree me here to stay.
If thou wilt say, that I shall live with thee;
Here shall my endless Tabernacle be:
If not, (as banisht) I will live alone
There, where no language ever yet was known.

On himselfe.

Love-sick I am, and must endure
A desp'rate grief, that finds no cure.
Ah me! I try; and trying, prove,
No Herbs have power to cure Love.
Only one Soveraign salve, I know,
And that is Death, the end of Woe.

Vertue is sensible of suffering.

Though a wise man all pressures can sustaine;
His vertue still is sensible of paine:
Large shoulders though he has, and well can beare,
He feeles when Packs do pinch him; and the where.

The cruell Maid.

And cruell Maid, because I see
You scornfull of my love, and me:
I'll trouble you no more; but goe
My way, where you shall never know
What is become of me: there I
Will find me out a path to die;
Or learne some way how to forget
You, and your name, for ever: yet
Ere I go hence; know this from me,
What will, in time, your Fortune be:
This to your coynesse I will tell;
And having spoke it once, Farewell.
The Lillie will not long endure;
Nor the Snow continue pure:
The Rose, the Violet, one day
See, both these Lady-flowers decay:
And you must fade, as well as they.
And it may chance that Love may turn,
And (like to mine) make your heart burn
And weep to see't; yet this thing doe,
That my last Vow commends to you:
When you shall see that I am dead,
For pitty let a teare be shed;
And (with your Mantle o're me cast)
Give my cold lips a kisse at last:
If twice you kisse, you need not feare,
That I shall stir, or live more here.
Next, hollow out a Tombe to cover
Me; me, the most despised Lover:
And write thereon, *This, Reader, know,*
Love kill'd this man. No more but so.

To Dianeme.

Sweet, be not proud of those two eyes,
Which Star-like sparkle in their skies:
Nor be you proud, that you can see
All hearts your captives; yours, yet free:
Be you not proud of that rich haire,
Which wantons with the Love-sick aire:
When as that Rubie, which you weare,
Sunk from the tip of your soft eare,
Will last to be a precious Stone,
When all your world of Beautie's gone.

To the King,
To cure the Evill.

To find that Tree of Life, whose Fruits did feed,
And Leaves did heale, all sick of humane seed:
To finde Bethesda, and an Angel there,
Stirring the waters, I am come; and here,
At last, I find, (after my much to doe)
The Tree, Bethesda, and the Angel too:
And all in Your Blest Hand, which has the powers
Of all those suppling-healing herbs and flowers.
To that soft Charm, that Spell, that Magick Bough,
That high Enchantment I betake me now:
And to that Hand, (the Branch of Heavens faire Tree)
I kneele for help; O! lay that hand on me,
Adored Cesar! and my Faith is such,
I shall be heal'd, if that my King but touch.
The Evill is not Yours: my sorrow sings,
Mine is the Evill, but the Cure, the Kings.

His misery in a Mistresse.

Water, Water I espie:
Come, and coole ye; all who frie
In your loves; but none as I.

Though a thousand showres be
Still a falling, yet I see
Not one drop to light on me.

Happy you, who can have seas
For to quench ye, or some ease
From your kinder Mistresses.

I have one, and she alone,
Of a thousand thousand known,
Dead to all compassion.

Such an one, as will repeat
Both the cause, and make the heat
More by Provocation great.

Gentle friends, though I despaire
Of my cure, doe you beware
Of those Girles, which cruell are.

To a Gentlewoman objecting to him his gray haires.

Am I despis'd, because you say,
And I dare sweare, that I am gray?
Know, Lady, you have but your day:
And time will come when you shall weare
Such frost and snow upon your haire:
And when (though long it comes to passe)
You question with your Looking-glasse;
And in that sincere Christall seek,
But find no Rose-bud in your cheek:
Nor any bed to give the shew
Where such a rare Carnation grew.
Ah! then too late, close in your chamber keeping,
     It will be told
     That you are old;
By those true teares y'are weeping.

To Cedars.

If 'mongst my many Poems, I can see
One, onely, worthy to be washt by thee:
I live for ever; let the rest all lye
In dennes of Darkness, or condemn'd to die.

Upon Cupid.

Love, like a Gypsie, lately came;
    And did me much importune
To see my hand; that by the same
    He might fore-tell my Fortune.

He saw my Palme; and then, said he,
    I tell thee, by this score here;
That thou, within few months, shalt be
    The youthfull Prince D'Amour here.

I smil'd; and bade him once more prove,
    And by some crosse-line show it;
That I co'd ne'r be Prince of Love,
    Though here the Princely Poet.

How Primroses came green.

Virgins, time-past, known were these,
Troubled with Green-sicknesses,
Turn'd to flowers: Stil the hieu,
Sickly Girles, they beare of you.

To Jos: Lo: Bishop of Exeter.

Whom sho'd I feare to write to, if I can
Stand before you, my learn'd Diocesan?
And never shew blood-guiltinesse, or feare
To see my Lines Excathedrated here.
Since none so good are, but you may condemne;
Or here so bad, but you may pardon them.
If then, (my Lord) to sanctifie my Muse
One onely Poem out of all you'l chuse;
And mark it for a Rapture nobly writ,
'Tis Good Confirm'd; for you have Bishop't it.

Upon a black Twist, rounding the Arme of the Countesse of
Carlile.

I saw about her spotlesse wrist,
Of blackest silk, a curious twist;
Which, circumvolving gently, there
Enthrall'd her Arme, as Prisoner.
Dark was the Jayle; but as if light
Had met t'engender with the night;
Or so, as Darknesse made a stay
To shew at once, both night and day.
One fancie more! but if there be
Such Freedome in Captivity;
I beg of Love, that ever I
May in like Chains of Darknesse lie.

On himselfe.

I feare no Earthly Powers;
But care for crowns of flowers:
And love to have my Beard
With Wine and Oile besmear'd
This day I'll drowne all sorrow;
Who knowes to live to morrow?

Upon Pagget.

Pagget, a School-boy, got a Sword, and then
He vow'd Destruction both to Birch, and Men:
Who wo'd not think this Yonker fierce to fight?
Yet comming home, but somewhat late, (last night)
Untrusse, his Master bade him; and that word
Made him take up his shirt, lay down his sword.

A Ring presented to Julia.

Julia, I bring
To thee this Ring.
Made for thy finger fit;
To shew by this,
That our love is
(Or sho'd be) like to it.

Close though it be,
The joynt is free:
So when Love's yoke is on,
It must not gall,
Or fret at all
With hard oppression.

But it must play
Still either way;
And be, too, such a yoke,
As not too wide,
To over-slide;
Or be so strait to choak.

So we, who beare,
This beame, must reare
Our selves to such a height:
As that the stay
Of either may
Create the burden light.

And as this round
Is no where found
To flaw, or else to sever:
So let our love
As endless prove;
And pure as Gold for ever.

To the Detracter.

Where others love, and praise my Verses; still
Thy long-black-Thumb-nail marks 'em out for ill:
A fellon take it, or some Whit-flaw come
For to unslate, or to untile that thumb!
But cry thee Mercy: Exercise thy nailes
To scratch or claw, so that thy tongue not railes:
Some numbers prurient are, and some of these
Are wanton with their itch; scratch, and 'twill please.

Upon the same.

I ask't thee oft, what Poets thou hast read,
And lik'st the best? Still thou reply'st, The dead.
I shall, ere long, with green turfs cover'd be;
Then sure thou't like, or thou wilt envie me.

Julia's *Petticoat*

Thy Azure Robe I did behold,
As airy as the leaves of gold,
Which, erring here, and wand'ring there,
Pleas'd with transgression everywhere:
Sometimes 'twould pant, and sigh, and heave,
As if to stir it scarce had leave:
But having got it; thereupon
'Twould make a brave expansion.
And pound'd with stars it show'd to me
Like a *Celestiall Canopie*.
Sometimes 'twould blaze, and then abate,
Like to a flame grown moderate:
Sometimes away 'twould wildly fling,
Then to thy thighs so closely cling
That some conceit did melt me down,
As lovers fall into a swoon:
And, all confus'd, I there did lie
Drown'd in Delights, but could not die.
That Leading Cloud I follow'd still,
Hoping t'have seen of it my fill;
But ah! I could not: should it move
To Life Eternal, I could love.

To Musick.

Begin to charme, and as thou stroak'st mine eares
With thy enchantment, melt me into tears.
Then let thy active hand scu'd o're thy Lyre:
And make my spirits frantick with the fire.
That done, sink down into a silv'rie straine;
And make me smooth as Balme, and Oile againe.

Distrust.

To safe-guard Man from wrongs, there nothing must
Be truer to him, then a wise Distrust.
And to thy selfe be best this sentence knowne,
Heare all men speak; but credit few or none.

Corinna's going a Maying.

Get up, get up for shame, the Blooming Morne
Upon her wings presents the god unshorne.
    See how Aurora throwes her faire
    Fresh-quilted colours through the aire:
    Get up, sweet-Slug-a-bed, and see
    The Dew-bespangling Herbe and Tree.
Each Flower has wept, and bow'd toward the East,
Above an houre since; yet you not drest,
    Nay! not so much as out of bed?
    When all the Birds have Mattens seyd,
    And sung their thankfull Hymnes: 'tis sin,
    Nay, profanation to keep in,
When as a thousand Virgins on this day,
Spring, sooner then the Lark, to fetch in May.

Rise; and put on your Foliage, and be seene
To come forth, like the Spring-time, fresh and greene;
    And sweet as Flora. Take no care
    For Jewels for your Gowne, or Haire:
    Feare not; the leaves will strew
    Gemms in abundance upon you:
Besides, the childhood of the Day has kept,
Against you come, some Orient Pearls unwept:
    Come, and receive them while the light
    Hangs on the Dew-locks of the night:
    And Titan on the Eastern hill
    Retires himselfe, or else stands still
Till you come forth. Wash, dresse, be briefe in praying:
Few Beads are best, when once we goe a Maying.

Come, my Corinna, come; and comming, marke
How each field turns a street; each street a Parke
    Made green, and trimm'd with trees: see how
    Devotion gives each House a Bough,
    Or Branch: Each Porch, each doore, ere this,
    An Arke a Tabernacle is
Made up of white-thorn neatly enterwove;

As if here were those cooler shades of love.
    Can such delights be in the street,
    And open fields, and we not see't?
    Come, we'll abroad; and let's obay
    The Proclamation made for May:
And sin no more, as we have done, by staying;
But my Corinna, come, let's goe a Maying.

There's not a budding Boy, or Girle, this day,
But is got up, and gone to bring in May.
    A deale of Youth, ere this, is come
    Back, and with White-thorn laden home.
    Some have dispatcht their Cakes and Creame,
    Before that we have left to dreame:
And some have wept, and woo'd, and plighted Troth,
And chose their Priest, ere we can cast off sloth:
    Many a green-gown has been given;
    Many a kisse, both odde and even:
    Many a glance too has been sent
    From out the eye, Loves Firmament:
Many a jest told of the Keyes betraying
This night, and Locks pickt, yet w'are not a Maying.

Come, let us goe, while we are in our prime;
And take the harmlesse follie of the time.
    We shall grow old apace, and die
    Before we know our liberty.
    Our life is short; and our dayes run
    As fast away as do's the Sunne:
And as a vapour, or a drop of raine
Once lost, can ne'r be found againe:
    So when or you or I are made
    A fable, song, or fleeting shade;
    All love, all liking, all delight
    Lies drown'd with us in endlesse night.
Then while time serves, and we are but decaying;
Come, my Corinna, come, let's goe a Maying.

On Julia's breath.

Breathe, Julia, breathe, and I'll protest,
    Nay more, I'll deeply sweare,
That all the Spices of the East
    Are circumfused there.

Upon a Child.
An Epitaph.

But borne, and like a short Delight,
I glided by my Parents sight.
That done, the harder Fates deny'd
My longer stay, and so I dy'd.
If pittying my sad Parents Teares,
You'l spil a tear, or two with theirs:
And with some flowrs my grave bestrew,
Love and they'l thank you for't. Adieu.

A Dialogue betwixt Horace and Lydia,
Translated Anno 1627. and set by Mr. Ro: Ramsey.

Hor. While, Lydia, I was lov'd of thee,
Nor any was preferr'd 'fore me
To hug thy whitest neck: Then I,
The Persian King liv'd not more happily.

Lyd. While thou no other didst affect,
Nor Cloe was of more respect;
Then Lydia, far-fam'd Lydia,
I flourish't more then Roman Ilia.

Hor. Now Thracian Cloe governs me,
Skilfull i'th' Harpe, and Melodie:
For whose affection, Lydia, I
(So Fate spares her) am well content to die.

Lyd. My heart now set on fire is
By Ornithes sonne, young Calais;
For whose commutuall flames here I
(To save his life) twice am content to die.

Hor. Say our first loves we sho'd revoke,
And sever'd, joyne in brazen yoke:
Admit I Cloe put away,
And love againe love-cast-off Lydia?

Lyd. Though mine be brighter then the Star;
Thou lighter then the Cork by far:
Rough as th'Adratick sea, yet I
Will live with thee, or else for thee will die.

The captiv'd Bee:
or, The little Filcher.

As Julia once a-slumb'ring lay,
It chanc't a Bee did flie that way,
(After a dew, or dew-like shower)
To tipple freely in a flower.
For some rich flower, he took the lip
Of Julia, and began to sip;
But when he felt he suckt from thence
Hony, and in the quintessence:
He drank so much he scarce co'd stir;
So Julia took the Pilferer.
And thus surpriz'd (as Filchers use)
He thus began himselfe t'excuse:
Sweet Lady-Flower, I never brought .
Hither the least one theeving thought:
But taking those rare lips of yours
For some fresh, fragrant, luscious flowers:
I thought I might there take a taste,
Where so much sirrop ran at waste.
Besides, know this, I never sting
The flower that gives me nourishing:
But with a kisse, or thanks, doe pay
For Honie, that I beare away.
This said, he laid his little scrip
Of hony, 'fore her Ladiship:
And told her, (as some tears did fall)
That, that he took, and that was all.
At which she smil'd; and bade him goe
And take his bag; but thus much know,
When next he came a pilfring so,
He sho'd from her full lips derive,
Hony enough to fill his hive.

Upon Prig.

Prig now drinks Water, who before drank Beere:
What's now the cause? we know the case is cleere:
Look in Prig's purse, the chev'rell there tells you
Prig mony wants, either to buy, or brew.

An Ode to Master Endymion Porter,
upon his Brothers death.

Not all thy flushing Sunnes are set,
      Herrick, as yet:
Nor doth this far-drawn Hemisphere
Frown, and look sullen ev'ry where.
Daies may conclude in nights; and Suns may rest,
As dead, within the West;
Yet the next Morne, re-guild the fragrant East.

Alas for me! that I have lost
      E'en all almost:
Sunk is my sight; set is my Sun;
And all the loome of life undone:
The staffe, the Elme, the prop, the shelt'ring wall
Whereon my Vine did crawle,
Now, now, blowne downe; needs must the old stock fall.

Yet, Porter, while thou keep'st alive,
      In death I thrive:
And like a Phenix re-aspire
From out my Narde, and Fun'rall fire:
And as I prune my feather'd youth, so I
Do mar'l how I co'd die,
When I had Thee, my chiefe Preserver, by.

I'm up, I'm up, and blesse that hand,
      Which makes me stand
Now as I doe; and but for thee,
I must confesse, I co'd not be.
The debt is paid: for he who doth resigne
Thanks to the gen'rous Vine;
Invites fresh Grapes to fill his Presse with Wine.

To his dying Brother, Master
William Herrick.

Life of my life, take not so soone thy flight,
But stay the time till we have bade Good night.
Thou hast both Wind and Tide with thee; Thy way
As soone dispatcht is by the Night, as Day.
Let us not then so rudely henceforth goe
Till we have wept, kist, sigh't, shook hands, or so.
There's paine in parting; and a kind of hell,
When once true-lovers take their last Fare-well.
What? shall we two our endlesse leaves take here
Without a sad looke, or a solemne teare?
He knowes not Love, that hath not this truth proved,
Love is most loth to leave the thing beloved.
Pay we our Vowes, and goe; yet when we part,
Then, even then, I will bequeath my heart
Into thy loving hands: For I'll keep none
To warme my Breast, when thou my Pulse art gone.
No, here I'll last, and walk (a harmless shade)
About this Urne, wherein thy Dust is laid,
To guard it so, as nothing here shall be
Heavy, to hurt those sacred seeds of thee.

The Olive Branch.

Sadly I walk't within the field,
To see what comfort it wo'd yeeld:
And as I went my private way,
An Olive-branch before me lay:
And seeing it, I made a stay.
And took it up, and view'd it; then
Kissing the Omen, said Amen:
Be, be it so, and let this be
A Divination unto me:
That in short time my woes shall cease;
And Love shall crown my End with Peace.

Upon Much-more. Epigram.

Much-more, provides, and hoords up like an Ant;
Yet Much-more still complains he is in want.
Let Much-more justly pay his tythes; then try
How both his Meale and Oile will multiply.

To Cherry-blossomes.

Ye may simper, blush, and smile,
And perfume the aire a while:
But (sweet things) ye must be gone;
Fruit, ye know, is comming on:
Then, Ah! Then, where is your grace,
When as Cherries come in place?

How Lillies came white.

White though ye be; yet, Lillies, know,
From the first ye were not so:
But I'll tell ye
What befell ye;
Cupid and his Mother lay
In a Cloud; while both did play,
He with his pretty finger prest
The rubie niplet of her breast;
Out of the which, the creame of light,
Like to a Dew,
Fell downe on you,
And made ye white.

To Pansies.

Ah, cruell Love! must I endure
Thy many scorns, and find no cure?
Say, are thy medicines made to be
Helps to all others, but to me?
I'll leave thee, and to Pansies come;
Comforts you'l afford me some:
You can ease my heart, and doe
What Love co'd ne'r be brought unto.

On Gelli-flowers begotten.

What was't that fell but now
    From that warme kisse of ours?
Look, look, by Love I vow
    They were two Gelli-flowers.

Let's kisse, and kisse agen;
    For if so be our closes
Make Gelli-flowers, then
    I'm sure they'l fashion Roses.

The Lilly in a Christal.

You have beheld a smiling Rose
  When Virgins hands have drawn
  O'r it a Cobweb-Lawne:
And here, you see, this Lilly shows,
  Tomb'd in a Christal stone,
More faire in this transparent case,
  Then when it grew alone;
  And had but single grace.

You see how Creame but naked is;
  Nor daunces in the eye
  Without a Strawberrie:
Or some fine tincture, like to this,
  Which draws the sight thereto,
More by that wantoning with it;
  Then when the paler hieu
  No mixture did admit.

You see how Amber through the streams
  More gently stroaks the sight,
  With some conceal'd delight;
Then when he darts his radiant beams
  Into the boundlesse aire:
Where either too much light his worth
  Doth all at once impaire,
  Or set it little forth.

Put Purple Grapes, or Cherries in-
  To Glasse, and they will send
  More beauty to commend
Them, from that cleane and subtile skin,
  Then if they naked stood,
And had no other pride at all,
  But their own flesh and blood,
  And tinctures naturall.

Thus Lillie, Rose, Grape, Cherry, Creame,

And Straw-berry do stir
More love, when they transfer
A weak, a soft, a broken beame;
Then if they sho'd discover
At full their proper excellence;
Without some Scean cast over,
To juggle with the sense.

Thus let this Christal'd Lillie be
A Rule, how far to teach,
Your nakednesse must reach:
And that, no further, then we see
Those glaring colours laid
By Arts wise hand, but to this end
They sho'd obey a shade;
Lest they too far extend.

So though y'are white as Swan, or Snow,
And have the power to move
A world of men to love:
Yet, when your Lawns & Silks shal flow;
And that white cloud divide
Into a doubtful Twi-light; then,
Then will your hidden Pride
Raise greater fires in men.

To his Booke.

Like to a Bride, come forth my Book, at last,
With all thy richest jewels over-cast:
Say, if there be 'mongst many jems here; one
Deservelesse of the name of Paragon:
Blush not at all for that; since we have set
Some Pearls on Queens, that have been counterfet.

Upon some women.

Thou who wilt not love, doe this;
Learne of me what Woman is.
Something made of thred and thrumme;
A meere Botch of all and some.
Pieces, patches, ropes of haire;
In-laid Garbage ev'ry where.
Out-side silk, and out-side Lawne;
Sceanes to cheat us neatly drawne.
False in legs, and false in thighes;
False in breast, teeth, haire, and eyes:
False in head, and false enough;
Onely true in shreds and stuffe.

Upon Batt.

Batt he gets children, not for love to reare 'em;
But out of hope his wife might die to beare 'em.

Supreme fortune falls soonest.

While leanest Beasts in Pastures feed,
The fattest Oxe the first must bleed.

Upon Gubbs. Epigram.

Gubbs call's his children Kitlings: and wo'd bound
(Some say) for joy, to see those Kitlings drown'd.

Safety on the Shore.

What though the sea be calme? Trust to the shore:
Ships have been drown'd, where late they danc't before.

The Welcome to Sack.

So soft streams meet, so springs with gladder smiles
Meet after long divorcement by the Iles:
When Love (the child of likenesse) urgeth on
Their Christal natures to an union.
So meet stolne kisses, when the Moonie nights
Call forth fierce Lovers to their wisht Delights:
So Kings & Queens meet, when Desire convinces
All thoughts, but such as aime at getting Princes,
As I meet thee. Soule of my life, and fame!
Eternall Lamp of Love! whose radiant flame
Out-glares the Heav'ns Osiris; and thy gleams
Out-shine the splendour of his mid-day beams. Sun
Welcome, O welcome my illustrious Spouse;
Welcome as are the ends unto my Vowes:
I! far more welcome then the happy soile,
The Sea-scourg'd Merchant, after all his toile,
Salutes with tears of joy; when fires betray
The smoakie chimneys of his Ithaca.
Where hast thou been so long from my embraces,
Poore pittyed Exile? Tell me, did thy Graces
Flie discontented hence, and for a time
Did rather choose to blesse another clime?
Or went'st thou to this end, the more to move me,
By thy short absence, to desire and love thee?
Why frowns my Sweet? Why won't my Saint confer
Favours on me, her fierce Idolater?
Why are Those Looks, Those Looks the which have been
Time-past so fragrant, sickly now drawn in
Like a dull Twi-light? Tell me; and the fault
I'll expiate with Sulphur, Haire, and Salt:
And with the Christal humour of the spring,
Purge hence the guilt, and kill this quarrelling.
Wo't thou not smile, or tell me what's amisse?
Have I been cold to hug thee, too remisse,
Too temp'rate in embracing? Tell me, ha's desire
To thee-ward dy'd i'th'embers, and no fire
Left in this rak't-up Ash-heap, as a mark

To testifie the glowing of a spark?
Have I divorc't thee onely to combine
In hot Adult'ry with another Wine?
True, I confesse I left thee, and appeale
'Twas done by me, more to confirme my zeale,
And double my affection on thee; as doe those,
Whose love growes more enflam'd, by being Foes.
But to forsake thee ever, co'd there be
A thought of such like possibilitie?
When thou thy selfe dar'st say, thy Iles shall lack
Grapes, before Herrick leaves Canarie Sack.
Thou mak'st me ayrie, active to be born,
Like Iphyclus, upon the tops of Corn.
Thou mak'st me nimble, as the winged howers,
To dance and caper on the heads of flowers,
And ride the Sun-beams. Can there be a thing
Under the heavenly Isis, that can bring The Moon
More love unto my life, or can present
My Genius with a fuller blandishment?
Illustrious Idoll! co'd th'AEgyptians seek
Help from the Garlick, Onyon, and the Leek,
And pay no vowes to thee? who wast their best
God, and far more transcendent then the rest?
Had Cassius, that weak Water-drinker, known
Thee in thy Vine, or had but tasted one
Small Chalice of thy frantick liquor; He
As the wise Cato had approv'd of thee.
Had not Joves son, that brave Tyrinthian Swain, Hercules
(Invited to the Thesbian banquet) ta'ne
Full goblets of thy gen'rous blood; his spright
Ne'r had kept heat for fifty Maids that night.
Come, come and kisse me; Love and lust commends
Thee, and thy beauties; kisse, we will be friends,
Too strong for Fate to break us: Look upon
Me, with that full pride of complexion,
As Queenes, meet Queenes; or come thou unto me,
As Cleopatra came to Anthonie;
When her high carriage did at once present
To the Triumvir, Love and Wonderment.
Swell up my nerves with spirit; let my blood

Run through my veines, like to a hasty flood.
Fill each part full of fire, active to doe
What thy commanding soule shall put it to.
And till I turne Apostate to thy love,
Which here I vow to serve, doe not remove
Thy Fiers from me; but Apollo's curse
Blast these-like actions, or a thing that's worse;
When these Circumstants shall but live to see
The time that I prevaricate from thee.
Call me The sonne of Beere, and then confine
Me to the Tap, the Tost, the Turfe; Let Wine
Ne'r shine upon me; May my Numbers all
Run to a sudden Death, and Funerall.
And last, when thee (deare Spouse) I disavow,
Ne'r may Prophetique Daphne crown my Brow.

Impossibilities to his friend.

My faithful friend, if you can see
The Fruit to grow up, or the Tree:
If you can see the colour come
Into the blushing Peare, or Plum:
If you can see the water grow
To cakes of Ice, or flakes of Snow:
If you can see, that drop of raine
Lost in the wild sea, once againe:
If you can see, how Dreams do creep
Into the Brain by easie sleep:
Then there is hope that you may see
Her love me once, who now hates me.

Upon Luggs. Epigram.

Luggs, by the Condemnation of the Bench,
Was lately whipt for lying with a Wench.
Thus Paines and Pleasures turne by turne succeed:
He smarts at last, who do's not first take heed.

To live merrily, and to trust to
Good Verses.

Now is the time for mirth,
    Nor cheek, or tongue be dumbe:
For with the flowrie earth,
    The golden pomp is come.

The golden Pomp is come;
    For now each tree do's weare
(Made of her Pap and Gum)
    Rich beads of Amber here.

Now raignes the Rose, and now
    Th'Arabian Dew besmears
My uncontrolled brow,
    And my retorted haires.

Homer, this Health to thee,
    In Sack of such a kind,
That it wo'd make thee see,
    Though thou wert ne'r so blind.

Next, Virgil, I'll call forth,
    To pledge this second Health
In Wine, whose each cup's worth
    An Indian Common-wealth.

A Goblet next I'll drink
    To Ovid; and suppose,
Made he the pledge, he'd think
    The world had all one Nose.

Then this immensive cup
    Of Aromatike wine,
Catullus, I quaffe up
    To that Terce Muse of thine.

Wild I am now with heat;
    O Bacchus! coole thy Raies!
Or frantick I shall eate
    Thy Thyrse, and bite the Bayes.

Round, round, the roof do's run;
    And being ravisht thus,
Come, I will drink a Tun
    To my Propertius.

Now, to Tibullus, next,
    This flood I drink to thee:
But stay; I see a Text,
    That this presents to me.

Behold, Tibullus lies
    Here burnt, whose smal return
Of ashes, scarce suffice
    To fill a little Urne.

Trust to good Verses then;
    They onely will aspire,
When Pyramids, as men,
    Are lost, i'th'funerall fire.

And when all Bodies meet
    In Lethe to be drown'd;
Then onely Numbers sweet,
    With endless life are crown'd.

Faire dayes: or, Dawnes deceitfull.

Faire was the Dawne; and but e'ne now the Skies
Shew'd like to Creame, enspir'd with Strawberries:
But on a sudden, all was chang'd and gone
That smil'd in that first-sweet complexion.
Then Thunder-claps and Lightning did conspire
To teare the world, or set it all on fire.
What trust to things below, when as we see,
As Men, the Heavens have their Hypocrisie?

Lips Tonguelesse.

For my part, I never care
For those lips, that tongue-ty'd are:
Tell-tales I wo'd have them be
Of my Mistresse, and of me.
Let them prattle how that I
Sometimes freeze, and sometimes frie:
Let them tell how she doth move
Fore- or backward in her love:
Let them speak by gentle tones,
One and th'others passions:
How we watch, and seldome sleep;
How by Willowes we doe weep:
How by stealth we meet, and then
Kisse, and sigh, so part agen.
This the lips we will permit
For to tell, not publish it.

To the Fever, not to trouble Julia.

Th'ast dar'd too farre; but Furie now forbeare
To give the least disturbance to her haire:
But lesse presume to lay a Plait upon
Her skins most smooth, and cleare expansion.
'Tis like a Lawnie-Firmament as yet
Quite dispossest of either fray, or fret.
Come thou not neere that Filmne so finely spred,
Where no one piece is yet unlevelled.
This if thou dost, woe to thee Furie, woe,
I'll send such Frost, such Haile, such Sleet, and Snow,
Such Flesh-quakes, Palsies, and such fears as shall
Dead thee to th'most, if not destroy thee all.
And thou a thousand thousand times shalt be
More shak't thy selfe, then she is scorch't by thee.

To Violets.

Welcome Maids of Honour,
    You doe bring
    In the Spring;
And wait upon her.

She has Virgins many,
    Fresh and faire;
    Yet you are
More sweet then any.

Y'are the Maiden Posies,
    And so grac't,
    To be plac't,
'Fore Damask Roses.

Yet though thus respected,
    By and by
    Ye doe lie,
Poore Girles, neglected.

Upon Bunce. Epigram.

Mony thou ow'st me; Prethee fix a day
For payment promis'd, though thou never pay:
Let it be Doomes-day; nay, take longer scope;
Pay when th'art honest; let me have some hope.

To Carnations. A Song.

Stay while ye will, or goe;
    And leave no scent behind ye:
Yet trust me, I shall know
    The place, where I may find ye.

Within my Lucia's cheek,
    (Whose Livery ye weare)
Play ye at Hide or Seek,
    I'm sure to find ye there

To the Virgins, to make much of Time.

Gather ye Rose-buds while ye may,
    Old Time is still a flying:
And this same flower that smiles to day,
    To morrow will be dying.

The glorious Lamp of Heaven, the Sun,
    The higher he's a getting;
The sooner will his Race be run,
    And neerer he's to Setting.

That Age is best, which is the first,
    When Youth and Blood are warmer;
But being spent, the worse, and worst
    Times, still succeed the former.

Then be not coy, but use your time;
    And while ye may, goe marry:
For having lost but once your prime,
    You may for ever tarry.

Safety to look to ones selfe.

For my neighbour I'll not know,
Whether high he builds or no:
Onely this I'll look upon,
Firm be my foundation.
Sound, or unsound, let it be;
'Tis the lot ordain'd for me.
He who to the ground do's fall,
Has not whence to sink at all.

To his Friend, on the untuneable Times.

Play I co'd once; but (gentle friend) you see
My Harp hung up, here on the Willow tree.
Sing I co'd once; and bravely too enspire
(With luscious Numbers) my melodious Lyre.
Draw I co'd once (although not stocks or stones,
Amphion-like) men made of flesh and bones,
Whether I wo'd; but (ah!) I know not how,
I feele in me, this transmutation now.
Griefe, (my deare friend) has first my Harp unstrung;
Wither'd my hand, and palsie-struck my tongue.

His Poetrie his Pillar.

Onely a little more
    I have to write,
    Then I'll give o're,
And bid the world Good-night.

'Tis but a flying minute,
    That I must stay,
    Or linger in it;
And then I must away.

O time that cut'st down all!
    And scarce leav'st here
    Memoriall
Of any men that were.

How many lye forgot
    In Vaults beneath?
    And piece-meale rot
Without a fame in death?

Behold this living stone,
    I reare for me,
    Ne'r to be thrown
Downe, envious Time by thee.

Pillars let some set up,
    (If so they please)
    Here is my hope,
And my Pyramides.

A Pastorall upon the birth of Prince Charles, Presented to the King, and Set by Mr. Nic: Laniere.

The Speakers, Mirtillo, Amintas, and Amarillis.

Amin. Good day, Mirtillo. Mirt. And to you no lesse:
And all faire Signs lead on our Shepardesse.
  Amar. With all white luck to you. Mirt. But say, what news
Stirs in our Sheep-walk? Amin. None, save that my Ewes,
My Weathers, Lambes, and wanton Kids are well,
Smooth, faire, and fat; none better I can tell:
Or that this day Menalchas keeps a feast
For his Sheep-shearers. Mir. True, these are the least.
But dear Amintas, and sweet Amarillis,
Rest but a while here, by this bank of Lillies,
And lend a gentle eare to one report
The Country has. Amint. From whence? Amar. From whence?
Mir. The Court Three dayes before the shutting in of May,
(With whitest Wool be ever crown'd that day!)
To all our joy, a sweet-fac't child was borne,
More tender then the childhood of the Morne.
  Chor. Pan pipe to him, and bleats of lambs and sheep,
Let Lullaby the pretty Prince asleep!
  Mirt. And that his birth sho'd be more singular,
At Noone of Day, was seene a silver Star,
Bright as the Wise-men's Torch, which guided them
To Gods sweet Babe, when borne at Bethlehem;
While Golden Angels (some have told to me)
Sung out his Birth with Heav'nly Minstralsie.
  Amint. O rare! But is't a trespasse if we three
Sho'd wend along his Baby-ship to see?
  Mir. Not so, not so. Chor. But if it chance to prove
At most a fault, 'tis but a fault of love.
  Amar. But deare Mirtillo, I have heard it told,
Those learned men brought Incense, Myrrhe, and Gold,
From Countries far, with Store of Spices, (sweet)
And laid them downe for Offrings at his feet.
  Mirt. 'Tis true indeed; and each of us will bring
Unto our smiling, and our blooming King,

A neat, though not so great an Offering.

  Amar. A Garland for my Gift shall be
Of flowers, ne'r suckt by th'theeving Bee:
And all most sweet; yet all lesse sweet then he.

  Amint. And I will beare along with you
Leaves dropping downe the honyed dew,
With oaten pipes, as sweet, as new.

  Mirt. And I a Sheep-hook will bestow,
To have his little King-ship know,
As he is Prince, he's Shepherd too.

  Chor. Come let's away, and quickly let's be drest,
And quickly give, The swiftest Grace is best.
And when before him we have laid our treasures,
We'll blesse the Babe, Then back to Countrie pleasures.

To the Lark.

Good speed, for I this day
Betimes my Mattens say:
  Because I doe
  Begin to wooe:
  Sweet singing Lark,
  Be thou the Clark,
  And know thy when
  To say, Amen.
  And if I prove
  Blest in my love;
  Then thou shalt be
  High-Priest to me,
  At my returne,
  To Incense burne;
And so to solemnize
Love's, and my Sacrifice.

The Bubble. A Song.

To my revenge, and to her desp'rate feares,
Flie thou made Bubble of my sighs, and tears.
In the wild aire, when thou hast rowl'd about,
And (like a blasting Planet) found her out;
Stoop, mount, passe by to take her eye, then glare
Like to a dreadfull Comet in the Aire:
Next, when thou dost perceive her fixed sight,
For thy revenge to be most opposite;
Then like a Globe, or Ball of Wild-fire, flie,
And break thy self in shivers on her eye.

A Meditation For His Mistress

You are a *Tulip* seen today,
But (Dearest) of so short a stay
That where you grew scarce man can say.

You are a lovely *July-flower*
Yet one rude wind or ruffling shower
Will force you hence, (and in an hour.)

You are a sparkling *Rose* in' th'bud,
Yet lost ere that chaste flesh and blood
Can show where you or grew or stood.

You are a full-spread, fair-set Vine,
And can with Tendrils love entwine,
Yet dry'd, ere you distil your Wine.

You are like Balme enclosed (well)
In *Amber*, or some *Crystal* shell,
Yet lost ere you transfuse your smell.

You are a dainty *Violet*,
Yet whither'd ere you can be set
Within a Virgin's Coronet.

You are the *Queen* all flowers among,
But die you must (fair Maid) ere long,
As He, the maker of this song.

The bleeding hand: or, The sprig of Eglantine given to a maid.

From this bleeding hand of mine,
Take this sprig of Eglantine.
Which (though sweet unto your smell)
Yet the fretfull bryar will tell,
He who plucks the sweets shall prove
Many thorns to be in Love.

Lyrick for Legacies.

Gold I've none, for use or show,
Neither Silver to bestow
At my death; but thus much know,
That each Lyrick here shall be
Of my love a Legacie,
Left to all posterity.
Gentle friends, then doe but please,
To accept such coynes as these;
As my last Remembrances.

A Dirge upon the Death of the Right Valiant Lord,
Bernard Stuart.

Hence, hence, profane; soft silence let us have;
While we this Trentall sing about thy Grave.

Had Wolves or Tigers seen but thee,
They wo'd have shew'd civility;
And in compassion of thy yeeres,
Washt those thy purple wounds with tears.
But since th'art slaine; and in thy fall,
The drooping Kingdome suffers all.

Chor. This we will doe; we'll daily come
And offer Tears upon thy Tomb:
And if that they will not suffice,
Thou shalt have soules for sacrifice.

Sleepe in thy peace, while we with spice perfume thee,
And Cedar wash thee, that no times consume thee.

Live, live thou dost, and shalt; for why?
Soules doe not with their bodies die:
Ignoble off-springs, they may fall
Into the flames of Funerall:
When as the chosen seed shall spring
Fresh, and for ever flourishing.

Cho. And times to come shall, weeping, read thy glory,
Lesse in these Marble stones, then in thy story.

To Perenna, a Mistresse.

Deare Perenna, prethee come,
And with Smallage dresse my Tomb:
Adde a Cypresse-sprig thereto,
With a teare; and so Adieu.

Great boast, small rost.

Of Flanks and Chines of Beefe doth Gorrell boast
He has at home; but who tasts boil'd or rost?
Look in his Brine-tub, and you shall find there
Two stiffe-blew-Pigs-feet, and a sow's cleft eare.

The Fairie Temple: or, Oberons Chappell.
Dedicated to Mr. John Merrifield, Counsellor at Law.

Rare Temples thou hast seen, I know,
And rich for in and outward show:
Survey this Chappell, built, alone,
Without or Lime, or Wood, or Stone:
Then say, if one th'ast seene more fine
Then this, the Fairies once, now Thine.

The Temple.

A way enchac't with glasse & beads
There is, that to the Chappel leads:
Whose structure (for his holy rest)
Is here the Halcion's curious nest:
Into the which who looks shall see
His Temple of Idolatry:
Where he of God-heads has such store,
As Rome's Pantheon had not more.
His house of Rimmon, this he calls,
Girt with small bones, instead of walls.
First, in a Neech, more black than jet,
His Idol-Cricket there is set:
Then in a Polisht Ovall by
There stands his Idol-Beetle-flie:
Next in an Arch, akin to this,
His Idol-Canker seated is:
Then in a Round, is plac't by these,
His golden god, Cantharides.
So that where ere ye look, ye see,
No Capitoll, no Cornish free,
Or Freeze, from this fine Fripperie.
Now this the Fairies wo'd have known,
Theirs is a mixt Religion.
And some have heard the Elves it call
Part Pagan, part Papisticall.
If unto me all Tongues were granted,
I co'd not speak the Saints here painted.

Saint Tit, Saint Nit, Saint Is, Saint Itis,
Who 'gainst Mabs-state plac't here right is.
Saint Will o'th' Wispe (of no great bignes)
But alias call'd here Fatuus ignis.
Saint Frip, Saint Trip, Saint Fill, S. Fillie,
Neither those other-Saint-ships will I
Here goe about for to recite
Their number (almost) infinite,
Which one by one here set downe are
In this most curious Calendar.
First, at the entrance of the gate,
A little-Puppet-Priest doth wait,
Who squeaks to all the commers there,
Favour your tongues, who enter here.
Pure hands bring hither, without staine.
A second pules, Hence, hence, profane.
Hard by, i'th'shell of halfe a nut,
The Holy-water there is put:
A little brush of Squirrils haires,
(Compos'd of odde, not even paires)
Stands in the Platter, or close by,
To purge the Fairie Family.
Neere to the Altar stands the Priest,
There off'ring up the Holy-Grist:
Ducking in Mood, and perfect Tense,
With (much-good-do't him) reverence.
The Altar is not here foure-square,
Nor in a forme Triangular;
Nor made of glasse, or wood, or stone,
But of a little Transverce bone;
Which boyes, and Bruckel'd children call
(Playing for Points and Pins) Cockall.
Whose Linnen-Drapery is a thin
Subtile and ductile Codlin's skin;
Which o're the board is smoothly spred,
With little Seale-work Damasked.
The Fringe that circumbinds it too,
Is Spangle-work of trembling dew,
Which, gently gleaming, makes a show,
Like Frost-work glitt'ring on the Snow.

Upon this fetuous board doth stand
Something for Shew-bread, and at hand
(Just in the middle of the Altar)
Upon an end, the Fairie-Psalter,
Grac't with the Trout-flies curious wings,
Which serve for watched Ribbanings.
Now, we must know, the Elves are led
Right by the Rubrick, which they read.
And if Report of them be true,
They have their Text for what they doe;
I, and their Book of Canons too.
And, as Sir Thomas Parson tells,
They have their Book of Articles:
And if that Fairie Knight not lies,
They have their Book of Homilies:
And other Scriptures, that designe
A short, but righteous discipline.
The Bason stands the board upon
To take the Free-Oblation:
A little Pin-dust; which they hold
More precious, then we prize our gold:
Which charity they give to many
Poore of the Parish, (if there's any)
Upon the ends of these neat Railes
(Hatcht, with the Silver-light of snails)
The Elves, in formall manner, fix
Two pure, and holy Candlesticks:
In either which a small tall bent
Burns for the Altars ornament.
For sanctity, they have, to these,
Their curious Copes and Surplices
Of cleanest Cobweb, hanging by
In their Religious Vesterie.
They have their Ash-pans, & their Brooms
To purge the Chappel and the rooms:
Their many mumbling Masse-priests here,
And many a dapper Chorister.
There ush'ring Vergers, here likewise,
Their Canons, and their Chaunteries:
Of Cloyster-Monks they have enow,

I, and their Abby-Lubbers too:
And if their Legend doe not lye,
They much affect the Papacie:
And since the last is dead, there's hope,
Elve Boniface shall next be Pope.
They have their Cups and Chalices;
Their Pardons and Indulgences:
Their Beads of Nits, Bels, Books, & Wax
Candles (forsooth) and other knacks:
Their Holy Oyle, their Fasting-Spittle;
Their sacred Salt here, (not a little.)
Dry chips, old shooes, rags, grease, & bones;
Beside their Fumigations,
To drive the Devill from the Cod-piece
Of the Fryar, (of work an odde-piece.)
Many a trifle too, and trinket,
And for what use, scarce man wo'd think it.
Next, then, upon the Chanters side
An Apples-core is hung up dry'd,
With ratling Kirnils, which is rung
To call to Morn, and Even-Song.
The Saint, to which the most he prayes
And offers Incense Nights and dayes,
The Lady of the Lobster is,
Whose foot-pace he doth stroak and kisse:
And, humbly, chives of Saffron brings,
For his most cheerfull offerings.
When, after these, h'as paid his vows,
He lowly to the Altar bows:
And then he dons the Silk-worms shed,
(Like a Turks Turbant on his head)
And reverently departeth thence,
Hid in a cloud of Frankincense:
And by the glow-worms light wel guided,
Goes to the Feast that's now provided.

To Mistresse Katherine Bradshaw, the lovely,
that crowned him with Laurel.

My Muse in Meads has spent her many houres,
Sitting, and sorting severall sorts of flowers,
To make for others garlands; and to set
On many a head here, many a Coronet:
But, amongst All encircled here, not one
Gave her a day of Coronation;
Till you (sweet Mistresse) came and enterwove
A Laurel for her, (ever young as love)
You first of all crown'd her; she must of due,
Render for that, a crowne of life to you.

The Plaudite, or end of life.

If after rude and boystrous seas,
My wearyed Pinnace here finds ease:
If so it be I've gain'd the shore
With safety of a faithful Ore:
If having run my Barque on ground,
Ye see the aged Vessell crown'd:
What's to be done? but on the Sands
Ye dance, and sing, and now clap hands.
The first Act's doubtfull, (but we say)
It is the last commends the Play.

To the most vertuous Mistresse Pot,
who many times entertained him.

When I through all my many Poems look,
And see your selfe to beautifie my Book;
Me thinks that onely lustre doth appeare
A Light ful-filling all the Region here.
Guild still with flames this Firmament, and be
A Lamp Eternall to my Poetrie.
Which if it now, or shall hereafter shine,
'Twas by your splendour (Lady) not by mine.
The Oile was yours; and that I owe for yet:
He payes the halfe, who do's confesse the Debt.

To Musique, to becalme his Fever.

Charm me asleep, and melt me so
　　With thy Delicious Numbers;
That being ravisht, hence I goe
　　Away in easie slumbers.
　　　　Ease my sick head,
　　　　And make my bed,
Thou Power that canst sever
　　From me this ill:
　　　　And quickly still:
　　　　Though thou not kill
　　　　　　My Fever.

Thou sweetly canst convert the same
　　From a consuming fire,
Into a gentle-licking flame,
　　And make it thus expire.
　　　　Then make me weep
　　　　My paines asleep;
And give me such reposes,
　　That I, poore I,
　　　　May think, thereby,
　　　　I live and die
　　　　　　'Mongst Roses.

Fall on me like a silent dew,
　　Or like those Maiden showrs,
Which, by the peepe of day, doe strew
　　A Baptime o're the flowers.
　　　　Melt, melt my paines,
　　　　With thy soft straines;
That having ease me given,
　　With full delight,
　　　　I leave this light;
　　　　And take my flight
　　　　　　For Heaven.

Upon a Gentlewoman with a sweet Voice.

So long you did not sing, or touch your Lute,
We knew 'twas Flesh and Blood, that there sate mute.
But when your Playing, and your Voice came in,
'Twas no more you then, but a Cherubin.

Upon Cupid.

As lately I a Garland bound,
'Mongst Roses, I there Cupid found:
I took him, put him in my cup,
And drunk with Wine, I drank him up.
Hence then it is, that my poore brest
Co'd never since find any rest.

Upon Julia's breasts.

Display thy breasts, my Julia, there let me
Behold that circummortall purity:
Betweene whose glories, there my lips I'll lay,
Ravisht, in that faire Via Lactea.

Best to be merry.

Fooles are they, who never know
How the times away doe goe:
But for us, who wisely see
Where the bounds of black Death be:
Let's live merrily, and thus
Gratifie the Genius.

The Changes to Corinna.

Be not proud, but now encline
Your soft eare to Discipline.
You have changes in your life,
Sometimes peace, and sometimes strife:
You have ebbes of face and flowes,
As your health or comes, or goes;
You have hopes, and doubts, and feares
Numberlesse, as are your haires.
You have Pulses that doe beat
High, and passions lesse of heat.
You are young, but must be old,
And, to these, ye must be told,
Time, ere long, will come and plow
Loathed Furrowes in your brow:
And the dimnesse of your eye
Will no other thing imply,
But you must die
As well as I.

No Lock against Letcherie.

Barre close as you can, and bolt fast too your doore,
To keep out the Letcher, and keep in the whore:
Yet, quickly you'l see by the turne of a pin,
The Whore to come out, or the Letcher come in.

Upon a Bleare-ey'd woman.

Wither'd with yeeres, and bed-rid Mumma lyes;
Dry-rosted all, but raw yet in her eyes.

Neglect.

Art quickens Nature; Care will make a face:
Neglected beauty perisheth apace.

Upon Sudds a Laundresse.

Sudds Launders Bands in pisse; and starches them
Both with her Husband's, and her own tough fleame.

Upon himselfe.

Mop-ey'd I am, as some have said,
Because I've liv'd so long a maid:
But grant that I sho'd wedded be,
Sho'd I a jot the better see?
No, I sho'd think, that Marriage might,
Rather then mend, put out the light.

Upon a Physitian.

Thou cam'st to cure me (Doctor) of my cold,
And caught'st thy selfe the more by twenty fold:
Prethee goe home; and for thy credit be
First cur'd thy selfe; then come and cure me.

To the Rose. Song.

Goe happy Rose, and enterwove
With other Flowers, bind my Love.
Tell her too, she must not be,
Longer flowing, longer free,
That so oft has fetter'd me.

Say (if she's fretfull) I have bands
Of Pearle, and Gold, to bind her hands:
Tell her, if she struggle still,
I have Mirtle rods, (at will)
For to tame, though not to kill.

Take thou my blessing, thus, and goe,
And tell her this, but doe not so,
Lest a handsome anger flye,
Like a Lightning, from her eye,
And burn thee 'up, as well as I.

Upon Guesse. Epigram.

Guesse cuts his shooes, and limping, goes about
To have men think he's troubled with the Gout:
But 'tis no Gout (beleeve it) but hard Beere,
Whose acrimonious humour bites him here.

To his Booke.

Thou art a plant sprung up to wither never,
But like a Laurell, to grow green for ever.

Upon a painted Gentlewoman.

Men say y'are faire; and faire ye are, 'tis true;
But (Hark!) we praise the Painter now, not you.

Upon a crooked Maid.

Crooked you are, but that dislikes not me;
So you be straight, where Virgins straight sho'd be.

Draw Gloves.

At Draw-Gloves we'l play,
And prethee, let's lay
A wager, and let it be this;
Who first to the Summe
Of twenty shall come,
Shall have for his winning a kisse.

To Musick, to becalme a sweet-sick-youth.

Charms, that call down the moon from out her sphere,
On this sick youth work your enchantments here:
Bind up his senses with your numbers, so,
As to entrance his paine, or cure his woe.
Fall gently, gently, and a while him keep
Lost in the civill Wildernesse of sleep:
That done, then let him, dispossest of paine,
Like to a slumbring Bride, awake againe.

To the High and Noble Prince, GEORGE,
Duke, Marquesse, and Earle of Buckingham.

Never my Book's perfection did appeare,
Til I had got the name of Villars here.
Now 'tis so full, that when therein I look,
I see a Cloud of Glory fills my Book.
Here stand it stil to dignifie our Muse,
Your sober Hand-maid; who doth wisely chuse,
Your Name to be a Laureat Wreathe to Hir,
Who doth both love and feare you Honour'd Sir.

His Recantation.

       Love, I recant,
        And pardon crave,
That lately I offended,
       But 'twas,
       Alas,
     To make a brave,
But no disdaine intended.

       No more I'll vaunt,
       For now I see,
Thou onely hast the power,
       To find,
       And bind
     A heart that's free,
And slave it in an houre.

The coming of good luck.

So Good-luck came, and on my roofe did light,
Like noyse-lesse Snow; or as the dew of night:
Not all at once, but gently, as the trees
Are, by the Sun-beams, tickel'd by degrees.

The Present: or, The Bag of the Bee.

Fly to my Mistresse, pretty pilfring Bee,
And say, thou bring'st this Hony-bag from me:
When on her lip, thou hast thy sweet dew plac't,
Mark, if her tongue, but slily, steale a taste.
If so, we live; if not, with mournfull humme,
Tole forth my death; next, to my buryall come.

On Love.

Love bade me aske a gift,
    And I no more did move,
But this, that I might shift
    Still with my clothes, my Love:
That favour granted was;
    Since which, though I love many,
Yet so it comes to passe,
    That long I love not any.

The Hock-Cart, or Harvest Home:
To the Right Honourable, Mildmay, Earle of Westmorland.

Come Sons of Summer, by whose toile,
We are the Lords of Wine and Oile:
By whose tough labours, and rough hands,
We rip up first, then reap our lands.
Crown'd with the eares of corne, now come,
And, to the Pipe, sing Harvest home.
Come forth, my Lord, and see the Cart
Drest up with all the Country Art.
See, here a Maukin, there a sheet,
As spotlesse pure, as it is sweet:
The Horses, Mares, and frisking Fillies,
(Clad, all, in Linnen, white as Lillies.)
The Harvest Swaines, and Wenches bound
For joy, to see the Hock-cart crown'd.
About the Cart, heare, how the Rout
Of Rurall Younglings raise the shout;
Pressing before, some coming after,
Those with a shout, and these with laughter.
Some blesse the Cart; some kisse the sheaves;
Some prank them up with Oaken leaves:
Some crosse the Fill-horse; some with great
Devotion, stroak the home-borne wheat:
While other Rusticks, lesse attent
To Prayers, then to Merryment,
Run after with their breeches rent.
Well, on, brave boyes, to your Lords Hearth,
Glitt'ring with fire; where, for your mirth,
Ye shall see first the large and cheefe
Foundation of your Feast, Fat Beefe:
With Upper Stories, Mutton, Veale
And Bacon, (which makes full the meale)
With sev'rall dishes standing by,
As here a Custard, there a Pie,
And here all tempting Frumentie.
And for to make the merry cheere,
If smirking Wine be wanting here,

There's that, which drowns all care, stout Beere;
Which freely drink to your Lords health,
Then to the Plough, (the Common-wealth)
Next to your Flailes, your Fanes, your Fatts;
Then to the Maids with Wheaten Hats:
To the rough Sickle, and crookt Sythe,
Drink frollick boyes, till all be blythe.
Feed, and grow fat; and as ye eat,
Be mindfull, that the lab'ring Neat
(As you) may have their fill of meat.
And know, besides, ye must revoke
The patient Oxe unto the Yoke,
And all goe back unto the Plough
And Harrow, (though they'r hang'd up now.)
And, you must know, your Lords word's true,
Feed him ye must, whose food fils you.
And that this pleasure is like raine,
Not sent ye for to drowne your paine,
But for to make it spring againe.

The Perfume.

To-morrow, Julia, I betimes must rise,
For some small fault, to offer sacrifice:
The Altar's ready; Fire to consume
The fat; breathe thou, and there's the rich perfume.

To Musick. A Song.

Musick, thou Queen of Heaven, Care-charming-spel,
    That strik'st a stilnesse into hell:
Thou that tam'st Tygers, and fierce storms (that rise)
    With thy soule-melting Lullabies:
Fall down, down, down, from those thy chiming spheres,
To charme our soules, as thou enchant'st our eares.

Not to love.

He that will not love, must be
My Scholar, and learn this of me:
There be in Love as many feares,
As the Summers Corne has eares:
Sighs, and sobs, and sorrowes more
Then the sand, that makes the shore:
Freezing cold, and firie heats,
Fainting swoones, and deadly sweats;
Now an Ague, then a Fever,
Both tormenting Lovers ever.
Wods't thou know, besides all these,
How hard a woman 'tis to please?
How crosse, how sullen, and how soone
She shifts and changes like the Moone.
How false, how hollow she's in heart;
And how she is her owne least part:
How high she's priz'd, and worth but small;
Little thou't love, or not at all.

To the Western wind.

Sweet Western Wind, whose luck it is,
    (Made rivall with the aire)
To give Perenn'as lip a kisse,
    And fan her wanton haire.

Bring me but one, I'll promise thee,
    Instead of common showers,
Thy wings shall be embalm'd by me,
    And all beset with flowers.

Upon the death of his Sparrow.
An Elegie.

Why doe not all fresh maids appeare
To work Love's Sampler onely here,
Where spring-time smiles throughout the yeare?
Are not here Rose-buds, Pinks, all flowers,
Nature begets by th'Sun and showers,
Met in one Hearce-cloth, to ore-spred
The body of the under-dead?
Phill, the late dead, the late dead Deare,
O! may no eye distill a Teare
For you once lost, who weep not here!
Had Lesbia (too-too-kind) but known
This Sparrow, she had scorn'd her own:
And for this dead which under-lies,
Wept out our heart, as well as eyes.
But endlesse Peace, sit here, and keep
My Phill, the time he has to sleep,
And thousand Virgins come and weep,
To make these flowrie Carpets show
Fresh, as their blood; and ever grow,
Till passengers shall spend their doome,
Not Virgil's Gnat had such a Tomb.

To Primroses fill'd with morning-dew.

Why doe ye weep, sweet Babes? can Tears
       Speak griefe in you,
       Who were but borne
     Just as the modest Morne
     Teem'd her refreshing dew?
Alas you have not known that shower,
       That marres a flower;
       Nor felt th'unkind
     Breath of a blasting wind;
     Nor are ye worne with yeares;
       Or warpt, as we,
     Who think it strange to see,
Such pretty flowers, (like to Orphans young)
To speak by Teares, before ye have a Tongue.

Speak, whimp'ring Younglings, and make known
       The reason, why
       Ye droop, and weep;
     Is it for want of sleep?
     Or childish Lullabie?
Or that ye have not seen as yet
       The Violet?
       Or brought a kisse
     From that Sweet-heart, to this?
     No, no, this sorrow shown
       By your teares shed,
     Wo'd have this Lecture read,
That things of greatest, so of meanest worth,
Conceiv'd with grief are, and with teares brought forth.

How Roses came red.

Roses at first were white,
　　Till they co'd not agree,
Whether my Sappho's breast,
　　Or they more white sho'd be.

But being vanquisht quite,
　　A blush their cheeks bespred;
Since which (beleeve the rest)
　　The Roses first came red.

Comfort to a Lady upon the Death
of her Husband.

Dry your sweet cheek, long drown'd with sorrows raine;
Since Clouds disperst, Suns guild the Aire again.
Seas chafe and fret, and beat, and over-boile;
But turne soone after calme, as Balme, or Oile.
Winds have their time to rage; but when they cease,
The leavie-trees nod in a still-born peace.
Your storme is over; Lady, now appeare
Like to the peeping spring-time of the yeare.
Off then with grave clothes; put fresh colours on;
And flow, and flame, in your Vermillion.
Upon your cheek sate Ysicles awhile;
Now let the Rose raigne like a Queene, and smile.

How Violets came blew.

Love on a day (wise Poets tell)
    Some time in wrangling spent,
Whether the Violets sho'd excell,
    Or she, in sweetest scent.

But Venus having lost the day,
    Poore Girles, she fell on you;
And beat ye so, (as some dare say)
    Her blowes did make ye blew.

Upon Groynes. Epigram.

Groynes, for his fleshly Burglary of late,
Stood in the Holy-Forum Candidate:
The word is Roman; but in English knowne:
Penance, and standing so, are both but one.

To the Willow-tree.

Thou art to all lost love the best,
    The onely true plant found,
Wherewith young men and maids distrest,
    And left of love, are crown'd.

When once the Lovers Rose is dead,
    Or laid aside forlorne;
Then Willow-garlands, 'bout the head,
    Bedew'd with teares, are worne.

When with Neglect, (the Lovers bane)
    Poore Maids rewarded be,
For their love lost; their onely gaine
    Is but a Wreathe from thee.

And underneath thy cooling shade,
    (When weary of the light)
The love-spent Youth, and love-sick Maid,
    Come to weep out the night.

Mrs. Eliz. Wheeler, under the name of the lost Shepardesse.

Among the Mirtles, as I walkt,
Love and my sighs thus intertalkt:
Tell me, said I, in deep distresse,
Where I may find my Shepardesse.
Thou foole, said Love, know'st thou not this?
In every thing that's sweet, she is.
In yond' Carnation goe and seek,
There thou shalt find her lip and cheek:
In that ennamel'd Pansie by,
There thou shalt have her curious eye:
In bloome of Peach, and Roses bud,
There waves the Streamer of her blood.
'Tis true, said I, and thereupon
I went to pluck them one by one,
To make of parts an union;
But on a sudden all were gone.
At which I stopt; Said Love, these be
The true resemblances of thee;
For as these flowers, thy joyes must die,
And in the turning of an eye;
And all thy hopes of her must wither,
Like those short sweets ere knit together.

To the King.

If when these Lyricks (Cesar) You shall heare,
And that Apollo shall so touch Your eare,
As for to make this, that, or any one
Number, Your owne, by free Adoption;
That Verse, of all the Verses here, shall be
The Heire to This great Realme of Poetry.

To the Queen.

Goddesse of Youth, and Lady of the Spring,
(Most fit to be the Consort to a King)
Be pleas'd to rest you in This Sacred Grove,
Beset with Mirtles; whose each leafe drops Love.
Many a sweet-fac't Wood-Nymph here is seene,
Of which chast Order You are now the Queene:
Witnesse their Homage, when they come and strew
Your Walks with Flowers, and give their Crowns to you.
Your Leavie-Throne (with Lilly-work) possesse;
And be both Princesse here, and Poetresse.

The Poets good wishes for the most hopefull and handsome
Prince, the Duke of Yorke.

May his pretty Duke-ship grow
Like t'a Rose of Jericho:
Sweeter far, then ever yet
Showrs or Sun-shines co'd beget.
May the Graces, and the Howers
Strew his hopes, and Him with flowers:
And so dresse him up with Love,
As to be the Chick of Jove.
May the thrice-three-Sisters sing
Him the Soveraigne of their Spring:
And entitle none to be
Prince of Hellicon, but He.
May his soft foot, where it treads,
Gardens thence produce and Meads:
And those Meddowes full be set
With the Rose, and Violet.
May his ample Name be knowne
To the last succession:
And his actions high be told
Through the world, but writ in gold.

The Poets good wishes for the most hopefull and handsome
Prince, the Duke of Yorke.

May his pretty Duke-ship grow
Like t'a Rose of Jericho:
Sweeter far, then ever yet
Showrs or Sun-shines co'd beget.
May the Graces, and the Howers
Strew his hopes, and Him with flowers:
And so dresse him up with Love,
As to be the Chick of Jove.
May the thrice-three-Sisters sing
Him the Soveraigne of their Spring:
And entitle none to be
Prince of Hellicon, but He.
May his soft foot, where it treads,
Gardens thence produce and Meads:
And those Meddowes full be set
With the Rose, and Violet.
May his ample Name be knowne
To the last succession:
And his actions high be told
Through the world, but writ in gold.

To Anthea, who may command him any thing.

Bid me to live, and I will live
    Thy Protestant to be:
Or bid me love, and I will give
    A loving heart to thee.

A heart as soft, a heart as kind,
    A heart as sound and free,
As in the whole world thou canst find,
    That heart I'll give to thee.

Bid that heart stay, and it will stay,
    To honour thy Decree:
Or bid it languish quite away,
    And't shall doe so for thee.

Bid me to weep, and I will weep,
    While I have eyes to see:
And having none, yet I will keep
    A heart to weep for thee.

Bid me despaire, and I'll despaire,
    Under that Cypresse tree:
Or bid me die, and I will dare
    E'en Death, to die for thee.

Thou art my life, my love, my heart,
    The very eyes of me:
And hast command of every part,
    To live and die for thee.

Upon her Voice.

Let but thy voice engender with the string,
And Angels will be borne, while thou dost sing.

Prevision, or Provision.

That Prince takes soone enough the Victors roome,
Who first provides, not to be overcome.

Obedience in Subjects.

The Gods to Kings the Judgement give to sway:
The Subjects onely glory to obay.

More potent, lesse peccant.

He that may sin, sins least; Leave to transgresse
Enfeebles much the seeds of wickednesse.

Upon a maid that dyed the day she was marryed.

That Morne which saw me made a Bride,
The Ev'ning witnest that I dy'd.
Those holy lights, wherewith they guide
Unto the bed the bashfull Bride;
Serv'd, but as Tapers, for to burne,
And light my Reliques to their Urne.
This Epitaph, which here you see,
Supply'd the Epithalamie.

Upon Pink an ill-fac'd Painter. Epigram.

To paint the Fiend, Pink would the Devill see;
And so he may, if he'll be rul'd by me:
Let but Pink's face i'th' Looking-glasse be showne,
And Pink may paint the Devill's by his owne.

Upon Brock. Epigram.

To clense his eyes, Tom Brock makes much adoe,
But not his mouth (the fouler of the two.)
A clammie Reume makes loathsome both his eyes:
His mouth worse furr'd with oathes and blasphemies.

To Meddowes.

Ye have been fresh and green,
    Ye have been fill'd with flowers:
And ye the Walks have been
    Where Maids have spent their houres.

You have beheld, how they
    With Wicker Arks did come
To kisse, and beare away
    The richer Couslips home.

Y'ave heard them sweetly sing,
    And seen them in a Round:
Each Virgin, like a Spring,
    With Hony-succles crown'd.

But now, we see, none here,
    Whose silv'rie feet did tread,
And with dishevell'd Haire,
    Adorn'd this smoother Mead.

Like Unthrifts, having spent,
    Your stock, and needy grown,
Y'are left here to lament
    Your poore estates, alone.

Crosses.

Though good things answer many good intents;
Crosses doe still bring forth the best events.

Miseries.

Though hourely comforts from the Gods we see,
No life is yet life-proofe from miserie.

Laugh and lie downe.

Y'ave laught enough (sweet) vary now your Text;
And laugh no more; or laugh, and lie down next.

To his Houshold Gods.

Rise, Houshold-gods, and let us goe;
But whither, I my selfe not know.
First, let us dwell on rudest seas;
Next, with severest Salvages;
Last, let us make our best abode,
Where humane foot, as yet, n'er trod:
Search worlds of Ice; and rather there
Dwell, then in lothed Devonshire.

To the Nightingale, and Robin-Red-brest.

When I departed am, ring thou my knell,
Thou pittifull, and pretty Philomel:
And when I'm laid out for a Corse; then be
Thou Sexton (Red-brest) for to cover me.

To the Yew and Cypresse to grace his Funerall.

     Both you two have
     Relation to the grave:
       And where
The Fun'rall-Trump sounds, you are there.

     I shall be made
     Ere long a fleeting shade:
       Pray come,
And doe some honour to my Tomb.

     Do not deny
     My last request; for I
       Will be
Thankfull to you, or friends, for me.

I call and I call.

I call, I call, who doe ye call?
The Maids to catch this Cowslip-ball:
But since these Cowslips fading be,
Troth, leave the flowers, and Maids, take me.
Yet, if that neither you will doe,
Speak but the word, and I'll take you.

On a perfum'd Lady.

You say y'are sweet; how sho'd we know
Whether that you be sweet or no?
From Powders and Perfumes keep free;
Then we shall smell how sweet you be.

A Nuptiall Song, or Epithalamie, on Sir
Clipseby Crew and his Lady.

What's that we see from far? the spring of Day
Bloom'd from the East, or faire Injewel'd May
    Blowne out of April; or some New-
      Star fill'd with glory to our view,
        Reaching at heaven,
To adde a nobler Planet to the seven?
      Say, or doe we not descrie
Some Goddesse, in a cloud of Tiffanie
      To move, or rather the
      Emergent Venus from the Sea?

'Tis she! 'tis she! or else some more Divine
Enlightned substance; mark how from the Shrine
    Of holy Saints she paces on,
    Treading upon Vermilion
        And Amber; Spice-
ing the Chaste Aire with fumes of Paradise.
    Then come on, come on, and yeeld
A savour like unto a blessed field,
      When the bedabled Morne
    Washes the golden eares of corne.

See where she comes; and smell how all the street
Breathes Vine-yards and Pomgranats: O how sweet!
    As a fir'd Altar, is each stone,
    Perspiring pounded Cynamon.
      The Phenix nest,
Built up of odours, burneth in her breast.
    Who therein wo'd not consume
His soule to Ash-heaps in that rich perfume?
      Bestroaking Fate the while
    He burnes to Embers on the Pile.

Himen, O Himen! Tread the sacred ground;
Shew thy white feet, and head with Marjoram crown'd:
    Mount up thy flames, and let thy Torch

Display the Bridegroom in the porch,
            In his desires
More towring, more disparkling then thy fires:
        Shew her how his eyes do turne
And roule about, and in their motions burne
            Their balls to Cindars: haste,
        Or else to ashes he will waste.

Glide by the banks of Virgins then, and passe
The Shewers of Roses, lucky-foure-leav'd grasse:
        The while the cloud of younglings sing,
        And drown yee with a flowrie Spring:
            While some repeat
Your praise, and bless you, sprinkling you with Wheat:
        While that others doe divine;
Blest is the Bride, on whom the Sun doth shine;
        And thousands gladly wish
        You multiply, as doth a Fish.

And beautious Bride we do confess y'are wise,
In dealing forth these bashfull jealousies:
        In Lov's name do so; and a price
        Set on your selfe, by being nice:
            But yet take heed;
What now you seem, be not the same indeed,
        And turne Apostate: Love will
Part of the way be met; or sit stone-still.
        On then, and though you slow-
        ly go, yet, howsoever, go.

And now y'are enter'd; see the Codled Cook
Runs from his Torrid Zone, to prie, and look,
        And blesse his dainty Mistresse: see,
        The Aged point out, This is she,
            Who now must sway
The House (Love shield her) with her Yea and Nay:
        And the smirk Butler thinks it
Sin, in's Nap'rie, not to express his wit;
        Each striving to devise
        Some gin, wherewith to catch your eyes.

To bed, to bed, kind Turtles, now, and write
This the short'st day, and this the longest night;
  But yet too short for you: 'tis we,
  Who count this night as long as three,
    Lying alone,
Telling the Clock strike Ten, Eleven, Twelve, One.
  Quickly, quickly then prepare;
And let the Young-men and the Bride-maids share
    Your Garters; and their joynts
  Encircle with the Bride-grooms Points.

By the Brides eyes, and by the teeming life
Of her green hopes, we charge ye, that no strife,
  (Farther then Gentlenes tends) gets place
  Among ye, striving for her lace:
    O doe not fall
Foule in these noble pastimes, lest ye call
  Discord in, and so divide
The youthfull Bride-groom, and the fragrant Bride:
    Which Love fore-fend; but spoken,
  Be't to your praise, no peace was broken.

Strip her of Spring-time, tender-whimpring-maids,
Now Autumne's come, when all those flowrie aids
  Of her Delayes must end; Dispose
  That Lady-smock, that Pansie, and that Rose
    Neatly apart;
But for Prick-madam, and for Gentle-heart;
  And soft-Maidens-blush, the Bride
Makes holy these, all others lay aside:
    Then strip her, or unto her
  Let him come, who dares undo her.

And to enchant yee more, see every where
About the Roofe a Syren in a Sphere;
  (As we think) singing to the dinne
  Of many a warbling Cherubim:
    O marke yee how
The soule of Nature melts in numbers: now

See, a thousand Cupids flye,
To light their Tapers at the Brides bright eye.
      To Bed; or her they'l tire,
    Were she an Element of fire.

And to your more bewitching, see, the proud
Plumpe Bed beare up, and swelling like a cloud,
    Tempting the two too modest; can
    Yee see it brusle like a Swan,
        And you be cold
To meet it, when it woo's and seemes to fold
    The Armes to hugge it? throw, throw
Your selves into the mighty over-flow
      Of that white Pride, and Drowne
    The night, with you, in floods of Downe.

The bed is ready, and the maze of Love
Lookes for the treaders; every where is wove
    Wit and new misterie; read, and
    Put in practise, to understand
        And know each wile,
Each hieroglyphick of a kisse or smile;
    And do it to the full; reach
High in your own conceit, and some way teach
      Nature and Art, one more
    Play then they ever knew before.

If needs we must for Ceremonies-sake,
Blesse a Sack-posset; Luck go with it; take
    The Night-Charme quickly; you have spells,
    And magicks for to end, and hells,
        To passe; but such
And of such Torture as no one would grutch
    To live therein for ever: Frie
And consume, and grow again to die,
      And live, and in that case,
    Love the confusion of the place.

But since It must be done, dispatch, and sowe
Up in a sheet your Bride, and what if so

It be with Rock, or walles of Brasse,
Ye Towre her up, as Danae was;
        Thinke you that this,
Or hell it selfe a powerfull Bulwarke is?
    I tell yee no; but like a
Bold bolt of thunder he will make his way,
       And rend the cloud, and throw
    The sheet about, like flakes of snow.

All now is husht in silence; Midwife-moone,
With all her Owle-ey'd issue begs a boon
      Which you must grant; that's entrance; with
      Which extract, all we can call pith
         And quintiscence
Of Planetary bodies; so commence
    All faire Constellations
Looking upon yee, That two Nations
      Springing from two such Fires,
    May blaze the vertue of their Sires.

The silken Snake.

For sport my Julia threw a Lace
Of silke and silver at my face:
Watchet the silke was; and did make
A shew, as if 't 'ad been a snake:
The suddenness did me affright;
But though it scar'd, it did not bite.

Upon himselfe.

I am Sive-like, and can hold
Nothing hot, or nothing cold.
Put in Love, and put in too
Jealousie, and both will through:
Put in Feare, and hope, and doubt;
What comes in, runnes quickly out:
Put in secrecies withall,
What ere enters, out it shall:
But if you can stop the Sive,
For mine own part I'de as lieve,
Maides sho'd say, or Virgins sing,
Herrick keeps, as holds nothing.

Upon Love.

Love's a thing, (as I do heare)
Ever full of pensive feare;
Rather then to which I'll fall,
Trust me, I'll not like at all:
If to love I should entend,
Let my haire then stand an end:
And that terrour likewise prove,
Fatall to me in my love.
But if horrour cannot slake
Flames, which wo'd an entrance make;
Then the next thing I desire,
Is to love, and live i'th fire.

Reverence to Riches.

Like to the Income must be our expence;
Man's Fortune must be had in reverence.

Devotion makes the Deity.

Who formes a Godhead out of Gold or Stone,
Makes not a God; but he that prayes to one.

The Eyes.

'Tis a known principle in War,
The eies be first, that conquer'd are.

To All Young Men That Love.

I could wish you all, who love,
That ye could your thoughts remove
From your Mistresses, and be,
Wisely wanton (like to me.)
I could wish you dispossest
Of that Fiend that marres your rest;
And with Tapers comes to fright
Your weake senses in the night.
I co'd wish, ye all, who frie
Cold as Ice, or coole as I.
But if flames best like ye, then
Much good do't ye Gentlemen.
I a merry heart will keep,
While you wring your hands and weep.

No Fault In Women.

No fault in women to refuse
The offer, which they most wo'd chuse.
No fault in women, to confesse
How tedious they are in their dresse.
No fault in women, to lay on
The tincture of Vermillion:
And there to give the cheek a die
Of white, where nature doth deny.
No fault in women, to make show
Of largeness, when th'are nothing so:
(When true it is, the out-side swels
With inward Buckram, little else.)
No fault in women, though they be
But seldome from suspition free:
No fault in womankind, at all,
If they but slip, and never fall.

Upon Shark. Epigram.

Shark, when he goes to any publick feast,
Eates to ones thinking, of all there, the least.
What saves the master of the House thereby?
When if the servants search, they may descry
In his wide Codpiece, (dinner being done)
Two Napkins cram'd up, and a silver Spoone.

Oberons Feast.

Shapcot! To thee the Fairy State
I with discretion, dedicate.
Because thou prizest things that are
Curious, and un-familiar.
Take first the feast; these dishes gone;
Wee'l see the Fairy-Court anon.

A little mushroome table spred,
After short prayers, they set on bread;
A Moon-parcht grain of purest wheat,
With some small glit'ring gritt, to eate
His choyce bitts with; then in a trice
They make a feast lesse great then nice.
But all this while his eye is serv'd,
We must not thinke his eare was sterv'd:
But that there was in place to stir
His Spleen, the chirring Grasshopper;
The merry Cricket, puling Flie,
The piping Gnat for minstralcy.
And now, we must imagine first,
The Elves present to quench his thirst
A pure seed-Pearle of Infant dew,
Brought and besweetned in a blew
And pregnant violet; which done,
His kitling eyes begin to runne
Quite through the table, where he spies
The hornes of paperie Butterflies,
Of which he eates, and tastes a little
Of that we call the Cuckoes spittle.
A little Fuz-ball-pudding stands
By, yet not blessed by his hands,
That was too coorse; but then forthwith
He ventures boldly on the pith
Of sugred Rush, and eates the sagge
And well bestrutted Bees sweet bagge:
Gladding his pallat with some store
Of Emits eggs; what wo'd he more?

But Beards of Mice, a Newt's stew'd thigh,
A bloated Earewig, and a Flie;
With the Red-capt worme, that's shut
Within the concave of a Nut,
Browne as his Tooth. A little Moth,
Late fatned in a piece of cloth:
With withered cherries; Mandrakes eares;
Moles eyes; to these, the slain-Stags teares:
The unctuous dewlaps of a Snaile;
The broke-heart of a Nightingale
Ore-come in musicke; with a wine,
Ne're ravisht from the flattering Vine,
But gently prest from the soft side
Of the most sweet and dainty Bride,
Brought in a dainty daizie, which
He fully quaffs up to bewitch
His blood to height; this done, commended
Grace by his Priest; The feast is ended.

Event of things not in our power.

By Time, and Counsell, doe the best we can,
Th'event is never in the power of man.

Upon her blush.

When Julia blushes, she do's show
Cheeks like to Roses, when they blow.

Merits make the man.

Our Honours, and our Commendations be
Due to the Merits, not Authoritie.

Vertue.

Each must, in vertue, strive for to excell;
That man lives twice, that lives the first life well.

To Virgins.

Heare ye Virgins, and I'll teach,
What the times of old did preach.
Rosamond was in a Bower
Kept, as Danae in a Tower:
But yet Love (who subtile is)
Crept to that, and came to this.
Be ye lockt up like to these,
Or the rich Hesperides;
Or those Babies in your eyes,
In their Christall Nunneries;
Notwithstanding Love will win,
Or else force a passage in:
And as coy be, as you can,
Gifts will get ye, or the man.

The Bell-man.

From noise of Scare-fires rest ye free,
From Murders *Benedicitie*.
From all mischances, that may fright
Your pleasing slumbers in the night:
Mercie secure ye all, and keep
The Goblin from ye, while ye sleep.
Past one aclock, and almost two,
My Masters all, Good day to you

To the most accomplisht Gentleman, Master Edward Norgate,
Clark of the Signet to His Majesty. Epigram.

For one so rarely tun'd to fit all parts;
For one to whom espous'd are all the Arts;
Long have I sought for: but co'd never see
Them all concenter'd in one man, but Thee.
Thus, thou, that man art, whom the Fates conspir'd
To make but One (and that's thy selfe) admir'd.

Upon Prudence Baldwin her sicknesse.

Prue, my dearest Maid, is sick,
Almost to be Lunatick:
Aesculapius! come and bring
Means for her recovering;
And a gallant Cock shall be
Offer'd up by Her, to Thee.

To Apollo. A short Hymne.

Phoebus! when that I a Verse,
Or some numbers more rehearse;
Tune my words, that they may fall,
Each way smoothly Musicall:
For which favour, there shall be
Swans devoted unto thee.

A Hymne to Bacchus.

Bacchus, let me drink no more;
Wild are Seas, that want a shore.
When our drinking has no stint,
There is no one pleasure in't.
I have drank up for to please
Thee, that great cup Hercules:
Urge no more; and there shall be
Daffadills g'en up to Thee.

Upon Bungie.

Bungie do's fast; looks pale; puts Sack-cloth on;
Not out of Conscience, or Religion:
Or that this Yonker keeps so strict a Lent,
Fearing to break the Kings Commandement:
But being poore, and knowing Flesh is deare,
He keeps not one, but many Lents i'th' yeare.

On himselfe.

Here down my wearyed limbs I'll lay;
My Pilgrims staffe; my weed of grey:
My Palmers hat; my Scallops shell;
My Crosse; my Cord; and all farewell.
For having now my journey done,
(Just at the setting of the Sun)
Here I have found a Chamber fit,
(God and good friends be thankt for it)
Where if I can a lodger be
A little while from Tramplers free;
At my up-rising next, I shall,
If not requite, yet thank ye all.
Meane while, the Holy-Rood hence fright
The fouler Fiend, and evill Spright,
From scaring you or yours this night.

Bashfulnesse.

Of all our parts, the eyes expresse
The sweetest kind of bashfulnesse.

Casualties.

Good things, that come of course, far lesse doe please,
Then those, which come by sweet contingences.

Bribes and Gifts get all.

Dead falls the Cause, if once the Hand be mute;
But let that speak, the Client gets the suit.

The end.

If well thou hast begun, goe on fore-right;
It is the End that crownes us, not the Fight.

Upon a child that dyed.

Here she lies, a pretty bud,
Lately made of flesh and blood:
Who, as soone, fell fast asleep,
As her little eyes did peep.
Give her strewings; but not stir
The earth, that lightly covers her.

Content, not cates.

'Tis not the food, but the content
That makes the Tables merriment.
Where Trouble serves the board, we eate
The Platters there, as soone as meat.
A little Pipkin with a bit
Of Mutton, or of Veale in it,
Set on my Table, (Trouble-free)
More then a Feast contenteth me.

The Entertainment: or, Porch-verse, at the
Marriage of Mr. Hen. Northly, and
the most witty Mrs. Lettice Yard.

Welcome! but yet no entrance, till we blesse
First you, then you, and both for white successe.
Profane no Porch young man and maid, for fear
Ye wrong the Threshold-god, that keeps peace here:
Please him, and then all good-luck will betide
You, the brisk Bridegroome, you the dainty Bride.
Do all things sweetly, and in comely wise;
Put on your Garlands first, then Sacrifice:
That done; when both of you have seemly fed,
We'll call on Night, to bring ye both to Bed:
Where being laid, all Faire signes looking on,
Fish-like, encrease then to a million:
And millions of spring-times may ye have,
Which spent, one death, bring to ye both one Grave.

The Good-night or Blessing.

Blessings, in abundance come,
To the Bride, and to her Groome;
May the Bed, and this short night,
Know the fulness of delight!
Pleasures, many here attend ye,
And ere long, a Boy Love send ye
Curld and comely, and so trimme,
Maides (in time) may ravish him.
Thus a dew of Graces fall
On ye both; Goodnight to all.

Upon Leech.

Leech boasts, he has a Pill, that can alone,
With speed give sick men their salvation:
'Tis strange, his Father long time has been ill,
And credits Physick, yet not trusts his Pill:
And why? he knowes he must of Cure despaire,
Who makes the slie Physitian his Heire.

To Daffadills.

Faire Daffadills, we weep to see
    You haste away so soone:
As yet the early-rising Sun
    Has not attain'd his Noone.
      Stay, stay,
    Untill the hasting day
        Has run
    But to the Even-song;
And, having pray'd together, we
    Will goe with you along.

We have short time to stay, as you,
    We have as short a Spring;
As quick a growth to meet Decay,
    As you, or any thing.
      We die,
    As your hours doe, and drie
        Away,
    Like to the Summers raine;
Or as the pearles of Mornings dew
    Ne'r to be found againe.

Upon Sneape. Epigram.

Sneape has a face so brittle, that it breaks
Forth into blushes, whensoere he speaks.

To a Maid.

You say, you love me; that I thus must prove;
If that you lye, then I will sweare you love.

Gold, before Goodnesse.

How rich a man is, all desire to know;
But none enquires if good he be, or no.

Upon a Lady that dyed in child-bed, and left
a daughter behind her.

As Gilly flowers do but stay
To blow, and seed, and so away;
So you sweet Lady (sweet as May)
The gardens-glory liv'd a while,
To lend the world your scent and smile.
But when your own faire print was set
Once in a Virgin Flosculet,
(Sweet as your selfe, and newly blown)
To give that life, resign'd your own:
But so, as still the mothers power
Lives in the pretty Lady-flower.

A New-yeares gift sent to Sir Simeon Steward

No newes of Navies burnt at Seas;
No noise of late spawn'd Tittyries:
No closset plot, or open vent,
That frights men with a Parliament:
No new devise, or late found trick,
To read by th'Starres, the Kingdoms sick:
No ginne to catch the State, or wring
The free-born Nosthrill of the King,
We send to you; but here a jolly
Verse crown'd with Yvie, and with Holly:
That tels of Winters Tales and Mirth,
That Milk-maids make about the hearth,
Of Christmas sports, the Wassell-boule,
That tost up, after Fox-i'th'hole:
Of Blind-man-buffe, and of the care
That young men have to shooe the Mare:
Of Twelf-tide Cakes, of Pease, and Beanes
Wherewith ye make those merry Sceanes,
When as ye chuse you King and Queen,
And cry out, Hey, for our town green.
Of Ash-heapes, in the which ye use
Husbands and Wives by streakes to chuse:
Of crackling Laurell, which fore-sounds,
A Plentious harvest to your grounds:
Of these, and such like things, for shift,
We send in stead of New-yeares gift.
Read then, and when your faces shine
With bucksome meat and capring Wine:
Remember us in Cups full crown'd,
And let our Citie-health go round,
Quite through the young maids and the men,
To the ninth number, if not tenne;
Untill the fired Chesnuts leape
For joy, to see the fruits ye reape,
From the plumpe Challice, and the Cup,
That tempts till it be tossed up:
Then as ye sit about your embers,

Call not to mind those fled Decembers;
But think on these, that are t'appeare,
As Daughters to the instant yeare:
Sit crown'd with Rose-buds, and carouse,
Till Liber Pater twirles the house
About your eares; and lay upon
The yeare (your cares) that's fled and gon.
And let the russet Swaines the Plough
And Harrow hang up resting now;
And to the Bag-pipe all addresse;
Till sleep takes place of wearinesse.
And thus, throughout, with Christmas playes
Frolick the full twelve Holy-dayes.

Mattens, or morning Prayer.

When with the Virgin morning thou do'st rise,
Crossing thy selfe; come thus to sacrifice:
First wash thy heart in innocence, then bring
Pure hands, pure habits, pure, pure every thing.
Next to the Altar humbly kneele, and thence,
Give up thy soule in clouds of frankinsence.
Thy golden Censors fil'd with odours sweet,
Shall make thy actions with their ends to meet.

Evensong.

Begin with Jove; then is the worke halfe done;
And runnes most smoothly, when tis well begunne.
Jove's is the first and last: The Morn's his due,
The midst is thine; but Joves the Evening too;
As sure a Mattins do's to him belong,
So sure he layes claime to the Evensong.

The Braclet to Julia.

Why I tye about thy wrist,
    Julia, this my silken twist;
    For what other reason is't,
But to shew thee how in part,
Thou my pretty Captive art?
But thy Bondslave is my heart:
'Tis but silke that bindeth thee,
Knap the thread, and thou art free:
But 'tis otherwise with me;
I am bound, and fast bound so,
That from thee I cannot go;
If I co'd, I wo'd not so.

The Christian Militant.

A man prepar'd against all ills to come,
That dares to dead the fire of martirdome:
That sleeps at home; and sayling there at ease,
Feares not the fierce sedition of the Seas:
That's counter-proofe against the Farms mis-haps,
Undreadfull too of courtly thunderclaps:
That weares one face (like heaven) and never showes
A change, when Fortune either comes, or goes:
That keepes his own strong guard, in the despight
Of what can hurt by day, or harme by night:
That takes and re-delivers every stroake
Of Chance, (as made up all of rock, and oake:)
That sighs at others death; smiles at his own
Most dire and horrid crucifixion.
Who for true glory suffers thus; we grant
Him to be here our Christian militant.

A short Hymne to Larr.

Though I cannot give thee fires
Glit'ring to my free desires:
These accept, and I'll be free,
Offering Poppy unto thee.

Another to Neptune.

Mighty Neptune, may it please
Thee, the Rector of the Seas,
That my Barque may safely runne
Through thy watrie-region;
And a Tunnie-fish shall be
Offer'd up, with thanks to thee.

Upon Greedy. Epigram.

An old, old widow Greedy needs wo'd wed,
Not for affection to her, or her Bed;
But in regard, 'twas often said, this old
Woman wo'd bring him more then co'd be told,
He tooke her; now the jest in this appeares,
So old she was, that none co'd tell her yeares.

His embalming to Julia.

For my embalming, Julia, do but this,
Give thou my lips but their supreamest kiss:
Or else trans-fuse thy breath into the chest,
Where my small reliques must for ever rest:
That breath the Balm, the myrrh, the Nard shal be,
To give an incorruption unto me.

The admonition.

Seest thou those Diamonds which she weares
    In that rich Carkanet;
Or those on her dishevel'd haires,
    Faire Pearles in order set?
Beleeve young man all those were teares
    By wretched Wooers sent,
In mournfull Hyacinths and Rue,
    That figure discontent;
Which when not warmed by her view,
    By cold neglect, each one,
Congeal'd to Pearle and stone;
    Which precious spoiles upon her,
    She weares as trophees of her honour.
Ah then consider! What all this implies;
She that will weare thy teares, wo'd weare thine eyes.

The Kisse. A Dialogue.

Among thy Fancies, tell me this,
What is the thing we call a kisse?
I shall resolve ye, what it is.

It is a creature born and bred
Between the lips, (all cherrie-red,)
By love and warme desires fed,
Chor. And makes more soft the Bridall Bed.

It is an active flame, that flies,
First, to the Babies of the eyes;
And charmes them there with lullabies;
Chor. And stils the Bride too, when she cries.

Then to the chin, the cheek, the eare,
It frisks, and flyes, now here, now there,
'Tis now farre off, and then tis nere;
Chor. And here, and there, and every where.

Ha's it a speaking virtue? Yes;
How speaks it, say? Do you but this,
Part your joyn'd lips, then speaks your kisse;
Chor. And this loves sweetest language is.

Has it a body? I, and wings
With thousand rare encolourings:
And as it flyes, it gently sings,
Chor. Love, honie yeelds; but never stings.

To his honoured kinsman Sir William Soame. Epigram.

I can but name thee, and methinks I call
All that have been, or are canonicall
For love and bountie, to come neare, and see,
Their many vertues volum'd up in thee;
In thee Brave Man! Whose incorrupted fame,
Casts forth a light like to a Virgin flame:
And as it shines, it throwes a scent about,
As when a Rain-bow in perfumes goes out.
So vanish hence, but leave a name, as sweet,
As Benjamin, and Storax, when they meet.

On himselfe.

Aske me, why I do not sing
To the tension of the string,
As I did, not long ago,
When my numbers full did flow?
Griefe (ay me!) hath struck my Lute,
And my tongue at one time mute.

To Larr.

No more shall I, since I am driven hence,
Devote to thee my graines of Frankinsence:
No more shall I from mantle-trees hang downe,
To honour thee, my little Parsly crown:
No more shall I (I feare me) to thee bring
My chives of Garlick for an offering:
No more shall I, from henceforth, heare a quire
Of merry Crickets by my Country fire,
Go where I will, thou luckie Larr stay here,
Warme by a glit'ring chimnie all the yeare.

The departure of the good Demon.

What can I do in Poetry,
Now the good Spirit's gone from me?
Why nothing now, but lonely sit,
And over-read what I have writ.

Clemency.

For punishment in warre, it will suffice,
If the chiefe author of the faction dyes;
Let but few smart, but strike a feare through all:
Where the fault springs, there let the judgement fall.

His age, dedicated to his peculiar friend, M. John
Wickes, under the name of Posthumus.

Ah Posthumus! Our yeares hence flye,
And leave no sound; nor piety,
          Or prayers, or vow
Can keepe the wrinkle from the brow:
          But we must on,
As Fate do's lead or draw us; none,
None, Posthumus, co'd ere decline
The doome of cruell Proserpine.

The pleasing wife, the house, the ground
Must all be left, no one plant found
          To follow thee,
Save only the Curst-Cipresse tree:
          A merry mind
Looks forward, scornes what's left behind:
Let's live, my Wickes, then, while we may,
And here enjoy our Holiday.

W'ave seen the past-best Times, and these
Will nere return, we see the Seas,
          And Moons to wain;
But they fill up their Ebbs again:
          But vanisht man,
Like to a Lilly-lost, nere can,
Nere can repullulate, or bring
His dayes to see a second Spring.

But on we must, and thither tend,
Where Anchus and rich Tullus blend
          Their sacred seed:
Thus has Infernall Jove decreed;
          We must be made,
Ere long, a song, ere long, a shade.
Why then, since life to us is short,
Lets make it full up, by our sport.

Crown we our Heads with Roses then,
And 'noint with Tirian Balme; for when
        We two are dead,
The world with us is buried.
        Then live we free,
As is the Air, and let us be
Our own fair wind, and mark each one
Day with the white and Luckie stone.

We are not poore; although we have
No roofs of Cedar, nor our brave
        Baië, nor keep
Account of such a flock of sheep;
        Nor Bullocks fed
To lard the shambles: Barbels bred
To kisse our hands, nor do we wish
For Pollio's Lampries in our dish.

If we can meet, and so conferre,
Both by a shining Salt-seller;
        And have our Roofe,
Although not archt, yet weather proofe,
        And seeling free,
From that cheape Candle baudery:
We'le eate our Beane with that full mirth,
As we were Lords of all the earth.

Well then, on what Seas we are tost,
Our comfort is, we can't be lost.
        Let the winds drive
Our Barke; yet she will keepe alive
        Amidst the deepes;
'Tis constancy (my Wickes) which keepes
The Pinnace up; which though she erres
I'th' Seas, she saves her passengers.

Say, we must part (sweet mercy blesse
Us both i'th' Sea, Camp, Wildernesse)
        Can we so farre
Stray, to become lesse circular,

Then we are now?
No, no, that selfe same heart, that vow,
Which made us one, shall ne'r undoe;
Or ravell so, to make us two.

Live in thy peace; as for my selfe,
When I am bruised on the Shelfe
          Of Time, and show
My locks behung with frost and snow:
          When with the reume,
The cough, the ptisick, I consume
Unto an almost nothing; then,
The Ages fled, I'll call agen:

And with a teare compare these last
Lame, and bad times, with those are past,
          While Baucis by,
My old leane wife, shall kisse it dry:
          And so we'l sit
By'th'fire, foretelling snow and slit,
And weather by our aches, grown
Now old enough to be our own

True Calenders, as Pusses eare
Washt o're, to tell what change is neare
          Then to asswage
The gripings of the chine by age;
          I'll call my young
I,lus to sing such a song
I made upon my Julia's brest;
And of her blush at such a feast.

Then shall he read that flowre of mine
Enclos'd within a christall shrine:
          A Primrose next;
A piece, then of a higher text:
          For to beget
In me a more transcendant heate,
Then that insinuating fire,
Which crept into each aged Sire.

When the faire Hellen, from her eyes,
Shot forth her loving Sorceries:
   At which I'll reare
Mine aged limbs above my chaire:
   And hearing it,
Flutter and crow, as in a fit
Of fresh concupiscence, and cry,
No lust theres like to Poetry.

Thus frantick crazie man (God wot)
I'll call to mind things half forgot:
   And oft between,
Repeat the Times that I have seen!
   Thus ripe with tears,
And twisting my I̦lus hairs;
Doting, I'll weep and say (In Truth)
Baucis, these were my sins of youth.

Then next I'll cause my hopefull Lad
(If a wild Apple can be had)
   To crown the Hearth,
(Larr thus conspiring with our mirth)
   Then to infuse
Our browner Ale into the cruse:
Which sweetly spic't, we'l first carouse
Unto the Genius of the house.

Then the next health to friends of mine
(Loving the brave Burgundian wine)
   High sons of Pith,
Whose fortunes I have frolickt with:
   Such as co'd well
Bear up the Magick bough, and spel:
And dancing 'bout the Mystick Thyrse,
Give up the just applause to verse:

To those, and then agen to thee
We'l drink, my Wickes, untill we be
   Plump as the cherry,

Though not so fresh, yet full as merry
　　　　　As the crickit;
The untam'd Heifer, or the Pricket,
Untill our tongues shall tell our ears,
W'are younger by a score of years.

Thus, till we see the fire lesse shine
From th'embers, then the kitlings eyne,
　　　　　We'l still sit up,
Sphering about the wassail cup,
　　　　　To all those times,
Which gave me honour for my Rhimes,
The cole once spent, we'l then to bed,
Farre more then night bewearied.

A short hymne to Venus.

Goddesse, I do love a Girle
Rubie-lipt, and tooth'd with Pearl:
If so be, I may but prove
Luckie in this Maide I love:
I will promise there shall be
Mirtles offer'd up to Thee.

To a Gentlewoman on just dealing.

True to your self, and sheets, you'l have me swear,
You shall; if righteous dealing I find there.
Do not you fall through frailty; I'll be sure
To keep my Bond still free from forfeiture.

Upon a delaying Lady.

Come come away,
Or let me go;
Must I here stay,
Because y'are slow;
And will continue so?
Troth Lady, no.

I scorne to be
A slave to state:
And since I'm free,
I will not wait,
Henceforth at such a rate,
For needy Fate.

If you desire
My spark sho'd glow,
The peeping fire
You must blow;
Or I shall quickly grow,
To Frost or Snow.

To the Lady Mary Villars, Governesse to
the Princesse Henretta

When I of Villars doe but heare the name,
It calls to mind, that mighty Buckingham,
Who was your brave exalted Uncle here,
(Binding the wheele of Fortune to his Sphere)
Who spurn'd at Envie; and co'd bring, with ease,
An end to all his stately purposes.
For his love then, whose sacred Reliques show
Their Resurrection, and their growth in you:
And for my sake, who ever did prefer
You, above all Those Sweets of Westminster:
Permit my Book to have a free accesse
To kisse your hand, most Dainty Governesse.

Upon his Julia.

Will ye heare, what I can say
Briefly of my Julia?
Black and rowling is her eye,
Double chinn'd, and forehead high:
Lips she has, all Rubie red,
Cheeks like Creame Enclarited:
And a nose that is the grace
And Proscenium of her face.
So that we may guesse by these,
The other parts will richly please.

To Flowers.

In time of life, I grac't ye with my Verse;
Doe now your flowrie honours to my Herse.
You shall not languish, trust me: Virgins here
Weeping, shall make ye flourish all the yeere.

To my ill Reader.

Thou say'st my lines are hard;
    And I the truth will tell;
They are both hard, and marr'd,
    If thou not read'st them well.

The hand and tongue.

Two parts of us successively command;
The tongue in peace; but then in warre the hand.

The power in the people.

Let Kings Command, and doe the best they may,
The saucie Subjects still will beare the sway.

Her Legs.

Fain would I kiss my Julia's dainty Leg,
Which is as white and hair-less as an egge.

A Hymne to Venus, and Cupid.

Sea-born Goddesse, let me be,
By thy sonne thus grac't, and thee;
That when ere I wooe, I find
Virgins coy, but not unkind.
Let me when I kisse a maid,
Taste her lips, so over-laid
With Loves-sirrop; that I may,
In your Temple, when I pray,
Kisse the Altar, and confess
Ther's in love, no bitterness.

On Julia's Picture.

How am I ravisht! When I do but see,
The Painters art in thy Sciography?
If so, how much more shall I dote thereon,
When once he gives it incarnation?

Her Bed.

See'st, thou that Cloud as silver cleare,
Plump, soft, & swelling every where?
Tis Julia's Bed, and she sleeps there.

Upon her Almes.

See how the poore do waiting stand,
For the expansion of thy hand.
A wafer Dol'd by thee, will swell
Thousands to feed by miracle.

Rewards.

Still to our gains our chief respect is had;
Reward it is, that makes us good or bad.

Nothing new.

Nothing is New: we walk where others went.
Ther's no vice now, but has his president.

Long and lazie.

That was the Proverb. Let my mistresse be
Lasie to others, but be long to me.

Upon Ralph. Epigram.

Curse not the mice, no grist of thine they eat:
But curse thy children, they consume thy wheat.

The Rainbow.

Look, how the Rainbow doth appeare
But in one onely Hemisphere:
So likewise after our disseace,
No more is seen the Arch of Peace.
That Cov'nant's here; The under-bow,
That nothing shoots, but war and woe.

The meddow verse or Aniversary to Mistris Bridget Lowman.

Come with the Spring-time, forth Fair Maid, and be
This year again, the medows Deity.
Yet ere ye enter, give us leave to set
Upon your Head this flowry Coronet:
To make this neat distinction from the rest;
You are the Prime, and Princesse of the Feast:
To which, with silver feet lead you the way,
While sweet-breath Nimphs, attend on you this Day.
This is your houre; and best you may command,
Since you are Lady of this Fairie land.
Full mirth wait on you; and such mirth as shall
Cherrish the cheek, but make none blush at all.

The parting verse, the feast there ended.

Loth to depart, but yet at last, each one
Back must now go to's habitation:
Not knowing thus much, when we once do sever,
Whether or no, that we shall meet here ever.
As for my self, since time a thousand cares
And griefs hath fil'de upon my silver hairs;
'Tis to be doubted whether I next yeer,
Or no, shall give ye a re-meeting here.
If die I must, then my last vow shall be,
You'l with a tear or two, remember me,
Your sometime Poet; but if fates do give
Me longer date, and more fresh springs to live:
Oft as your field, shall her old age renew,
Herrick shall make the meddow-verse for you.

Upon Judith. Epigram.

Judith has cast her old-skin, and got new;
And walks fresh varnisht to the publick view.
Foule Judith was; and foule she will be known,
For all this fair Transfiguration.

To the right honourable, Philip, Earle of Pembroke, and
Montgomerie.

How dull and dead are books, that cannot show
A Prince or Pembroke, and that Pembroke, you!
You, who are High born, and a Lord no lesse
Free by your fate, then Fortunes mightinesse,
Who hug our Poems (Honourd Sir) and then
The paper gild, and Laureat the pen.
Nor suffer you the Poets to sit cold,
But warm their wits, and turn their lines to gold.
Others there be, who righteously will swear
Those smooth-pac't Numbers, amble every where;
And these brave Measures go a stately trot;
Love those, like these; regard, reward them not.
But you, my Lord, are One, whose hand along
Goes with your mouth, or do's outrun your tongue;
Paying before you praise; and cockring wit,
Give both the Gold and Garland unto it.

An hymne to Juno.

Stately Goddesse, do thou please,
Who art chief at marriages,
But to dresse the Bridall-Bed,
When my Love and I shall wed:
And a Peacock proud shall be
Offerd up by us, to thee.

Upon Sappho, sweetly playing, and sweetly singing.

When thou do'st play, and sweetly sing,
Whether it be the voice or string,
Or both of them, that do agree
Thus to en-trance and ravish me:
This, this I know, I'm oft struck mute;
And dye away upon thy Lute.

Upon Paske a Draper.

Paske, though his debt be due upon the day
Demands no money by a craving way;
For why sayes he, all debts and their arreares,
Have reference to the shoulders, not the eares.

Chop-Cherry.

Thou gav'st me leave to kisse;
    Thou gav'st me leave to wooe;
Thou mad'st me thinke by this,
    And that, thou lov'dst me too.

But I shall ne'r forget,
    How for to make thee merry;
Thou mad'st me chop, but yet,
    Another snapt the Cherry.

To the most learned, wise, and Arch-Anti-
quary, M. John Selden.

I who have favour'd many, come to be
Grac't (now at last) or glorifi'd by thee.
Loe, I, the Lyrick Prophet, who have set
On many a head the Delphick Coronet,
Come unto thee for Laurell, having spent,
My wreaths on those, who little gave or lent.
Give me the Daphne, that the world may know it,
Whom they neglected, thou hast crown'd a Poet.
A City here of Heroes I have made,
Upon the rock, whose firm foundation laid,
Shall never shrink, where making thine abode,
Live thou a Selden, that's a Demi-god.

Upon himself.

Thou shalt not All die; for while Love's fire shines
Upon his Altar, men shall read thy lines;
And learn'd Musicians shall to honour Herricks
Fame, and his Name, both set, and sing his Lyricks.

Upon Mease. Epigram.

Mease brags of Pullets which he eats: but Mease
Ne'r yet set tooth in stump, or rump of these.

Upon wrinkles.

Wrinkles no more are, or no lesse,
Then beauty turn'd to sowernesse.

Upon Prigg.

Prigg, when he comes to houses, oft doth use
(Rather than fail) to steal from thence old shoes:
Sound or unsound, be they rent or whole,
Prigg bears away the body and the sole.

Upon Moon.

Moon is an Usurer, whose gain,
Seldome or never, knows a wain,
Onely Moons conscience, we confesse,
That ebs from pittie lesse and lesse.

Pray and prosper.

First offer Incense, then thy field and meads
Shall smile and smell the better by thy beads.
The spangling Dew dreg'd o're the grasse shall be
Turn'd all to Mell, and Manna there for thee.
Butter of Amber, Cream, and Wine, and Oile
Shall run, as rivers, all throughout thy soyl.
Wod'st thou to sincere-silver turn thy mold?
Pray once, twice pray; and turn thy ground to gold.

His Lachrimé or Mirth, turn'd to mourning.

Call me no more,
As heretofore,
The musick of a Feast;
Since now (alas)
The mirth, that was
In me, is dead or ceast.

Before I went
To banishment
Into the loathed West;
I co'd rehearse
A Lyrick verse,
And speak it with the best.

But time (Ai me)
Has laid, I see
My Organ fast asleep;
And turn'd my voice
Into the noise
Of those that sit and weep.

Upon Shift.

Shift now has cast his clothes: got all things new;
Save but his hat, and that he cannot mew.

Upon Cuts.

If wounds in clothes, Cuts calls his rags, 'tis cleere,
His linings are the matter running there.

Gain and Gettings.

When others gain much by the present cast,
The coblers getting time, is at the Last.

Upon his kinswoman Mistris Elizabeth Herrick.

Sweet virgin, that I do not set
The pillars up of weeping Jet,
Or mournfull Marble; let thy shade
Not wrathfull seem, or fright the Maide,
Who hither at her wonted howers
Shall come to strew thy earth with flowers.
No, know (Blest Maide) when there's not one
Remainder left of Brasse or stone,
Thy living Epitaph shall be,
Though lost in them, yet found in me.
Dear, in thy bed of Roses, then,
Till this world shall dissolve as men,
Sleep, while we hide thee from the light,
Drawing thy curtains round: Good night.

To the most fair and lovely Mistris,
Anne Soame, now Lady Abdie.

So smell those odours that do rise
From out the wealthy spiceries:
So smels the flowre of blooming Clove;
Or Roses smother'd in the stove:
So smells the Aire of spiced wine;
Or Essences of Jessimine:
So smells the Breath about the hives,
When well the work of hony thrives;
And all the busie Factours come
Laden with wax and hony home:
So smell those neat and woven Bowers,
All over-archt with Oringe flowers;
And Almond blossoms, that do mix
To make rich these Aromatikes:
So smell those bracelets, and those bands
Of Amber chaf't between the hands,
When thus enkindled they transpire
A noble perfume from the fire.
The wine of cherries, and to these,
The cooling breath of Respasses;
The smell of mornings milk, and cream;
Butter of Cowslips mixt with them;
Of rosted warden, or bak'd peare,
These are not to be reckon'd here;
When as the meanest part of her,
Smells like the maiden-Pomander.
Thus sweet she smells, or what can be
More lik'd by her, or lov'd by mee.

A Panegerick to Sir Lewis Pemberton.

Till I shall come again, let this suffice,
    I send my salt, my sacrifice
To Thee, thy Lady, younglings, and as farre
    As to thy Genius and thy Larre;
To the worn Threshold, Porch, Hall, Parlour, Kitchin,
    The fat-fed smoking Temple, which in
The wholsome savour of thy mighty Chines
    Invites to supper him who dines,
Where laden spits, warp't with large Ribbs of Beefe,
    Not represent, but give reliefe
To the lanke-Stranger, and the sowre Swain;
    Where both may feed, and come againe:
For no black-bearded Vigil from thy doore
    Beats with a button'd-staffe the poore:
But from thy warm-love-hatching gates each may
    Take friendly morsels, and there stay
To Sun his thin-clad members, if he likes,
    For thou no Porter keep'st who strikes.
No commer to thy Roofe his Guest-rite wants;
    Or staying there, is scourg'd with taunts
Of some rough Groom, who (yirkt with Corns) sayes, Sir
    Y'ave dipt too long i'th' Vinegar;
And with our Broth and bread, and bits; Sir, friend,
    Y'ave farced well, pray make an end;
Two dayes y'ave larded here; a third, yee know,
    Makes guests and fish smell strong; pray go
You to some other chimney, and there take
    Essay of other giblets; make
Merry at anothers hearth; y'are here
    Welcome as thunder to our beere:
    Manners knowes distance, and a man unrude
Wo'd soon recoile, and not intrude
    His Stomach to a second Meale. No, no,
Thy house, well fed and taught, can show
    No such crab'd vizard: Thou hast learnt thy Train,
With heart and hand to entertain:
    And by the Armes-full (with a Brest unhid)

As the old Race of mankind did,
 When eithers heart, and eithers hand did strive
To be the nearer Relative:
 Thou do'st redeeme those times; and what was lost
Of antient honesty, may boast
 It keeps a growth in thee; and so will runne
A course in thy Fames-pledge, thy Sonne.
 Thus, like a Roman Tribune, thou thy gate
Early setts ope to feast, and late:
 Keeping no currish Waiter to affright,
With blasting eye, the appetite,
 Which fain would waste upon thy Cates, but that
The Trencher-creature marketh what
 Best and more suppling piece he cuts, and by
Some private pinch tels danger's nie
 A hand too desp'rate, or a knife that bites
Skin deepe into the Porke, or lights
 Upon some part of Kid, as if mistooke,
When checked by the Butlers look.
 No, no, thy bread, thy wine, thy jocund Beere
Is not reserv'd for Trebius here,
 But all, who at thy table seated are,
Find equall freedome, equall fare;
 And Thou, like to that Hospitable God,
Jove, joy'st when guests make their abode
 To eate thy Bullocks thighs, thy Veales, thy fat
Weathers, and never grudged at.
 The *Phesant, Partridge, Gotwit, Reeve, Ruffe, Raile,*
The *Cock,* the *Curlew*, and the *Quaile;*
 These, and thy choicest viands do extend
Their taste unto the lower end
 Of thy glad table: not a dish more known
To thee, then unto any one:
 But as thy meate, so thy *immortall wine*
Makes the smirk face of each to shine,
 And spring fresh Rose-buds, while the salt, the wit
Flowes from the Wine, and graces it:
 While Reverence, waiting at the bashfull board,
Honours my Lady and my Lord.
 No scurrile jest; no open Sceane is laid

Here, for to make the face affraid;
    But temp'rate mirth dealt forth, and so discreet-
ly that it makes the meate more sweet;
    And adds perfumes unto the Wine, which thou
Do'st rather poure forth, then allow
    By cruse and measure; thus devoting Wine,
As the Canary Isles were thine:
    But with that wisdome, and that method, as
No One that's there his guilty glasse
    Drinks of distemper, or ha's cause to cry
Repentance to his liberty.
    No, thou know'st order, Ethicks, and ha's read
All Oeconomicks, know'st to lead
    A House-dance neatly, and can'st truly show,
How farre a Figure ought to go,
    Forward, or backward, side-ward, and what pace
Can give, and what retract a grace;
    What Gesture, Courtship; Comliness agrees,
With those thy primitive decrees,
    To give subsistance to thy house, and proofe,
What Genii support thy roofe,
    Goodnes and Greatnes; not the oaken Piles;
For these, and marbles have their whiles
    To last, but not their ever: Vertues Hand
It is, which builds, 'gainst Fate to stand.
    Such is thy house, whose firme foundations trust
Is more in thee, then in her dust,
    Or depth, these last may yeeld, and yearly shrinke,
When what is strongly built, no chinke
    Or yawning rupture can the same devoure,
But fixt it stands, by her own power,
    And well-laid bottome, on the iron and rock,
Which tryes, and counter-stands the shock,
    And Ramme of time and by vexation growes
The stronger: *Vertue dies when foes*
    Are wanting to her exercise, but great
And large she spreads by dust, and sweat.
    Safe stand thy Walls, and Thee, and so both will,
Since neithers height was rais'd by th'ill
    Of others; since no Stud, no Stone, no Piece,

Was rear'd up by the Poore-mans fleece:
    No Widowes Tenement was rackt to guild
Or fret thy Seeling, or to build
    A Sweating-Closset, to annoint the silke-
soft-skin, or bath in Asses milke:
    No Orphans pittance, left him, serv'd to set
The Pillars up of lasting Jet,
    For which their cryes might beate against thine eares,
Or in the dampe Jet read their Teares.
    No Planke from Hallowed Altar, do's appeale
To yond' Star-chamber, or do's seale
    A curse to Thee, or Thine; but all things even
Make for thy peace, and pace to heaven.
    Go on directly so, as just men may
A thousand times, more sweare, then say,
    This is that Princely Pemberton, who can
Teach man to keepe a God in man:
    And when wise Poets shall search out to see
Good men, They find them all in Thee.

To his Valentine, on S. Valentines day.

Oft have I heard both Youths and Virgins say,
Birds chuse their Mates, and couple too, this day:
But by their flight I never can divine,
When shall I couple with my Valentine.

Upon Doll. Epigram.

Doll she so soone began the wanton trade;
She ne'r remembers that she was a maide.

Upon Skrew. Epigram.

Skrew lives by shifts; yet sweares by no small oathes;
For all his shifts, he cannot shift his clothes.

Upon Linnit. Epigram.

Linnit playes rarely on the Lute, we know;
And sweetly sings, but yet his breath sayes no.

To his Nephew, to be prosperous in his
art of Painting.

On, as thou hast begunne, brave youth, and get
The Palme from Urbin, Titian, Tintarret,
Brugel and Coxu, and the workes out-doe,
Of Holben, and That mighty Ruben too.
So draw, and paint, as none may do the like,
No, not the glory of the World, Vandike.

Upon M. Ben. Johnson. Epigram.

After the rare Arch-Poet Johnson dy'd,
The Sock grew loathsome, and the Buskins pride,
Together with the Stages glory stood
Each like a poore and pitied widowhood.
The Cirque prophan'd was; and all postures rackt:
For men did strut, and stride, and stare, not act.
Then temper flew from words; and men did squeake,
Looke red, and blow, and bluster, but not speake:
No Holy-Rage, or frantick-fires did stirre,
Or flash about the spacious Theater.
No clap of hands, or shout, or praises-proofe
Did crack the Play-house sides, or cleave her roofe.
Artlesse the Sceane was; and that monstrous sin
Of deep and arrant ignorance came in;
Such ignorance as theirs was, who once hist
At thy unequal'd Play, the Alchymist:
Oh fie upon 'em! Lastly too, all witt
In utter darkenes did, and still will sit
Sleeping the lucklesse Age out, till that she
Her Resurrection ha's again with Thee.

Upon Glasse. Epigram.

Glasse, out of deepe, and out of desp'rate want,
Turn'd, from a Papist here, a Predicant.
A Vicarige at last Tom Glasse got here,
Just upon five and thirty pounds a yeare.
Adde to that thirty five, but five pounds more,
He'l turn a Papist, rancker then before.

A Vow to Mars.

Store of courage to me grant,
Now I'm turn'd a combatant:
Helpe me so, that I my shield,
(Fighting) lose not in the field.
That's the greatest shame of all,
That in warfare can befall.
Do but this; and there shall be
Offer'd up a Wolfe to thee.

To his maid Prew.

These Summer-Birds did with thy Master stay
The times of warmth; but then they flew away;
Leaving their Poet (being now grown old)
Expos'd to all the comming Winters cold.
But thou kind Prew did'st with my Fates abide,
As well the Winters, as the Summers Tide:
For which thy Love, live with thy Master here,
Not two, but all the seasons of the yeare.

A Canticle to Apollo.

Play Phoebus on thy Lute;
And we will, all sit mute:
By listning to thy Lire,
That sets all eares on fire.

Hark, harke, the God do's play!
And as he leads the way
Through heaven, the very Spheres,
As men, turne all to eares.

Another.

Thou had'st the wreath before, now take the Tree;
That henceforth none be Laurel crown'd but Thee.

A just man.

A Just man's like a Rock that turnes the wroth
Of all the raging Waves, into a froth.

Upon a hoarse Singer.

Sing me to death; for till thy voice be cleare,
'Twill never please the pallate of mine eare.

How Pansies or Heart-ease came first.

Frollick Virgins once these were,
Overloving, (living here:)
Being here their ends deny'd
Ran for Sweet-hearts mad, and dy'd.
Love in pitie of their teares,
And their losse in blooming yeares;
For their restlesse here-spent-houres,
Gave them Hearts-ease turn'd to Flow'rs.

To his peculiar friend Sir Edward Fish, Knight Baronet.

Since for thy full deserts (with all the rest
Of these chaste spirits, that are here possest
Of Life eternall) Time has made thee one,
For growth in this my rich Plantation:
Live here: But know 'twas vertue, & not chance,
That gave thee this so high inheritance.
Keepe it for ever; grounded with the good,
Who hold fast here an endlesse lively-hood.

Larr's portion, or the Poets part.

At my homely Country-seat,
I have there a little wheat;
Which I worke to Meale, and make
Therewithall a Holy-cake:
Part of which I give to Larr,
Part is my peculiar.

Upon man.

Man is compos'd here of a two-fold part;
The first of Nature, and the next of Art:
Art presupposes Nature; Nature shee
Prepares the way for mans docility.

Liberty.

Those ills that mortall men endure,
So long are capable of cure,
As they of freedome may be sure:
But that deni'd; a griefe, though small,
Shakes the whole Roofe, or ruines all.

Lots to be liked.

Learn this of me, where e'r thy Lot doth fall;
Short lot, or not, to be content with all.

Griefes.

Jove may afford us thousands of reliefs;
Since man expos'd is to a world of griefs.

Upon Eeles. Epigram.

Eeles winds and turnes, and cheats and steales; yet Eeles
Driving these sharking trades, is out at heels.

The Dreame.

By Dream I saw, one of the three
Sisters of Fate appeare to me.
Close to my Beds side she did stand
Shewing me there a fire brand;
She told me too, as that did spend,
So drew my life unto an end.
Three quarters were consum'd of it;
Onely remaind a little bit,
Which will be burnt up by and by,
Then Juha weep, for I must dy.

Upon Raspe Epigram.

Raspe playes at Nine-holes; and 'tis known he gets
Many a Teaster by his game, and bets:
But of his gettings there's but little sign;
When one hole wasts more then he gets by Nine.

Upon Center a Spectacle-maker with a flat nose.

Center is known weak sighted, and he sells
To others store of helpfull spectacles.
Why weres he none? Because we may suppose,
Where Leaven wants, there Levill lies the nose.

Clothes do but cheat and cousen us.

Away with silks, away with Lawn,
I'll have no Sceans, or Curtains drawn:
Give me my Mistresse, as she is,
Drest in her nak't simplicities:
For as my Heart, ene so mine Eye
Is wone with flesh, not Drapery.

To Dianeme.

Shew me thy feet; shew me thy legs, thy thighes;
Shew me Those Fleshie Principalities;
Shew me that Hill (where smiling Love doth sit)
Having a living Fountain under it.
Shew me thy waste; Then let me there withall,
By the Assention of thy Lawn, see All.

Upon Electra.

When out of bed my Love doth spring,
'Tis but as day a kindling:
But when She's up and fully drest,
'Tis then broad Day throughout the East.

To his Booke.

Have I not blest Thee? Then go forth; nor fear
Or spice, or fish, or fire, or close-stools here.
But with thy fair Fates leading thee, Go on
With thy most white Predestination.
Nor thinke these Ages that do hoarcely sing
The farting Tanner, and familiar King;
The dancing Frier, tatter'd in the bush;
Those monstrous lies of little Robin Rush:
Tom Chipperfeild, and pritty-lisping Ned,
That doted on a Maide of Gingerbred:
The flying Pilcher, and the frisking Dace,
With all the rabble of Tim-Trundells race,
(Bred from the dung-hils, and adulterous rhimes,)
Shall live, and thou not superlast all times?
No, no, thy Stars have destin'd Thee to see
The whole world die, and turn to dust with thee.
He's greedie of his life, who will not fall,
When as a publick ruine bears down All.

Of Love.

I do not love, nor can it be
Love will in vain spend shafts on me:
I did this God-head once defie;
Since which I freeze, but cannot frie.
Yet out alas! the deaths the same,
Kil'd by a frost or by a flame.

Upon himself.

I dislikt but even now;
Now I love I know not how.
Was I idle, and that while
Was I fier'd with a smile?
I'll too work, or pray; and then
I shall quite dislike agen.

Another.

Love he that will; it best likes me,
To have my neck from Loves yoke-free.

Upon Skinns. Epigram.

Skinns he din'd well to day; how do you think?
His Nails they were his meat, his Reume the drink.

Upon Pievish. Epigram.

Pievish doth boast, that he's the very first
Of English Poets, and 'tis thought the Worst.

Upon Jolly and Jilly, Epigram.

Jolly and Jillie, bite and scratch all day,
But yet get children (as the neighbours say.)
The reason is, though all the day they fight,
They cling and close, some minutes of the night.

The mad Maids song.

Good morrow to the Day so fair;
    Good morning Sir to you:
Good morrow to mine own torn hair
    Bedabled with the dew.

Good morning to this Prim-rose too;
    Good morrow to each maid;
That will with flowers the Tomb bestrew,
    Wherein my Love is laid.

Ah woe is me, woe, woe is me,
    Alack and welladay!
For pitty, Sir, find out that Bee,
    Which bore my Love away.

I'll seek him in your Bonnet brave;
    I'll seek him in your eyes;
Nay, now I think th'ave made his grave
    I'th'bed of strawburies.

I'll seek him there; I know, ere this,
    The cold, cold Earth doth shake him;
But I will go, or send a kisse
    By you, Sir, to awake him.

Pray hurt him not; though he be dead,
    He knowes well who do love him,
And who with green-turfes reare his head,
    And who do rudely move him.

He's soft and tender (Pray take heed)
    With bands of Cow-slips bind him;
And bring him home, but 'tis decreed,
    That I shall never find him.

To Springs and Fountains.

I heard ye co'd coole heat; and came
With hope you would allay the same:
Thrice I have washt, but feel no cold,
Nor find that true, which was foretold.
Me thinks like mine, your pulses beat;
And labour with unequall heat:
Cure, cure your selves, for I discrie,
Ye boil with Love, as well as I.

Upon Julia's unlacing herself.

Tell, if thou canst, (and truly) whence doth come
This Camphire, Storax, Spiknard, Galbanum:
These Musks, these Ambers, and those other smells
(Sweet as the Vestrie of the Oracles.)
I'll tell thee; while my Julia did unlace
Her silken bodies, but a breathing space:
The passive Aire such odour then assum'd,
As when to Jove Great Juno goes perfum'd.
Whose pure-Immortall body doth transmit
A scent, that fills both Heaven and Earth with it.

To Bacchus, a Canticle.

Whither dost thou whorry me,
Bacchus, being full of Thee?
This way, that way, that way, this,
Here, and there a fresh Love is.
That doth like me, this doth please;
Thus a thousand Mistresses,
I have now; yet I alone,
Having All, injoy not One.

The Lawne.

Wo'd I see Lawn, clear as the Heaven, and thin?
It sho'd be onely in my Julia's skin:
Which so betrayes her blood, as we discover
The blush of cherries, when a Lawn's cast over.

The Frankincense.

When my off'ring next I make,
Be thy hand the hallowed Cake:
And thy brest the Altar, whence
Love may smell the Frankincense.

Upon Patrick a footman, Epigram.

Now Patrick with his footmanship has done,
His eyes and ears strive which sho'd fastest run.

Upon Bridget. Epigram.

Of foure teeth onely Bridget was possest;
Two she spat out, a cough forc't out the rest.

To Sycamores.

I'm sick of Love; O let me lie
Under your shades, to sleep or die!
Either is welcome; so I have
Or here my Bed, or here my Grave.
Why do you sigh, and sob, and keep
Time with the tears, that I do weep?
Say, have ye sence, or do you prove
What Crucifixions are in Love?
I know ye do; and that's the why,
You sigh for Love, as well as I.

A Pastorall sung to the King:
Montano, Silvio, and Mirtillo, Shepheards.

Mon. Bad are the times. Sil. And wors then they are we.

Mon Troth, bad are both; worse fruit, and ill the tree:

The feast of Shepheards fail. Sil. None crowns the cup

Of Wassaile now, or sets the quintell up:

And He, who us'd to leade the Country-round,

Youthfull Mirtillo, Here he comes, Griefdrownd.

    Ambo. Lets cheer him up. Sil. Behold him weeping ripe.

    Mirt. Ah! Amarillis, farewell mirth and pipe;

Since thou art gone, no more I mean to play,

To these smooth Lawns, my mirthfull Roundelay. (sweet

Dear Amarillis! Mon. Hark! Sil. mark:Mir. this earth grew

Where, Amarillis, Thou didst set thy feet.

    Ambo. Poor pittied youth! Mir. And here the breth of kine

And sheep, grew more sweet, by that breth of Thine.

This flock of wooll, and this rich lock of hair,

This ball of Cow-slips, these she gave me here.

    Sil. Words sweet as Love it self. Montano, Hark.

    Mirt. This way she came, and this way too she went;

How each thing smells divinely redolent!

Like to a field of beans, when newly blown;

Or like a medow being lately mown.

    Mont. A sweet-sad passion.---

    Mirt. In dewie-mornings when she came this way,

Sweet Bents wode bow, to give my Love the day:

And when at night, she folded had her sheep,

Daysies wo'd shut, and closing, sigh and weep.

Besides (Ai me!) since she went hence to dwell,

The voices Daughter nea'r spake syllable.

But she is gone. Sil. Mirtillo, tell us whether,

    Mirt. Where she and I shall never meet together.

    Mont. Fore-fend it Pan, and Pales do thou please

To give an end: Mir. To what? Scil. Such griefs as these.

    Mirt. Never, O never! Still I may endure

The wound I suffer, never find a cure.

    Mont. Love for thy sake will bring her to these hills

And dales again: Mir. No I will languish still;

And all the while my part shall be to weepe;
And with my sighs, call home my bleating sheep:
And in the Rind of every comely tree
I'll carve thy name, and in that name kisse thee: (old
    Mont. Set with the Sunne, thy woes: Scil. The day grows
And time it is our full-fed flocks to fold.
    Chor. The shades grow great; but greater growes our sor,
        But lets go steepe
        Our eyes in sleepe;
        And meet to weepe
           To morrow.

The Poet loves a Mistresse, but not to marry.

I do not love to wed,
Though I do like to wooe;
And for a maidenhead
I'll beg, and buy it too.

I'll praise, and I'll approve
Those maids that never vary;
And fervently I'll love;
But yet I would not marry.

I'll hug, I'll kisse, I'll play,
And Cock-like Hens I'll tread:
And sport it any way;
But in the Bridall Bed:

For why? that man is poore,
Who hath but one of many;
But crown'd he is with store,
That single may have any.

Why then, say, what is he
(To freedome so unknown)
Who having two or three,
Will be content with one?

Upon Flimsey. Epigram.

Why walkes Nick Flimsey like a Male-content?
Is it because his money all is spent?
No, but because the Ding-thrift now is poore,
And knowes not where i'th world to borrow more.

Upon Shewbread. Epigram.

Last night thou didst invite me home to eate;
And shew'st me there much Plate, but little meat;
Prithee, when next thou do'st invite, barre State,
And give me meate, or give me else thy Plate.

The Willow Garland.

A willow Garland thou did'st send
     Perfum'd (last day) to me:
Which did but only this portend,
     I was forsooke by thee.

Since so it is; I'll tell thee what,
     To morrow thou shalt see
Me weare the Willow; after that,
     To dye upon the Tree.

As Beasts unto the Altars go
     With Garlands drest, so I
Will, with my Willow-wreath also,
     Come forth and sweetly dye.

A Hymne to Sir Clipseby Crew.

'Twas not Lov's Dart;
Or any blow
Of want, or foe,
Did wound my heart
With an eternall smart:

But only you,
My sometimes known
Companion,
(My dearest Crew,)
That me unkindly slew.

May your fault dye,
And have no name
In Bookes of fame;
Or let it lye
Forgotten now, as I.

We parted are,
And now no more,
As heretofore,
By jocund Larr,
Shall be familiar.

But though we Sever
My Crew shall see,
That I will be
Here faithlesse never;
But love my Clipseby ever.

Upon Roots. Epigram.

Roots had no money; yet he went o'th score
For a wrought Purse; can any tell wherefore?
Say, What sho'd Roots do with a Purse in print,
That h'ad nor Gold or Silver to put in't?

Upon Craw.

Craw cracks in sirrop; and do's stinking say,
Who can hold that (my friends) that will away?

Observation.

Who to the North, or South, doth set
His Bed, Male children shall beget.

Empires.

Empires of Kings, are now, and ever were,
(As Salust saith) co-incident to feare.

Felicity, quick of flight.

Every time seemes short to be,
That's measur'd by felicity:
But one halfe houre, that's made up here
With griefe; seemes longer then a yeare.

Putrefaction.

Putrefaction is the end
Of all that Nature doth entend.

Passion.

Were there not a Matter known,
There wo'd be no Passion.

Jack and Jill.

Since Jack and Jill both wicked be;
It seems a wonder unto me,
That they no better do agree.

Upon Parson Beanes.

Old Parson Beanes hunts six dayes of the week,
And on the seaventh, he has his Notes to seek.
Six dayes he hollows so much breath away,
That on the seaventh, he can nor preach, or pray.

The crowd and company.

In holy meetings, there a man may be
One of the crowd, not of the companie.

Short and long both likes.

This Lady's short, that Mistresse she is tall;
But long or short, I'm well content with all.

Pollicie in Princes.

That Princes may possesse a surer seat,
'Tis fit they make no One with them too great.

Upon Rook, Epigram.

Rook he sells feathers, yet he still doth crie
Fie on this pride, this Female vanitie.
Thus, though the Rooke do's raile against the sin,
He loves the gain that vanity brings in.

Upon the Nipples of Julia's Breast.

Have ye beheld (with much delight)
A red-Rose peeping through a white?
Or else a Cherrie (double grac't)
Within a Lillie? Center plac't?
Or ever mark't the pretty beam,
A Strawberry shewes halfe drown'd in Creame?
Or seen rich Rubies blushing through
A pure smooth Pearle, and Orient too?
So like to this, nay all the rest,
Is each neate Niplet of her breast.

To Daisies, not to shut so soone.

Shut not so soon; the dull-ey'd night
    Ha's not as yet begunne
To make a seisure on the light,
    Or to seale up the Sun.

No Marigolds yet closed are;
    No shadowes great appeare;
Nor doth the early Shepheards Starre
    Shine like a spangle here.

Stay but till my Julia close
    Her life-begetting eye;
And let the whole world then dispose
    It selfe to live or dye.

To the little Spinners.

Yee pretty Huswives, wo'd ye know
The worke that I wo'd put ye to?
This, this it sho'd be, for to spin,
A Lawn for me, so fine and thin,
As it might serve me for my skin.
For cruell Love ha's me so whipt,
That of my skin, I all am stript;
And shall dispaire, that any art
Can ease the rawnesse, or the smart;
Unlesse you skin again each part.
Which mercy if you will but do,
I call all Maids to witnesse too
What here I promise, that no Broom
Shall now, or ever after come
To wrong a Spinner or her Loome.

Oberons Palace.

After the Feast (my Shapcot) see,
The Fairie Court I give to thee:
Where we'le present our Oberon led
Halfe tipsie to the Fairie Bed,
Where Mab he finds; who there doth lie
Not without mickle majesty.
Which, done; and thence remov'd the light,
We'l wish both Them and Thee, good night.

Full as a Bee with Thyme, and Red,
As Cherry harvest, now high fed
For Lust and action; on he'l go,
To lye with Mab, though all say no.
Lust ha's no eares; He's sharpe as thorn;
And fretfull, carries Hay in's horne,
And lightning in his eyes; and flings
Among the Elves, (if mov'd) the stings
Of peltish wasps; we'l know his Guard
Kings though th'are hated, will be fear'd.
Wine lead him on. Thus to a Grove
(Sometimes devoted unto Love)
Tinseld with Twilight, He, and They
Lead by the shine of Snails; a way
Beat with their num'rous feet, which by
Many a neat perplexity,
Many a turn, and man' a crosse-
Track they redeem a bank of mosse
Spungie and swelling, and farre more
Soft then the finest Lemster Ore.
Mildly disparkling, like those fiers,
Which break from the Injeweld tyres
Of curious Brides; or like those mites
Of Candi'd dew in Moony nights.
Upon this Convex, all the flowers
(Nature begets by th'Sun, and showers,)
Are to a wilde digestion brought,
As if Loves Sampler here was wrought:

Or Citherea's Ceston, which
All with temptation doth bewitch.
Sweet Aires move here; and more divine
Made by the breath of great-ey'd kine,
Who as they lowe empearl with milk
The four-leav'd grasse, or mosse-like silk.
The breath of Munkies met to mix
With Musk-flies, are th'Aromaticks,
Which cense this Arch; and here and there,
And farther off, and every where,
Throughout that Brave Mosaick yard
Those Picks or Diamonds in the Card:
With peeps of Harts, of Club and Spade
Are here most neatly inter-laid.
Many a Counter, many a Die,
Half rotten, and without an eye,
Lies here abouts; and for to pave
The excellency of this Cave,
Squirrils and childrens teeth late shed,
Are neatly here enchequered.
With brownest Toadstones, and the Gum
That shines upon the blewer Plum.
The nails faln off by Whit-flawes: Art's
Wise hand enchasing here those warts,
Which we to others (from our selves)
Sell, and brought hither by the Elves.
The tempting Mole, stoln from the neck
Of the shie Virgin, seems to deck
The holy Entrance; where within
The roome is hung with the blew skin
Of shifted Snake: enfreez'd throughout
With eyes of Peacocks Trains, & Trout-
flies curious wings; and these among
Those silver-pence, that cut the tongue
Of the red infant, neatly hung.
The glow-wormes eyes; the shining scales
Of silv'rie fish; wheat-strawes, the snailes
Soft Candle-light; the Kitling's eyne;
Corrupted wood; serve here for shine.
No glaring light of bold-fac't Day,

Or other over radiant Ray
Ransacks this roome; but what weak beams
Can make reflected from these jems,
And multiply; Such is the light,
But ever doubtfull Day, or night.
By this quaint Taper-light he winds
His Errours up; and now he finds
His Moon-tann'd Mab, as somewhat sick,
And (Love knowes) tender as a chick.
Upon six plump Dandillions, high-
Rear'd, lyes her Elvish-majestie:
Whose woollie-bubbles seem'd to drowne
Hir Mab-ship in obedient Downe.
For either sheet, was spread the Caule
That doth the Infants face enthrall,
When it is born: (by some enstyl'd
The luckie Omen of the child)
And next to these two blankets ore-
Cast of the finest Gossamore.
And then a Rug of carded wooll,
Which, Spunge-like drinking in the dull-
Light of the Moon, seem'd to comply,
Cloud-like, the daintie Deitie.
Thus soft she lies: and over-head
A Spinners circle is bespread,
With Cob-web-curtains: from the roof
So neatly sunck, as that no proof
Of any tackling can declare
What gives it hanging in the Aire.
The Fringe about this, are those Threds
Broke at the Losse of Maiden-heads:
And all behung with these pure Pearls,
Dropt from the eyes of ravisht Girles
Or writhing Brides; when, (panting) they
Give unto Love the straiter way.
For Musick now; He has the cries
Of fained-lost-Virginities;
The which the Elves make to excite
A more unconquer'd appetite.
The Kings undrest; and now upon

The Gnats-watch-word the Elves are gone.
And now the bed, and Mab possest
Of this great-little-kingly-Guest.
We'll nobly think, what's to be done,
He'll do no doubt; This flax is spun.

To his peculiar friend Master Thomas
Shapcott, Lawyer.

I've paid Thee, what I promis'd; that's not All;
Besides I give Thee here a Verse that shall
(When hence thy Circum-mortall-part is gon)
Arch-like, hold up, Thy Name's Inscription.
Brave men can't die; whose Candid Actions are
Writ in the Poets Endlesse-Kalendar:
Whose velome, and whose volumne is the Skie,
And the pure Starres the praising Poetrie.
                    Farewell.

To Julia in the Temple.

Besides us two, i'th' Temple here's not one
To make up now a Congregation.
Let's to the Altar of perfumes then go,
And say short Prayers; and when we have done so,
Then we shall see, how in a little space,
Saints will come in to fill each Pew and Place.

To Oenone.

What Conscience, say, is it in thee
  When I a Heart had one,
To Take away that Heart from me,
  And to retain thy own?

For shame or pitty now encline
  To play a loving part;
Either to send me kindly thine,
  Or give me back my heart.

Covet not both; but if thou dost
  Resolve to part with neither;
Why! yet to shew that thou art just,
  Take me and mine together.

His weaknesse in woes.

I cannot suffer; And in this, my part
Of Patience wants. Grief breaks the stoutest Heart

Fame makes us forward.

To Print our Poems, the propulsive cause
Is Fame, (the breath of popular applause.)

To Groves.

Yee silent shades, whose each tree here
Some Relique of a Saint doth weare:
Who for some sweet-hearts sake, did prove
The fire, and martyrdome of love.
Here is the Legend of those Saints
That di'd for love; and their complaints:
Their wounded hearts; and names we find
Encarv'd upon the Leaves and Rind.
Give way, give way to me, who come
Scorch't with the selfe-same martyrdome:
And have deserv'd as much (Love knowes)
As to be canoniz'd 'mongst those,
Whose deeds, and deaths here written are
Within your Greenie-Kalendar:
By all those Virgins Fillets hung
Upon your Boughs, and Requiems sung
For Saints and Soules departed hence,
(Here honour'd still with Frankincense)
By all those teares that have been shed,
As a Drink-offering, to the dead:
By all those True-love-knots, that be
With Motto's carv'd on every tree,
By sweet S. Phillis; pitie me:
By deare S. Iphis; and the rest,
Of all those other Saints now blest;
Me, me, forsaken, here admit
Among your Mirtles to be writ:
That my poore name may have the glory
To live remembred in your story.

An Epitaph upon a Virgin.

Here a solemne Fast we keepe,
While all beauty lyes asleep
Husht be all things; (no noyse here)
But the toning of a teare:
Or a sigh of such as bring
Cowslips for her covering.

To live Freely.

Let's live in hast; use pleasures while we may:
Co'd life return, 'twod never lose a day.

To the right gratious Prince, Lodwick, Duke
of Richmond and Lenox.

Of all those three-brave-brothers, faln i'th' Warre,
(Not without glory) Noble Sir, you are,
Despite of all concussions left the Stem
To shoot forth Generations like to them.
Which may be done, if (Sir) you can beget
Men in their substance, not in counterfeit.
Such Essences as those Three Brothers; known
Eternall by their own production.
Of whom, from Fam's white Trumpet, This I'll Tell,
Worthy their everlasting Chronicle,
Never since first Bellona us'd a Shield,
Such Three brave Brothers fell in Mars his Field.
These were those Three Horatii Rome did boast,
Rom's were these Three Horatii we have lost.
One Cordelion had that Age long since;
This, Three; which Three, you make up Foure Brave Prince.

To Jealousie.

O Jealousie, that art
The Canker of the heart:
    And mak'st all hell
    Where thou do'st dwell;
    For pitie be
No Furie, or no Fire-brand to me.

Farre from me I'll remove
All thoughts of irksome Love:
    And turn to snow,
    Or Christall grow;
    To keep still free
(O! Soul-tormenting Jealousie,) from Thee.

Upon Spunge. Epigram.

Spunge makes his boasts that he's the onely man
Can hold of Beere and Ale an Ocean;
Is this his Glory? then his Triumph's Poore;
I know the Tunne of Hidleberge holds more.

To live Freely.

Let's live in hast; use pleasures while we may:
Co'd life return, 'twod never lose a day.

His Almes.

Here, here I live,
And somewhat give,
Of what I have,
To those, who crave.
Little or much,
My Almnes is such:
But if my deal
Of Oyl and Meal
Shall fuller grow,
More I'll bestow:
Mean time be it
E'en but a bit,
Or else a crum,
The scrip hath some.

Upon himself.

Come, leave this loathed Country-life, and then
Grow up to be a Roman Citizen.
Those mites of Time, which yet remain unspent,
Waste thou in that most Civill Government.
Get their comportment, and the gliding tongue
Of those mild Men, thou art to live among:
Then being seated in that smoother Sphere,
Decree thy everlasting Topick there.
And to the Farm-house nere return at all;
Though Granges do not love thee, Cities shall.

To enjoy the Time.

While Fates permits us, let's be merry;
Passe all we must the fatall Ferry:
And this our life too whirles away,
With the Rotation of the Day.

Upon Love.

Love, I have broke
    Thy yoke;
The neck is free:
But when I'm next
    Love vext,
Then shackell me.

'Tis better yet
    To fret
The feet or hands;
Then to enthrall,
    Or gall
The neck with bands.

To the right Honourable Mildmay, Earle of Westmorland.

You are a Lord, an Earle, nay more, a Man,
Who writes sweet Numbers well as any can:
If so, why then are not These Verses hurld,
Like Sybels Leaves, throughout the ample world?
What is a Jewell if it be not set
Forth by a Ring, or some rich Carkanet?
But being so; then the beholders cry,
See, see a Jemme (as rare as Belus eye.)
Then publick praise do's runne upon the Stone,
For a most rich, a rare, a precious One.
Expose your jewels then unto the view,
That we may praise Them, or themselves prize You.
Vertue conceal'd (with Horace you'l confesse)
Differs not much from drowzie slothfullnesse.

The Plunder.

I am of all bereft;
Save but some few Beanes left,
Whereof (at last) to make
For me, and mine a Cake:
Which eaten, they and I
Will say our grace, and die.

Littlenesse no cause of Leannesse.

One feeds on Lard, and yet is leane;
And I but feasting with a Beane,
Grow fat and smooth: The reason is,
Jove prospers my meat, more then his.

Upon Huncks. Epigram.

Huncks ha's no money (he do's sweare, or say)
About him, when the Taverns shot's to pay.
If he ha's none in's pockets, trust me, Huncks
Ha's none at home, in Coffers, Desks, or Trunks.

The parting Verse, or charge to his supposed
Wife when he travelled.

Go hence, and with this parting kisse,
Which joyns two souls, remember this;
Though thou beest young, kind, soft, and faire,
And may'st draw thousands with a haire:
Yet let these glib temptations be
Furies to others, Friends to me.
Looke upon all; and though on fire
Thou set'st their hearts, let chaste desire
Steere Thee to me; and thinke (me gone)
In having all, that thou hast none.
Nor so immured wo'd I have
Thee live, as dead and in thy grave;
But walke abroad, yet wisely well
Stand for my comming, Sentinell.
And think (as thou do'st walke the street)
Me, or my shadow thou do'st meet.
I know a thousand greedy eyes
Will on thy Feature tirannize,
In my short absence; yet behold
Them like some Picture, or some Mould
Fashion'd like Thee; which though 'tave eares
And eyes, it neither sees or heares.
Gifts will be sent, and Letters, which
Are the expressions of that itch,
And salt, which frets thy Suters; fly
Both, lest thou lose thy liberty:
For that once lost, thou't fall to one,
Then prostrate to a million.
But if they wooe thee, do thou say,
(As that chaste Queen of Ithaca
Did to her suitors) this web done
(Undone as oft as done) I'm wonne;
I will not urge Thee, for I know,
Though thou art young, thou canst say no,
And no again, and so deny,
Those thy Lust-burning Incubi.

Let them enstile Thee Fairest faire,
The Pearle of Princes, yet despaire
That so thou art, because thou must
Believe, Love speaks it not, but Lust:
And this their Flatt'rie do's commend
Thee chiefly for their pleasures end.
I am not jealous of thy Faith,
Or will be; for the Axiome saith,
He that doth suspect, do's haste
A gentle mind to be unchaste.
No, live thee to thy selfe, and keep
Thy thoughts as cold, as is thy sleep:
And let thy dreames be only fed
With this, that I am in thy bed.
And thou then turning in that Sphere,
Waking shalt find me sleeping there.
But yet if boundlesse Lust must skaile
Thy Fortress, and will needs prevaile;
And wildly force a passage in,
Banish consent, and 'tis no sinne
Of Thine; so Lucrece fell, and the
Chaste Syracusian Cyane.
So Medullina fell, yet none
Of these had imputation
For the least trespasse; 'cause the mind
Here was not with the act combin'd.
The body sins not, 'tis the Will
That makes the Action, good, or ill.
And if thy fall sho'd this way come,
Triumph in such a Martirdome.
I will not over-long enlarge
To thee, this my religious charge.
Take this compression, so by this
Means, I shall know what other kisse
Is mixt with mine; and truly know,
Returning, if 't be mine or no;
Keepe it till then; and now my Spouse,
For my wisht safety pay thy vowes,
And prayers to Venus; if it please
The Great-blew-ruler of the seas;

Not many full-fac't-moons shall waine,
Lean-horn'd, before I come again
As one triumphant; when I find
In thee, all faith of Woman-kind.
Nor wo'd I have thee thinke, that Thou
Had'st power thy selfe to keep this vow;
But having scapt temptations shelfe,
Know vertue taught thee, not thy selfe.

The Jimmall Ring, or True-love-knot.

Thou sent'st to me a True-love-knot; but I
Return'd a Ring of Jimmals, to imply
Thy Love had one knot, mine a triple tye.

To his Kinsman, Sir Tho. Soame.

Seeing thee Soame, I see a Goodly man,
And in that Good, a great Patrician.
Next to which Two; among the City-Powers,
And Thrones, thy selfe one of Those Senatours:
Not wearing Purple only for the show;
(As many Conscripts of the Citie do)
But for True Service, worthy of that Gowne,
The Golden chain too, and the Civick Crown.

To Blossoms.

Faire pledges of a fruitfull Tree,
      Why do yee fall so fast?
      Your date is not so past;
But you may stay yet here a while,
      To blush and gently smile;
        And go at last.

What, were yee borne to be
      An houre or half's delight;
      And so to bid goodnight?
'Twas pitie Nature brought yee forth
      Meerly to shew your worth,
        And lose you quite.

But you are lovely Leaves, where we
      May read how soon things have
      Their end, though ne'r so brave:
And after they have shown their pride,
      Like you a while: They glide
        Into the Grave.

Mans dying-place uncertain.

Man knowes where first he ships himselfe; but he
Never can tell, where shall his Landing be.

Upon one who said she was alwayes young.

You say y'are young; but when your Teeth are told
To be but three, Black-ey'd, wee'l thinke y'are old.

Nothing Free-cost.

Nothing comes Free-cost here; Jove will not let
His gifts go from him; if not bought with sweat.

Few fortunate.

Many we are, and yet but few possesse
Those Fields of everlasting happinesse.

To Perenna.

How long, Perenna, wilt thou see
Me languish for the love of Thee?
Consent and play a friendly part
To save; when thou may'st kill a heart.

To the Ladyes.

Trust me Ladies, I will do
Nothing to distemper you;
If I any fret or vex,
Men they shall be, not your sex.

The old Wives Prayer.

Holy-Rood come forth and shield
Us i'th' Citie, and the Field:
Safely guard us, now and aye,
From the blast that burns by day;
And those sounds that us affright
In the dead of dampish night.
Drive all hurtfull Feinds us fro,
By the Time the Cocks first crow.

Upon a cheap Laundresse. Epigram.

Feacie (some say) doth wash her clothes i'th' Lie
That sharply trickles from her either eye.
The Laundresses, They envie her good-luck,
Who can with so small charges drive the buck.
What needs she fire and ashes to consume,
Who can scoure Linnens with her own salt reeume?

Upon his departure hence.

Thus I
Passe by,
And die:
As One,
Unknown,
And gon:
I'm made
A shade,
And laid
I'th grave,
There have
My Cave.
Where tell
I dwell,
Farewell.

The Wassaile.

Give way, give way ye Gates, and win
An easie blessing to your Bin,
And Basket, by our entring in.

May both with manchet stand repleat;
Your Larders too so hung with meat,
That though a thousand, thousand eat;

Yet, ere twelve Moones shall whirl about
Their silv'rie Spheres, ther's none may doubt,
But more's sent in, then was serv'd out.

Next, may your Dairies Prosper so,
As that your pans no Ebbe may know;
But if they do, the more to flow.

Like to a solemne sober Stream
Bankt all with Lillies, and the Cream
Of sweetest Cow-slips filling Them.

Then, may your Plants be prest with Fruit,
Nor Bee, or Hive you have be mute;
But sweetly sounding like a Lute.

Next may your Duck and teeming Hen
Both to the Cocks-tread say Amen;
And for their two egs render ten.

Last, may your Harrows, Shares and Ploughes,
Your Stacks, your Stocks, your sweetest Mowes,
All prosper by your Virgin-vowes.

Alas! we blesse, but see none here,
That brings us either Ale or Beere;
In a drie-house all things are neere.

Let's leave a longer time to wait,
Where Rust and Cobwebs bind the gate;
And all live here with needy Fate.

Where Chimneys do for ever weepe,
For want of warmth, and Stomachs keepe
With noise, the servants eyes from sleep.

It is in vain to sing, or stay
Our free-feet here; but we'l away:
Yet to the Lares this we'l say,

The time will come, when you'l be sad,
And reckon this for fortune bad,
T'ave lost the good ye might have had.

Upon a Lady faire, but fruitlesse.

Twice has Pudica been a Bride, and led
By holy Himen to the Nuptiall Bed.
Two Youths sha's known, thrice two, and twice 3. yeares;
Yet not a Lillie from the Bed appeares;
Nor will; for why, Pudica, this may know,
Trees never beare, unlesse they first do blow.

How Springs came first.

These Springs were Maidens once that lov'd,
But lost to that they most approv'd:
My Story tells, by Love they were
Turn'd to these Springs, which wee see here:
The pretty whimpering that they make,
When of the Banks their leave they take;
Tels ye but this, they are the same,
In nothing chang'd but in their name.

To Rosemary and Baies.

My wooing's ended: now my wedding's neere;
When Gloves are giving, Guilded be you there.

Upon Skurffe.

Skurffe by his Nine-bones sweares, and well he may,
All know a Fellon eate the Tenth away.

Upon a Scarre in a Virgins Face.

'Tis Heresie in others: In your face
That Scarr's no Schisme, but the sign of grace.

Upon his eye-sight failing him.

I beginne to waine in sight;
Shortly I shall bid goodnight:
Then no gazing more about,
When the Tapers once are out.

To his worthy Friend, M. Tho. Falconbirge.

Stand with thy Graces forth, Brave man, and rise
High with thine own Auspitious Destinies:
Nor leave the search, and proofe, till Thou canst find
These, or those ends, to which Thou wast design'd.
Thy lucky Genius, and thy guiding Starre,
Have made Thee prosperous in thy wayes, thus farre:
Nor will they leave Thee, till they both have shown
Thee to the World a Prime and Publique One.
Then, when Thou see'st thine Age all turn'd to gold,
Remember what thy Herrick Thee foretold,
When at the holy Threshold of thine house,
He Boded good-luck to thy Selfe and Spouse.
Lastly, be mindfull (when thou art grown great)
That Towrs high rear'd dread most the lightnings threat:
When as the humble Cottages not feare
The cleaving Bolt of Jove the Thunderer.

Upon Julia's haire fill'd with Dew.

Dew sate on Julia's haire,
    And spangled too,
Like Leaves that laden are
    With trembling Dew:
Or glitter'd to my sight,
    As when the Beames
Have their reflected light,
    Daunc't by the Streames.

Another on her.

How can I choose but love, and follow her,
Whose shadow smels like milder Pomander!
How can I chuse but kisse her, whence do's come
The Storax, Spiknard, Myrrhe, and Ladanum.

Losse from the least.

Great men by small meanes oft are overthrown:
He's Lord of thy life, who contemnes his own.

Reward and punishments.

All things are open to these two events,
Or to Rewards, or else to Punishments.

Shame, no Statist.

Shame is a bad attendant to a State:
He rents his Crown, That feares the Peoples hate.

To Sir Clisebie Crew.

Since to th'Country first I came,
I have lost my former flame:
And, methinks, I not inherit,
As I did, my ravisht spirit.
If I write a Verse, or two,
'Tis with very much ado;
In regard I want that Wine,
Which sho'd conjure up a line.
Yet, though now of Muse bereft,
I have still the manners left
For to thanke you (Noble Sir)
For those gifts you do conferre
Upon him, who only can
Be in Prose a gratefull man.

Upon himselfe.

I co'd never love indeed;
Never see mine own heart bleed:
Never crucifie my life;
Or for Widow, Maid, or Wife.

I co'd never seeke to please
One, or many Mistresses:
Never like their lips, to sweare
Oyle of Roses still smelt there.

I co'd never breake my sleepe,
Fold mine Armes, sob, sigh, or weep:
Never beg, or humbly wooe
With oathes, and lyes, (as others do.)

I co'd never walke alone;
Put a shirt of sackcloth on:
Never keep a fast, or pray
For good luck in love (that day.)

But have hitherto liv'd free,
As the aire that circles me:
And kept credit with my heart,
Neither broke i'th whole, or part.

Fresh Cheese and Cream.

Wo'd yee have fresh Cheese and Cream?
Julia's Breast can give you them:
And if more; Each Nipple cries,
To your Cream, her's Strawberries.

An Eclogue, or Pastorall between Endimion Porter
and Lycidas Herrick, set and sung.

Endym. Ah! Lycidas, come tell me why
    Thy whilome merry Oate
By thee doth so neglected lye;
    And never purls a Note?

I prithee speake: *Lyc.* I will. *End.* Say on:
    Lyc. 'Tis thou, and only thou,
That art the cause Endimion; *End.*
    For Loves-sake, tell me how.

Lyc. In this regard, that thou do'st play
    Upon an other Plain:
And for a Rurall Roundelay,
    Strik'st now a Courtly strain.

Thou leav'st our Hills, our Dales, our Bowers,
    Our finer fleeced sheep:
(Unkind to us) to spend thine houres,
    Where Shepheards sho'd not keep.

I meane the Court: Let Latmos be
    My lov'd Endymions Court;
End. But I the Courtly State wo'd see:
    Lyc. Then see it in report.

What ha's the Court to do with Swaines,
    Where Phillis is not known?
Nor do's it mind the Rustick straines
    Of us, or Coridon.

Breake, if thou lov'st us, this delay;
    End. Dear Lycidas, e're long,
I vow by Pan, to come away
    And Pipe unto thy Song.

Then Jessimine, with Florabell;

And dainty Amarillis,
With handsome-handed Drosomell
    Shall pranke thy Hooke with Lillies.

Lyc. Then Tityrus, and Coridon,
    And Thyrsis, they shall follow
With all the rest; while thou alone
    Shalt lead, like young Apollo.

And till thou com'st, thy Lycidas,
    In every Geniall Cup,
Shall write in Spice, Endimion 'twas
    That kept his Piping up.

And my most luckie Swain, when I shall live to see
Endimions Moon to fill up full, remember me:
Mean time, let Lycidas have leave to Pipe to thee.

To a Bed of Tulips.

Bright Tulips, we do know,
    You had your comming hither;
And Fading-time do's show,
    That Ye must quickly wither.

Your Sister-hoods may stay,
    And smile here for your houre;
But dye ye must away:
    Even as the meanest Flower.

Come Virgins then, and see
    Your frailties; and bemone ye;
For lost like these, 'twill be,
    As Time had never known ye.

A Caution.

That Love last long; let it thy first care be
To find a Wife, that is most fit for Thee.
Be She too wealthy, or too poore; be sure,
Love in extreames, can never long endure.

To the Water Nymphs, drinking at the Fountain.

Reach, with your whiter hands, to me,
    Some Christall of the Spring;
And I, about the Cup shall see
    Fresh Lillies flourishing

Or else sweet Nimphs do you but this;
    To'th' Glasse your lips encline;
And I shall see by that one kisse,
    The Water turn'd to Wine.

To his Honoured Kinsman, Sir Richard Stone.

To this white Temple of my Heroes, here
Beset with stately Figures (every where)
Of such rare Saint-ships, who did here consume
Their lives in sweets, and left in death perfume.
Come thou Brave man! And bring with Thee a Stone
Unto thine own Edification.
High are These Statues here, besides no lesse
Strong then the Heavens for everlastingnesse:
Where build aloft; and being fixt by These,
Set up Thine own eternall Images.

Upon a Flie.

A golden Flie one shew'd to me
Clos'd in a Box of Yvorie: (have
Where both seem'd proud; the Flie to
His buriall in an yvory grave:
The yvorie tooke State to hold
A Corps as bright as burnisht gold.
One Fate had both; both equall Grace;
The Buried, and the Burying-place.
Not Virgils Gnat, to whom the Spring
All Flowers sent to'is burying.
Not Marshals Bee, which in a Bead
Of Amber quick was buried.
Nor that fine Worme that do's interre
Her self i'th' silken Sepulchre.
Nor my rare Phil, that lately was Sparrow
With Lillies Tomb'd up in a Glasse;
More honour had, then this same Flie;
Dead, and closed up in Yvorie.

Upon Jack and Jill. Epigram.

When Jill complaines to Jack for want of meate;
Jack kisses Jill, and bids her freely eate:
Jill sayes, of what? sayes Jack, on that sweet kisse,
Which full of Nectar and Ambrosia is,
The food of Poets; so I thought sayes Jill,
That makes them looke so lanke, so Ghost-like still.
Let Poets feed on aire, or what they will;
Let me feed full, till that I fart, sayes Jill.

To Julia.

Julia, when thy Herrick dies,
Close thou up thy Poets eyes:
And his last breath, let it be
Taken in by none but Thee.

To Mistresse Dorothy Parsons.

If thou aske me (Deare) wherefore
I do write of thee no more:
I must answer (Sweet) thy part
Lesse is here, then in my heart.

Upon Parrat.

Parrat protests 'tis he, and only he
Can teach a man the Art of memory:
Believe him not; for he forgot it quite,
Being drunke, who 'twas that Can'd his Ribs last night.

How he would drinke his Wine.

Fill me my Wine in Christall; thus, and thus
I see't in's *puris naturalibus:*
Unmixt. I love to have it smirke and shine,
'Tis sin I know, 'tis sin to throtle Wine.
What Mad-man's he, that when it sparkles so,
Will coole his flames, or quench his fires with snow?

How Marigolds came yellow.

Jealous Girles these sometimes were,
While they liv'd, or lasted here:
Turn'd to Flowers, still they be
Yellow, markt for Jealousie.

The Broken Christall.

To Fetch me Wine my Lucia went,
Bearing a Christall continent:
But making haste, it came to passe,
She brake in two the purer Glasse,
Then smil'd, and sweetly chid her speed;
So with a blush, beshrew'd the deed.

To the right Honourable Edward Earle of Dorset.

If I dare write to You, my Lord, who are,
Of your own selfe, a Publick Theater.
And sitting, see the wiles, wayes, walks of wit,
And give a righteous judgement upon it.
What need I care, though some dislike me sho'd,
If Dorset say, what Herrick writes, is good?
We know y'are learn'd i'th' Muses, and no lesse
In our State-sanctions, deep, or bottomlesse.
Whose smile can make a Poet; and your glance
Dash all bad Poems out of countenance.
So, that an Author needs no other Bayes
For Coronation, then Your onely Praise.
And no one mischief greater then your frown,
To null his Numbers, and to blast his Crowne.
Few live the life immortall. He ensures
His Fame's long life, who strives to set up Yours.

Upon himself.

Th'art hence removing, (like a Shepherds Tent)
And walk thou must the way that others went:
Fall thou must first, then rise to life with These,
Markt in thy Book for faithfull Witnesses.

Hope well and Have well: or,
Faire after Foule weather.

What though the Heaven be lowring now,
And look with a contracted brow?
We shall discover, by and by,
A Repurgation of the Skie:
And when those clouds away are driven,
Then will appeare a cheerfull Heaven.

Upon Love.

I held Love's head while it did ake;
    But so it chanc't to be;
The cruell paine did his forsake,
    And forthwith came to me.

Ai me! How shal my griefe be stil'd?
    Or where else shall we find
One like to me, who must be kill'd
    For being too-too-kind?

To his Kinswoman, Mrs. Penelope Wheeler.

Next is your lot (Faire) to be number'd one,
Here, in my Book's Canonization:
Late you come in; but you a Saint shall be,
In Chiefe, in this Poetick Liturgie.

Another upon her.

First, for your shape, the curious cannot shew
Any one part that's dissonant in you:
And 'gainst your chast behaviour there's no Plea,
Since you are knowne to be Penelope.
Thus faire and cleane you are, although there be
A mighty strife 'twixt Forme and Chastitie.

Precepts.

Good Precepts we must firmly hold,
By daily Learning we wax old.

Kissing and bussing.

Kissing and bussing differ both in this;
We busse our Wantons, but our Wives we kisse.

�֎ 304

Crosse and Pile.

Faire and foule dayes trip Crosse and Pile; The faire
Far lesse in number, then our foule dayes are.

Change gives content.

What now we like, anon we disapprove:
The new successor drives away old Love.

To the Lady Crew, upon the death of her Child.

Why, Madam, will ye longer weep,
When as your Baby's lull'd asleep?
And (pretty Child) feeles now no more
Those paines it lately felt before.
All now is silent; groanes are fled:
Your Child lyes still, yet is not dead:
But rather like a flower hid here
To spring againe another yeare.

His Winding-sheet.

Come thou, who art the Wine, and wit
    Of all I've writ:
The Grace, the Glorie, and the best
    Piece of the rest.
Thou art of what I did intend
    The All, and End.
And what was made, was made to meet
    Thee, thee my sheet.
Come then, and be to my chast side
    Both Bed, and Bride.
We two (as Reliques left) will have
    One Rest, one Grave.
And, hugging close, we will not feare
    Lust entring here:
Where all Desires are dead, or cold
    As is the mould:
And all Affections are forgot,
    Or Trouble not.
Here, here the Slaves and Pris'ners be
    From Shackles free:
And weeping Widowes long opprest
    Doe here find rest.
The wronged Client ends his Lawes
    Here, and his Cause.
Here those long suits of Chancery lie
    Quiet, or die:
And all Star-chamber-Bils doe cease,
    Or hold their peace.
Here needs no Court for our Request,
    Where all are best;
All wise; all equall; and all just
    Alike i'th' dust.
Nor need we here to feare the frowne
    Of Court, or Crown.
Where Fortune bears no sway o're things
    There all are Kings.
In this securer place we'l keep,

As lull'd asleep;
Or for a little time we'l lye,
        As Robes laid by;
To be another day re-worne,
        Turn'd, but not torn:
Or like old Testaments ingrost,
        Lockt up, not lost:
And for a while lye here conceal'd,
        To be reveal'd
Next, at that great Platonick yeere,
        And then meet here.

To Mistresse Mary Willand.

One more by Thee, Love, and Desert have sent,
T'enspangle this expansive Firmament.
O Flame of Beauty! come, appeare, appeare
A Virgin Taper, ever shining here.

Upon Magot a frequenter of Ordinaries.

Magot frequents those houses of good-cheere,
Talkes most, eates most, of all the Feeders there.
He raves through leane, he rages through the fat;
(What gets the master of the Meal by that?)
He who with talking can devoure so much,
How wo'd he eate, were not his hindrance such?

On himselfe.

Borne I was to meet with Age,
And to walke Life's pilgrimage.
Much I know of Time is spent,
Tell I can't, what's Resident.
Howsoever, cares, adue;
I'll have nought to say to you:
But I'll spend my comming houres,
Drinking wine, & crown'd with flowres.

Fortune favours.

Fortune did never favour one
Fully, without exception;
Though free she be, ther's something yet
Still wanting to her Favourite.

To Phillis to love, and live with him.

Live, live with me, and thou shalt see
The pleasures I'll prepare for thee:
What sweets the Country can afford
Shall blesse thy Bed, and blesse thy Board.
The soft sweet Mosse shall be thy bed,
With crawling Woodbine over-spread:
By which the silver-shedding streames
Shall gently melt thee into dreames.
Thy clothing next, shall be a Gowne
Made of the Fleeces purest Downe.
The tongues of Kids shall be thy meate;
Their Milke thy drinke; and thou shalt eate
The Paste of Filberts for thy bread
With Cream of Cowslips buttered:
Thy Feasting-Tables shall be Hills
With Daisies spread, and Daffadils;
Where thou shalt sit, and Red-brest by,
For meat, shall give thee melody.
I'll give thee Chaines and Carkanets
Of Primroses and Violets.
A Bag and Bottle thou shalt have;
That richly wrought, and This as brave;
So that as either shall expresse
The Wearer's no meane Shepheardesse.
At Sheering-times, and yearely Wakes,
When Themilis his pastime makes,
There thou shalt be; and be the wit,
Nay more, the Feast, and grace of it.
On Holy-dayes, when Virgins meet
To dance the Heyes with nimble feet;
Thou shalt come forth, and then appeare
The Queen of Roses for that yeere.
And having danc't ('bove all the best)
Carry the Garland from the rest.
In Wicker-baskets Maids shal bring
To thee, (my dearest Shepharling)
The blushing Apple, bashfull Peare,

And shame-fac't Plum, (all simp'ring there).
Walk in the Groves, and thou shalt find
The name of Phillis in the Rind
Of every straight, and smooth-skin tree;
Where kissing that, I'll twice kisse thee.
To thee a Sheep-hook I will send,
Be-pranckt with Ribbands, to this end,
This, this alluring Hook might be
Lesse for to catch a sheep, then me.
Thou shalt have Possets, Wassails fine,
Not made of Ale, but spiced Wine;
To make thy Maids and selfe free mirth,
All sitting neer the glitt'ring Hearth.
Thou sha't have Ribbands, Roses, Rings,
Gloves, Garters, Stockings, Shooes, and Strings
Of winning Colours, that shall move
Others to Lust, but me to Love.
These (nay) and more, thine own shal be,
If thou wilt love, and live with me.

To his Kinswoman, Mistresse Susanna Herrick.

When I consider (Dearest) thou dost stay
But here awhile, to languish and decay;
Like to these Garden-glories, which here be
The Flowrie-sweet resemblances of Thee:
With griefe of heart, methinks, I thus doe cry,
Wo'd thou hast ne'r been born, or might'st not die.

Upon her Eyes.

Cleere are her eyes,
Like purest Skies.
Discovering from thence
A Babie there
That turns each Sphere,
Like an Intelligence.

Upon her feet.

Her pretty feet
Like snailes did creep
A little out, and then,
As if they started at Bo-peep,
Did soon draw in agen.

To his honoured friend, Sir John Mince.

For civill, cleane, and circumcised wit,
And for the comely carriage of it;
Thou art The Man, the onely Man best known,
Markt for the True-wit of a Million:
From whom we'l reckon. Wit came in, but since
The Calculation of thy Birth, Brave Mince.

Upon his gray haires.

Fly me not, though I be gray,
Lady, this I know you'l say;
Better look the Roses red,
When with white commingled.
Black your haires are; mine are white;
This begets the more delight,
When things meet most opposite:
As in Pictures we descry,
Venus standing Vulcan by.

Upon Mistresse Susanna Southwell, her cheeks.

Rare are thy cheeks Susanna, which do show
Ripe Cherries smiling, while that others blow.

Accusation.

If Accusation onely can draw blood,
None shall be guiltlesse, be he n'er so good.

Pride allowable in Poets.

As thou deserv'st, be proud; then gladly let
The Muse give thee the Delphick Coronet.

A Vow to Minerva.

Goddesse, I begin an Art;
Come thou in, with thy best part,
For to make the Texture lye
Each way smooth and civilly:
And a broad-fac't Owle shall be
Offer'd up with Vows to Thee.

On Jone.

Jone wo'd go tel her haires; and well she might,
Having but seven in all; three black, foure white.

Upon Dundrige.

Dundrige his Issue hath; but is not styl'd
For all his Issue, Father of one Child.

Discord not disadvantageous.

Fortune no higher Project can devise,
Then to sow Discord 'mongst the Enemies.

Ill Government.

Preposterous is that Government, (and rude)
When Kings obey the wilder Multitude.

Upon Letcher. Epigram.

Letcher was Carted first about the streets,
For false Position in his neighbours sheets:
Next, hang'd for Theeving: Now the people say,
His Carting was the Prologue to this Play.

To Electra.

    'Tis Ev'ning, my Sweet,
    And dark; let us meet;
Long time w'ave here been a toying:
    And never, as yet,
    That season co'd get,
Wherein t'ave had an enjoying.

    For pitty or shame,
    Then let not Love's flame,
Be ever and ever a spending;
    Since now to the Port
    The path is but short;
And yet our way has no ending.

    Time flyes away fast;
    Our houres doe waste:
The while we never remember,
    How soone our life, here,
    Growes old with the yeere,
That dyes with the next December.

To Marygolds.

Give way, and be ye ravisht by the Sun,
(And hang the head when as the Act is done)
Spread as He spreads; wax lesse as He do's wane;
And as He shuts, close up to Maids again.

To Dianeme.

Give me one kisse,
    And no more;
If so be, this
    Makes you poore;
To enrich you,
    I'll restore
For that one, two
    Thousand score.

To Julia, the Flaminica Dialis, or Queen-Priest.

Thou know'st, my Julia, that it is thy turne
This Mornings Incense to prepare, and burne.
The Chaplet, and Inarculum here be,
With the white Vestures, all attending Thee.
This day, the Queen-Priest, thou art made t'appease
Love for our very-many Trespasses.
One chiefe transgression is among the rest,
Because with Flowers her Temple was not drest:
The next, because her Altars did not shine
With daily Fyers: The last, neglect of Wine:
For which, her wrath is gone forth to consume
Us all, unlesse preserv'd by thy Perfume.
Take then thy Censer; Put in Fire, and thus,
O Pious-Priestresse! make a Peace for us.
For our neglect, Love did our Death decree,
That we escape. *Redemption comes by Thee.*

Anacreontike.

Born I was to be old,
    And for to die here:
After that, in the mould
    Long for to lye here.
But before that day comes,
    Still I be Bousing;
For I know, in the Tombs
    There's no Carousing.

Meat without mirth.

Eaten I have; and though I had good cheere,
I did not sup, because no friends were there.
Where Mirth and Friends are absent when we Dine
Or Sup, there wants the Incense and the Wine.

Large Bounds doe but bury us.

All things o'r-rul'd are here by Chance;
The greatest mans Inheritance.
Where ere the luckie Lot doth fall,
Serves but for place of Buriall.

An Ode to Sir Clipsebie Crew.

Here we securely live, and eate
      The Creame of meat;
    And keep eternal fires,
By which we sit, and doe Divine
        As Wine
    And Rage inspires.

If full we charme; then call upon
      Anacreon
    To grace the frantick Thyrse:
And having drunk, we raise a shout
      Throughout
    To praise his Verse.

Then cause we Horace to be read,
      Which sung, or seyd,
    A Goblet, to the brim,
Of Lyrick Wine, both swell'd and crown'd,
      A Round
    We quaffe to him.

Thus, thus, we live, and spend the houres
      In Wine and Flowers:
    And make the frollick yeere,
The Month, the Week, the instant Day
      To stay
    The longer here.

Come then, brave Knight, and see the Cell
      Wherein I dwell;
    And my Enchantments too;
Which Love and noble freedome is;
      And this
    Shall fetter you.

Take Horse, and come; or be so kind,
      To send your mind

(Though but in Numbers few)
And I shall think I have the heart,
               Or part
Of Clipseby Crew.

Upon Ursley.

Ursley, she thinks those Velvet Patches grace
The Candid Temples of her comely face:
But he will say, who e'r those Circlets seeth,
They be but signs of Ursleys hollow teeth.

To his worthy Kinsman, Mr. Stephen Soame.

Nor is my Number full, till I inscribe
Thee sprightly Soame, one of my righteous Tribe:
A Tribe of one Lip; Leven, and of One
Civil Behaviour, and Religion.
A Stock of Saints; where ev'ry one doth weare
A stole of white, (and Canonized here)
Among which Holies, be Thou ever known,
Brave Kinsman, markt out with the whiter stone:
Which seals Thy Glorie; since I doe prefer
Thee here in my eternall Calender.

To his Tomb-maker.

Go I must; when I am gone,
Write but this upon my Stone;
Chaste I liv'd, without a wife,
That's the Story of my life.
Strewings need none, every flower
Is in this word, Batchelour.

Great Spirits supervive.

Our mortall parts may wrapt in Seare-cloths lye:
Great Spirits never with their bodies dye.

None free from fault.

Out of the world he must, who once comes in:
No man exempted is from Death, or sinne.

Pitie to the prostrate.

Tis worse then barbarous cruelty to show
No part of pitie on a conquer'd foe.

Upon himselfe being buried.

Let me sleep this night away,
Till the Dawning of the day:
Then at th'opening of mine eyes,
I, and all the world shall rise.

Way in a crowd.

Once on a Lord-Mayors day, in Cheapside, when
Skulls co'd not well passe through that scum of men.
For quick dispatch, Sculls made no longer stay,
Then but to breath, and every one gave way:
For as he breath'd, the People swore from thence
A Fart flew out, or a Sir-reverence.

The credit of the Conquerer.

He who commends the vanquisht, speaks the Power,
And glorifies the worthy Conquerer.

His content in the Country.

Here, here I live with what my Board,
Can with the smallest cost afford.
Though ne'r so mean the Viands be,
They well content my Prew and me.
Or Pea, or Bean, or Wort, or Beet,
What ever comes, content makes sweet:
Here we rejoyce, because no Rent
We pay for our poore Tenement:
Wherein we rest, and never feare
The Landlord, or the Usurer.
The Quarter-day do's ne'r affright
Our Peacefull slumbers in the night.
We eate our own, and batten more,
Because we feed on no mans score:
But pitie those, whose flanks grow great,
Swel'd with the Lard of others meat.
We blesse our Fortunes, when we see
Our own beloved privacie:
And like our living, where w'are known
To very few, or else to none.

On himselfe.

Some parts may perish; dye thou canst not all:
The most of Thee shall scape the funerall.

Lines have their Linings, and Bookes their Buckram.

As in our clothes, so likewise he who lookes,
Shall find much farcing Buckram in our Books.

Upon one-ey'd Broomsted. Epigram.

Broomsted a lamenesse got by cold and Beere;
And to the Bath went, to be cured there:
His feet were helpt, and left his Crutch behind:
But home return'd, as he went forth, halfe blind.

The Fairies.

If ye will with Mab find grace,
Set each Platter in his place:
Rake the Fier up, and get
Water in, ere Sun be set.
Wash your Pailes, and clense your Dairies;
Sluts are loathsome to the Fairies:
Sweep your house: Who doth not so,
Mab will pinch her by the toe.

To his honoured friend, M. John Weare, Councellour.

Did I or love, or could I others draw
To the indulgence of the rugged Law:
The first foundation of that zeale sho'd be
By Reading all her Paragraphs in Thee.
Who dost so fitly with the Lawes unite,
As if You Two, were one Hermophrodite:
Nor courts thou Her because she's well attended
With wealth, but for those ends she was entended:
Which were, (and still her offices are known)
Law is to give to ev'ry one his owne.
To shore the Feeble up, against the strong;
To shield the Stranger, and the Poore from wrong:
This was the Founders grave and good intent,
To keepe the out-cast in his Tenement:
To free the Orphan from that Wolfe-like-man,
Who is his Butcher more then Guardian.
To drye the Widowes teares; and stop her Swoones,
By pouring Balme and Oyle into her wounds.
This was the old way; and 'tis yet thy course,
To keep those pious Principles in force.
Modest I will be; but one word I'll say
(Like to a sound that's vanishing away)
Sooner the in-side of thy hand shall grow
Hisped, and hairie, ere thy Palm shall know
A Postern-bribe tooke, or a Forked-Fee
To fetter Justice, when She might be free.
Eggs I'll not shave: But yet brave man, if I
Was destin'd forth to golden Soveraignty:
A Prince I'de be, that I might Thee preferre
To be my Counsell both, and Chanceller.

The Watch.

Man is a Watch, wound up at first, but never
Wound up again: Once down, He's down for ever.
The Watch once downe, all motions then do cease;
And Mans Pulse stopt, All Passions sleep in Peace.

Art above Nature, to Julia.

When I behold a Forrest spread
With silken trees upon thyhead;
And when I see that other Dresse
Of flowers set in comlinesse:
When I behold another grace
In the ascent of curious Lace,
Which like a Pinacle doth shew
The top, and the top-gallant too.
Then, when I see thy Tresses bound
Into an Ovall, square, or round;
And knit in knots far more then I
Can tell by tongue; or true-love tie:
Next, when those Lawnie Filmes I see
Play with a wild civility:
And all those airie silks to flow,
Alluring me, and tempting so:
I must confesse, mine eye and heart
Dotes less on Nature, then on Art.

Upon Sibilla.

With paste of Almonds, Syb her hands doth scoure;
Then gives it to the children to devoure.
In Cream she bathes her thighs (more soft then silk)
Then to the poore she freely gives the milke.

Upon his kinswoman Mistresse Bridget Herrick.

Sweet Bridget blusht, & therewithall,
Fresh blossoms from her cheekes did fall.
I thought at first 'twas but a dream,
Till after I had handled them;
And smelt them, then they smelt to me,
As Blossomes of the Almond Tree.

Upon Love.

I played with Love, as with the fire
    The wanton Satyre did;
Nor did I know, or co'd descry
    What under there was hid.

That Satyre he but burnt his lips;
    (But min's the greater smart)
For kissing Loves dissembling chips,
    The fire scorctht my heart.

Upon a comely, and curious Maide.

If Men can say that beauty dyes;
Marbles will sweare that here it lyes.
If Reader then thou canst forbeare,
In publique loss to shed a Teare:
The Dew of griefe upon this stone
Will tell thee Pitie thou hast none.

Upon the losse of his Finger.

One of the five straight branches of my hand
Is lopt already; and the rest but stand
Expecting when to fall: which soon will be;
First dyes the Leafe, the Bough next, next the Tree.

Upon Irene.

Angry if Irene be
But a Minutes life with me:
Such a fire I espie
Walking in and out her eye,
As at once I freeze, and frie.

Upon Tooly.

The Eggs of Pheasants wrie-nosed Tooly sells;
But ne'r so much as licks the speckled shells:
Only, if one prove addled, that he eates
With superstition, (as the Cream of meates.)
The Cock and Hen he feeds; but not a bone
He ever pickt (as yet) of any one.

A Hymne to the Graces.

When I love, (as some have told,
Love I shall when I am old)
O ye Graces! Make me fit
For the welcoming of it.
Clean my Roomes, as Temples be,
T'entertain that Deity.
Give me words wherewith to wooe,
Suppling and successefull too:
Winning postures; and withall,
Manners each way musicall:
Sweetnesse to allay my sowre
And unsmooth behaviour.
For I know you have the skill
Vines to prune, though not to kill,
And of any wood ye see,
You can make a Mercury.

To Silvia.

No more my Silvia, do I mean to pray
For those good dayes that ne'r will come away.
I want beliefe; O gentle Silvia, be
The patient Saint, and send up vowes for me.

Upon Blanch. Epigram.

I have seen many Maidens to have haire;
Both for their comely need, and some to spare:
But Blanch has not so much upon her head,
As to bind up her chaps when she is dead.

Upon Umber. Epigram.

Umber was painting of a Lyon fierce,
And working it, by chance from Umbers Erse
Flew out a crack, so mighty, that the Fart,
(As Umber sweares) did make his Lyon start.

The Poet hath lost his pipe.

I cannot pipe as I was wont to do,
Broke is my Reed, hoarse is my singing too:
My wearied Oat I'll hang upon the Tree,
And give it to the Silvan Deitie.

Upon Electra's Teares.

Upon her cheekes she wept, and from those showers
Sprang up a sweet Nativity of Flowres.

True Friendship.

Wilt thou my true Friend be?
Then love not mine, but me.

The Apparition of his Mistresse calling him to Elizium.

Desunt nonnulla —

Come then, and like two Doves with silv'rie wings,
Let our soules flie to' th'shades, where ever springs
Sit smiling in the Meads; where Balme and Oile,
Roses and Cassia crown the untill'd soyle.
Where no disease raignes, or infection comes
To blast the Aire, but Amber-greece and Gums.
This, that, and ev'ry Thicket doth transpire
More sweet, then Storax from the hallowed fire:
Where ev'ry tree a wealthy issue beares
Of fragrant Apples, blushing Plums, or Peares:
And all the shrubs, with sparkling spangles, shew
Like Morning-Sun-shine tinsilling the dew.
Here in green Meddowes sits eternall May,
Purfling the Margents, while perpetuall Day
So double gilds the Aire, as that no night
Can ever rust th'Enamel of the light.
Here, naked Younglings, handsome Striplings run
Their Goales for Virgins kisses; which when done,
Then unto Dancing forth the learned Round
Commixt they meet, with endlesse Roses crown'd.
And here we'l sit on Primrose-banks, and see
Love's Chorus led by Cupid; and we'l be
Two loving followers too unto the Grove,
Where Poets sing the stories of our love.
There thou shalt hear Divine Museus sing
Of Hero, and Leander; then I'll bring
Thee to the Stand, where honour'd Homer reades
His Odisees, and his high Iliads.
About whose Throne the crowd of Poets throng
To heare the incantation of his tongue:
To Linus, then to Pindar; and that done,
I'll bring thee Herrick to Anacreon,
Quaffing his full-crown'd bowles of burning Wine,
And in his Raptures speaking Lines of Thine,
Like to His subject; and as his Frantick-

Looks, shew him truly Bacchanalian like,
Besmear'd with Grapes; welcome he shall thee thither,
Where both may rage, both drink and dance together.
Then stately Virgil, witty Ovid, by
Whom faire Corinna sits, and doth comply
With Yvorie wrists, his Laureat head, and steeps
His eye in dew of kisses, while he sleeps.
Then soft Catullus, sharp-fang'd Martial,
And towring Lucan, Horace, Juvenal,
And Snakie Perseus, these, and those, whom Rage
(Dropt for the jarres of heaven) fill'd t'engage
All times unto their frenzies; Thou shalt there
Behold them in a spacious Theater.
Among which glories, (crown'd with sacred Bayes,
And flatt'ring Ivie) Two recite their Plaies,
Beumont and Fletcher, Swans, to whom all eares
Listen, while they (like Syrens in their Spheres)
Sing their Evadne; and still more for thee
There yet remaines to know, then thou can'st see
By glim'ring of a fancie: Doe but come,
And there I'll shew thee that capacious roome
In which thy Father Johnson now is plac't,
As in a Globe of Radiant fire, and grac't
To be in that Orbe crown'd (that doth include
Those Prophets of the former Magnitude)
And he one chiefe; But harke, I heare the Cock,
(The Bell-man of the night) proclaime the clock
Of late struck one; and now I see the prime
Of Day break from the pregnant East, 'tis time
I vanish; more I had to say;
But Night determines here, Away.

Life is the Bodies Light.

Life is the Bodies light; which once declining,
Those crimson clouds i'th'cheeks & lips leave shining.
Those counter-changed Tabbies in the ayre,
(The Sun once set) all of one colour are.
So, when Death comes, Fresh tinctures lose their place,
And dismall Darknesse then doth smutch the face.

Upon Urles. Epigram.

Urles had the Gout so, that he co'd not stand;
Then from his Feet, it shifted to his Hand:
When 'twas in's Feet, his Charity was small;
Now tis in's Hand, he gives no Almes at all.

Upon Franck.

Franck ne'r wore silk she sweares; but I reply,
She now weares silk to hide her blood-shot eye.

Love lightly pleased.

Let faire or foule my Mistresse be,
Or low, or tall, she pleaseth me:
Or let her walk, or stand, or sit,
The posture hers, I'm pleas'd with it.

Or let her tongue be still, or stir,
Gracefull is ev'ry thing from her.
Or let her Grant, or else Deny,
My Love will fit each Historie.

The Primrose.

    Aske me why I send you here
This sweet Infanta of the yeere?
    Aske me why I send to you
This Primrose, thus bepearl'd with dew?
    I will whisper to your eares,
The sweets of Love are mixt with tears.

    Ask me why this flower do's show
So yellow-green, and sickly too?
    Ask me why the stalk is weak
And bending, (yet it doth not break?)
    I will answer, These discover
What fainting hopes are in a Lover.

The Tythe. To the Bride.

If nine times you your Bride-groome kisse;
The tenth you know the Parsons is.
Pay then your Tythe; and doing thus,
Prove in your Bride-bed numerous.
If children you have ten, Sir John
Won't for his tenth part ask you one.

A Frolick.

Bring me my Rose-buds, Drawer come;
    So, while I thus sit crown'd;
I'll drink the aged Cecubum,
    Untill the roofe turne round.

Change common to all.

All things subjected are to Fate;
Whom this Morne sees most fortunate,
The Ev'ning sees in poore estate.

To Julia.

The Saints-bell calls; and, Julia, I must read
The Proper Lessons for the Saints now dead:
To grace which Service, Julia, there shall be
One Holy Collect, said or sung for Thee.
Dead when thou art, Deare Julia, thou shalt have
A Tentrall sung by Virgins o're thy Grave:
Meane time we two will sing the Dirge of these;
Who dead, deserve our best remembrances.

No luck in Love.

I doe love I know not what;
Sometimes this, & sometimes that:
All conditions I aime at.

But, as lucklesse, I have yet
Many shrewd disasters met,
To gaine her whom I wo'd get.

Therefore now I'll love no more,
As I've doted heretofore:
He who must be, shall be poore.

In the darke none dainty.

Night hides our thefts; all faults then pardon'd be:
All are alike faire, when no spots we see.
Lais and Lucrece, in the night time are
Pleasing alike; alike both singular:
Jone, and my Lady have at that time one,
One and the selfe-same priz'd complexion.
Then please alike the Pewter and the Plate;
The chosen Rubie, and the Reprobate.

A charme, or an allay for Love.

If so be a Toad be laid
In a Sheeps-skin newly flaid,
And that ty'd to man 'twil sever
Him and his affections ever.

Upon a free Maid, with a foule breath.

You say you'l kiss me, and I thanke you for it:
But stinking breath, I do as hell abhorre it.

Upon Coone. Epigram.

What is the reason Coone so dully smels?
His Nose is over-cool'd with Isicles.

To his Brother in Law Master John Wingfield

For being comely, consonant, and free
To most of men, but most of all to me:
For so decreeing, that thy clothes expence
Keepes still within a just circumference:
Then for contriving so to loade thy Board,
As that the Messes ne'r o'r-laid the Lord:
Next for Ordaining, that thy words not swell
To any one unsober syllable.
These I co'd praise thee for beyond another,
Wert thou a Winckfield onely, not a Brother.

The Head-ake.

My head doth ake,
O Sappho! take
　　Thy fillit,
And bind the paine;
Or bring some bane
　　To kill it.

But lesse that part,
Then my poore heart,
　　Now is sick:
One kisse from thee
Will counsell be,
　　And Physick.

On himselfe.

Live by thy Muse thou shalt; when others die
Leaving no Fame to long Posterity:
When Monarchies trans-shifted are, and gone;
Here shall endure thy vast Dominion.

Upon a Maide.

Hence a blessed soule is fled,
Leaving here the body dead:
Which (since here they can't combine)
For the Saint, we'l keep the Shrine.

�֍ 339

Upon Spalt.

Of Pushes Spalt has such a knottie race,
He needs a Tucker for to burle his face.

Of Horne a Comb-maker.

Horne sells to others teeth; but has not one
To grace his own Gums, or of Box, or bone.

Cruelty base in Commanders.

Nothing can be more loathsome, then to see
Power conjoyn'd with Natures Crueltie.

Upon a sowre-breath Lady. Epigram.

Fie, (quoth my Lady) what a stink is here?
When 'twas her breath that was the Carrionere.

Upon the troublesome times.

O! Times most bad,
Without the scope
 Of hope
Of better to be had!

Where shall I goe,
Or whither run
 To shun
This publique overthrow?

No places are
(This I am sure)
 Secure
In this our wasting Warre.

Some storms w'ave past;
Yet we must all
 Down fall,
And perish at the last.

Upon Lucia.

I askt my Lucia but a kisse;
And she with scorne deny'd me this:
Say then, how ill sho'd I have sped,
Had I then askt her Maidenhead?

Little and loud.

Little you are; for Womans sake be proud;
For my sake next, (though little) be not loud.

Ship-wrack.

He, who has suffer'd Ship-wrack, feares to saile
Upon the Seas, though with a gentle gale.

Paines without profit.

A long-lifes-day I've taken paines
For very little, or no gaines:
The Ev'ning's come; here now I'll stop,
And work no more; but shut up Shop.

To his Booke.

Be bold my Booke, nor be abasht, or feare
The cutting Thumb-naile, or the Brow severe.
But by the Muses sweare, all here is good,
If but well read; or ill read, understood.

His Prayer to Ben. Johnson.

When I a Verse shall make,
    Know I have praid thee,
For old Religions sake,
    Saint Ben to aide me.

Make the way smooth for me,
    When I, thy Herrick,
Honouring thee, on my knee
    Offer my Lyrick.

Candles I'll give to thee,
    And a new Altar;
And thou Saint Ben, shalt be
    Writ in my Psalter.

Poverty and Riches.

Give Want her welcome if she comes; we find,
Riches to be but burthens to the mind.

Again.

Who with a little cannot be content,
Endures an everlasting punishment.

The Covetous still Captives.

Let's live with that smal pittance that we have;
Who covets more, is evermore a slave.

Lawes.

When Lawes full power have to sway, we see
Little or no part there of Tyrannie.

Upon Lungs. Epigram.

Lungs (as some, say) ne'r sets him down to eate,
But that his breath do's Fly-blow all the meate.

Painting sometimes permitted.

If Nature do deny
Colours, let Art supply.

Of Love.

> I'll get me hence,
> Because no fence,
> Or Fort that I can make here;
> But Love by charmes,
> Or else by Armes
> Will storme, or starving take here.

To his Muse.

Go wooe young Charles no more to looke,
Then but to read this in my Booke:
How Herrick beggs, if that he can-
Not like the Muse; to love the man,
Who by the Shepheards, sung (long since)
The Starre-led-birth of Charles the Prince.

The bad season makes the Poet sad.

Dull to my selfe, and almost dead to these
My many fresh and fragrant Mistresses:
Lost to all Musick now; since every thing
Puts on the semblance here of sorrowing.
Sick is the Land to'th' heart; and doth endure
More dangerous faintings by her desp'rate cure.
But if that golden Age wo'd come again,
And Charles here Rule, as he before did Raign;
If smooth and unperplext the Seasons were,
As when the Sweet Maria lived here:
I sho'd delight to have my Curles halfe drown'd
In Tyrian Dewes, and Head with Roses crown'd.
And once more yet (ere I am laid out dead)
Knock at a Starre with my exalted Head.

To Vulcan.

Thy sooty Godhead, I desire
Still to be ready with thy fire:
That sho'd my Booke despised be,
Acceptance it might find of thee.

Like Pattern, like People.

This is the height of Justice, that to doe
Thy selfe, which thou put'st other men unto.
As great men lead; the meaner follow on,
Or to the good, or evill action.

❊ 346

Purposes.

No wrath of Men, or rage of Seas
Can shake a just mans purposes:
No threats of Tyrants, or the Grim
Visage of them can alter him;
But what he doth at first entend,
That he holds firmly to the end.

His own Epitaph.

As wearied Pilgrims, once possest
Of long'd-for lodging, go to rest:
So I, now having rid my way;
Fix here my Button'd Staffe and stay.
Youth (I confess) hath me mis-led;
But Age hath brought me right to Bed.

To the Maids to walke abroad.

Come sit we under yonder Tree,
Where merry as the Maids we'l be.
And as on Primroses we sit,
We'l venter (if we can) at wit:
If not, at Draw-gloves we will play;
So spend some minutes of the day:
Or else spin out the thread of sands,
Playing at Questions and Commands:
Or tell what strange Tricks Love can do,
By quickly making one of two.
Thus we will sit and talke; but tell
No cruell truths of Philomell,
Or Phyllis, whom hard Fate forc't on,
To kill her selfe for Demophon.
But Fables we'l relate; how Jove
Put on all shapes to get a Love:
As now a Satyr, then a Swan;
A Bull but then; and now a man.
Next we will act, how young men wooe;
And sigh, and kiss, as Lovers do:
And talke of Brides; & who shall make
That wedding-smock, this Bridal-Cake;
That Dress, this Sprig, that Leaf, this Vine;
That smooth and silken Columbine.
This done, we'l draw lots, who shall buy
And guild the Baies and Rosemary:
What Posies for our Wedding Rings;
What Gloves we'l give, and Ribanings:
And smiling at our selves, decree,
Who then the joyning Priest shall be.
What short sweet Prayers shall be said;
And how the Posset shall be made
With Cream of Lillies (not of Kine)
And Maiden's-blush, for spiced wine.
Thus, having talkt, we'l next commend
A kiss to each; and so we'l end.

A Nuptiall Verse to Mistresse Elizabeth Lee,
now Lady Tracie.

Spring with the Larke, most comely Bride, and meet
Your eager Bridegroome with auspitious feet.
The Morn's farre spent; and the immortall Sunne
Corrols his cheeke, to see those Rites not done.
Fie, Lovely maid! Indeed you are too slow,
When to the Temple Love sho'd runne, not go.
Dispatch your dressing then; and quickly wed:
Then feast, and coy't a little; then to bed.
This day is Loves day; and this busie night
Is yours, in which you challeng'd are to fight
With such an arm'd, but such an easie Foe,
As will if you yeeld, lye down conquer'd too.
The Field is pitcht; but such must be your warres,
As that your kisses must out-vie the Starres.
Fall down together vanquisht both, and lye
Drown'd in the bloud of Rubies there, not die.

The Night-Piece to Julia

Her Eyes the Glow-worm lend thee,
The Shooting Starres attend thee;
    And the Elves also,
    Whose little eyes glow
Like the sparks of fire, befriend thee.

No *Will-o'-the-Wispe* mislight thee,
Nor Snake or Slow-worm bite thee;
    But on, on thy way
    Not making a stay,
Since Ghost there's none to affright thee.

Let not the dark thee cumber:
What though the Moon does slumber?
    The Starres of the night
    Will lend thee their light
Like Tapers clear without number.

Then *Julia*, let me woo thee,
Thus, thus to come unto me;
    And when I shall meet
    Thy silv'ry feet
My soul I'll pour into thee.

Good Luck not lasting.

If well the Dice runne, lets applaud the cast:
The happy fortune will not alwayes last.

A Kisse.

What is a Kisse? Why this, as some approve;
The sure sweet-Sement, Glue, and Lime of Love.

Glorie.

I make no haste to have my Numbers read.
Seldome comes Glorie till a man be dead.

Poets.

Wantons we are; and though our words be such,
Our Lives do differ from our Lines by much.

Upon Cock.

Cock calls his Wife his Hen: when Cock goes too't,
Cock treads his Hen, but treads her under-foot.

No despight to the dead.

Reproach we may the living; not the dead:
'Tis cowardice to bite the buried.

To his Verses.

What will ye (my poor Orphans) do
When I must leave the World (and you)
Who'l give ye then a sheltring shed,
Or credit ye, when I am dead?
Who'l let ye by their fire sit?
Although ye have a stock of wit,
Already coin'd to pay for it.
I cannot tell; unlesse there be
Some Race of old humanitie
Left (of the large heart, and long hand)
Alive, as Noble Westmorland;
Or gallant Newark; which brave two
May fost'ring fathers be to you.
If not; expect to be no less
Ill us'd, then Babes left fatherless.

His charge to Julia at his death.

Dearest of thousands, now the time drawes neere,
That with my Lines, my Life must full-stop here.
Cut off thy haires; and let thy Teares be shed
Over my Turfe, when I am buried.
Then for effusions, let none wanting be,
Or other Rites that doe belong to me;
As Love shall helpe thee, when thou do'st go hence
Unto thy everlasting residence.

Upon Love.

In a Dreame, Love bad me go
To the Gallies there to Rowe;
In the Vision I askt, why?
Love as briefly did reply;
'Twas better there to toyle, then prove
The turmoiles they endure that love.
I awoke, and then I knew
What Love said was too too true:
Henceforth therefore I will be
As from Love, from trouble free.
None pities him that's in the snare,
And warn'd before, wo'd not beware.

The Coblers Catch.

Come sit we by the fires side;
    And roundly drinke we here;
Till that we see our cheekes Ale-dy'd
    And noses tann'd with Beere.

Upon Bran. Epigram.

What made that mirth last night? the neighbours
That Bran the Baker did his Breech bewray: (say,
I rather thinke (though they may speake the worst)
'Twas to his Batch, but Leaven laid there first.

Upon Snare, an Usurer.

Snare, ten i'th' hundred calls his wife; and why?
Shee brings in much, by carnall usury:
He by extortion brings in three times more:
Say, who's the worst, th'exactor, or the whore?

Upon Grudgings.

Grudgings turnes bread to stones, when to the Poore
He gives an almes, and chides them from his door

To his lovely Mistresses.

One night i'th' yeare, my dearest Beauties, come
And bring those dew-drink-offerings to my Tomb.
When thence ye see my reverend Ghost to rise,
And there to lick th'effused sacrifice:
Though palenes be the Livery that I weare,
Looke ye not wan, or colourlesse for feare.
Trust me I will not hurt ye; or once shew
The least grim looke, or cast a frown on you:
Nor shall the Tapers when I'm there, burn blew.
This I may do (perhaps) as I glide by,
Cast on my Girles a glance, and loving eye:
Or fold mine armes, and sigh, because I've lost
The world so soon, and in it, you the most.
Then these, no feares more on your Fancies fall,
Though then I smile, and speake no words at all.

Upon Gander. Epigram.

Since Gander did his prettie Youngling wed;
Gander (they say) doth each night pisse a Bed:
What is the cause? Why Gander will reply,
No Goose layes good eggs that is trodden drye.

Connubii Flores, or the well-wishes at Weddings.

Chorus Sacerdotum.

From the Temple to your home
May a thousand blessings come!
And a sweet concurring stream
Of all joyes, to joyn with them.

Chorus Juvenum.

    Happy day
    Make no long stay
        Here
    In thy Sphere;
But give thy place to night,
        That she,
        As Thee,
        May be
Partaker of this sight.
And since it was thy care
To see the Younglings wed;
'Tis fit that Night, the Paire,
Sho'd see safe brought to Bed.

Chorus Senum.

Go to your banquet then, but use delight,
So as to rise still with an appetite.
Love is a thing most nice; and must be fed
To such a height; but never surfeited.
What is beyond the mean is ever ill:
'Tis best to feed Love; but not over-fill:
Go then discreetly to the Bed of pleasure;
And this remember, Vertue keepes the measure.

Chorus Virginum.

Luckie signes we have discri'd

To encourage on the Bride;
And to these we have espi'd,
Not a kissing Cupid flyes
Here about, but has his eyes,
To imply your Love is wise

Chorus Pastorum.

Here we present a fleece
To make a peece
Of cloth;
Nor, Faire, must you be loth
Your Finger to apply
To huswiferie.
Then, then begin
To spin:
And (Sweetling) marke you, what a Web will come
Into your Chests, drawn by your painfull Thumb.

Chorus Matronarum.

Set you to your Wheele, and wax
Rich, by the Ductile Wool and Flax.
Yarne is an Income; and the Huswives thread
The Larder fills with meat; the Bin with bread.

Chorus Senum.

Let wealth come in by comely thrift,
And not by any sordid shift:
'Tis haste
Makes waste;
Extreames have still their fault;
The softest Fire makes the sweetest Mault.
Who gripes too hard the dry and slip'rie sand,
Holds none at all, or little in his hand.

Chorus Virginum.

Goddesse of Pleasure, Youth and Peace,

Give them the blessing of encrease:
And thou Lucina, that do'st heare
The vowes of those, that children beare:
When as her Aprill houre drawes neare,
Be thou then propitious there.

Chorus Juvenum.

Farre hence be all speech, that may anger move:
Sweet words must nourish soft and gentle Love.

Chorus omnium.

Live in the Love of Doves, and having told
The Ravens yeares, go hence more Ripe then old.

An end decreed.

Let's be jocund while we may;
All things have an ending day:
And when once the Work is done;
Fates revolve no Flax th'ave spun.

Upon Love.

A Christall Violl Cupid brought,
    Which had a juice in it:
Of which who drank, he said no thought
    Of Love he sho'd admit.

I greedy of the prize, did drinke,
    And emptied soon the glasse;
Which burnt me so, that I do thinke
    The fire of hell it was

Give me my earthen Cups again,
    The Christall I contemne;
Which, though enchas'd with Pearls, contain
    A deadly draught in them.

And thou O Cupid! come not to
    My Threshold, since I see,
For all I have, or else can do,
    Thou still wilt cozen me.

Upon a child.

Here a pretty Baby lies
Sung asleep with Lullabies:
Pray be silent, and not stirre
Th'easie earth that covers her.

The Beggar to Mab, the Fairie Queen.

Please your Grace, from out your Store,
Give an Almes to one that's poore,
That your mickle, may have more.
Black I'm grown for want of meat;
Give me then an Ant to eate;
Or the cleft eare of a Mouse
Over-sowr'd in drinke of Souce:
Or sweet Lady reach to me
The Abdomen of a Bee;
Or commend a Crickets-hip,
Or his Huckson, to my Scrip.
Give for bread, a little bit
Of a Pease, that 'gins to chit,
And my full thanks take for it.
Floure of Fuz-balls, that's too good
For a man in needy-hood:
But the Meal of Mill-dust can
Well content a craving man.
Any Orts the Elves refuse
Well will serve the Beggars use.
But if this may seem too much
For an Almes; then give me such
Little bits, that nestle there
In the Pris'ners Panier.
So a blessing light upon
You, and mighty Oberon:
That your plenty last till when,
I return your Almes agen.

Farwell Frost, or welcome the Spring.

Fled are the Frosts, and now the Fields appeare
Re-cloth'd in fresh and verdant Diaper.
Thaw'd are the snowes, and now the lusty Spring
Gives to each Mead a neat enameling.
The Palms put forth their Gemmes, and every Tree
Now swaggers in her Leavy gallantry.
The while the Daulian Minstrell sweetly sings,
With warbling Notes, her Tyrrean sufferings.
What gentle Winds perspire? As if here
Never had been the Northern Plunderer
To strip the Trees, and Fields, to their distresse,
Leaving them to a pittied nakednesse.
And look how when a frantick Storme doth tear
A stubborn Oake, or Holme (long growing there)
But lul'd to calmnesse, then succeeds a breeze
That scarcely stirs the nodding leaves of Trees:
So when this War (which tempest-like doth spoil
Our salt, our Corn, our Honie, Wine, and Oile)
Falls to a temper, and doth mildly cast
His inconsiderate Frenzie off (at last)
The gentle Dove may, when these turmoils cease,
Bring in her Bill, once more, the Branch of Peace.

The Hag.

The Hag is astride,
This night for to ride;
The Devill and shee together:
Through thick, and through thin,
Now out, and then in,
Though ne'r so foule be the weather.

A Thorn or a Burr
She takes for a Spurre:
With a lash of a Bramble she rides now,
Through Brakes and through Bryars,
O're Ditches, and Mires,
She followes the Spirit that guides now.

No Beast, for his food,
Dares now range the wood;
But husht in his laire he lies lurking:
While mischeifs, by these,
On Land and on Seas,
At noone of Night are a working.

The storme will arise,
And trouble the skies;
This night, and more for the wonder,
The ghost from the Tomb
Affrighted shall come,
Call'd out by the clap of the Thunder.

Upon an old man a Residenciarie.

Tread, Sirs, as lightly as ye can
Upon the grave of this old man.
Twice fortie (bating but one year,
And thrice three weekes) he lived here.
Whom gentle fate translated hence
To a more happy Residence.
Yet, Reader, let me tell thee this
(Which from his ghost a promise is)
If here ye will some few teares shed,
He'l never haunt ye now he's dead.

Upon Teares.

Teares, though th'are here below the sinners brine,
Above they are the Angels spiced wine.

Physitians.

Physitians fight not against men; but these
Combate for men, by conquering the disease.

Upon Cob. Epigram.

Cob clouts his shooes, and as the story tells,
His thumb-nailes-par'd, afford him sperrables.

Upon Lucie. Epigram.

Sound Teeth has Lucie, pure as Pearl, and small,
With mellow Lips, and luscious there withall.

The Primitie to Parents.

Our Houshold-gods our Parents be;
And manners good requires, that we
The first-Fruits give to them, who gave
Us hands to get what here we have.

Upon Skoles. Epigram.

Skoles stinks so deadly, that his Breeches loath
His dampish Buttocks furthermore to cloath:
Cloy'd they are up with Arse; but hope, one blast
Will whirle about, and blow them thence at last.

To Silvia.

I am holy, while I stand
Circum-crost by thy pure hand:
But when that is gone; Again,
I, as others, am Prophane.

To his Closet-Gods.

When I goe Hence ye Closet-Gods, I feare
Never againe to have ingression here:
Where I have had, what ever thing co'd be
Pleasant, and precious to my Muse and me.
Besides rare sweets, I had a Book which none
Co'd reade the Intext but my selfe alone.
About the Cover of this Book there went
A curious-comely clean Compartlement:
And, in the midst, to grace it more, was set
A blushing-pretty-peeping Rubelet:
But now 'tis clos'd; and being shut, & seal'd,
Be it, O be it, never more reveal'd!
Keep here still, Closet-Gods, 'fore whom I've set
Oblations oft, of sweetest Marmelet.

A Bacchanalian Verse.

Fill me a mighty Bowle
    Up to the brim:
    That I may drink
Unto my Johnsons soule.

Crowne it agen agen;
    And thrice repeat
    That happy heat;
To drink to Thee my Ben.

Well I can quaffe, I see,
    To th'number five,
    Or nine; but thrive
In frenzie ne'r like thee.

Long lookt for comes at last.

Though long it be, yeeres may repay the debt;
None loseth that, which he in time may get.

To Youth.

Drink Wine, and live here blithefull, while ye may:
The morrowes life too late is, Live to-day.

Never too late to dye.

No man comes late unto that place from whence
Never man yet had a regredience.

Ambition.

In wayes to greatnesse, think on this,
That slippery all Ambition is.

A Hymne to the Muses.

O! you the Virgins nine!
That doe our soules encline
To noble Discipline!
Nod to this vow of mine:
Come then, and now enspire
My violl and my lyre
With your eternall fire:
And make me one entire
Composer in your Quire.
Then I'll your Altars strew
With Roses sweet and new;
And ever live a true
Acknowledger of you.

On himselfe.

I'll sing no more, nor will I longer write
Of that sweet Lady, or that gallant Knight:
I'll sing no more of Frosts, Snowes, Dews and Showers;
No more of Groves, Meades, Springs, and wreaths of
I'll write no more, nor will I tell or sing (Flowers:
Of Cupid, and his wittie coozning:
I'll sing no more of death, or shall the grave
No more my Dirges, and my Trentalls have.

Upon Jone and Jane.

Jone is a wench that's painted;
Jone is a Girle that's tainted;
    Yet Jone she goes
    Like one of those
Whom purity had Sainted.

Jane is a Girle that's prittie;
Jane is a wench that's wittie;
    Yet, who wo'd think,
    Her breath do's stinke,
As so it doth? that's pittie.

To Momus.

Who read'st this Book that I have writ,
And can'st not mend, but carpe at it:
By all the muses! thou shalt be
Anathema to it, and me.

To Electra.

I dare not ask a kisse;
    I dare not beg a smile;
Lest having that, or this,
    I might grow proud the while.

No, no, the utmost share
    Of my desire, shall be
Onely to kisse that Aire,
    That lately kissed thee.

To his worthy friend, M. Arthur Bartly.

When after many Lusters thou shalt be
Wrapt up in Seare-cloth with thine Ancestrie:
When of thy ragg'd Escutcheons shall be seene
So little left, as if they ne'r had been:
Thou shalt thy Name have, and thy Fames best trust,
Here with the Generation of my Just.

The Country life, to the honoured M. End. Porter,
Groome of the Bed-Chamber to His Maj.

Sweet Country life, to such unknown,
Whose lives are others, not their own!
But serving Courts, and Cities, be
Less happy, less enjoying thee.
Thou never Plow'st the Oceans foame
To seek, and bring rough Pepper home:
Nor to the Eastern Ind dost rove
To bring from thence the scorched Clove.
Nor, with the losse of thy lov'd rest,
Bring'st home the Ingot from the West.
No, thy Ambition's Master-piece
Flies no thought higher then a fleece:
Or how to pay thy Hinds, and cleere
All scores; and so to end the yeere:
But walk'st about thine own dear bounds,
Not envying others larger grounds:
For well thou know'st, 'tis not th'extent
Of Land makes life, but sweet content.
When now the Cock (the Plow-mans Horne)
Calls forth the lilly-wristed Morne;
Then to thy corn-fields thou dost goe,
Which though well soyl'd, yet thou dost know,
That the best compost for the Lands
Is the wise Masters Feet, and Hands.
There at the Plough thou find'st thy Teame,
With a Hind whistling there to them:
And cheer'st them up, by singing how
The Kingdoms portion is the Plow.
This done, then to th'enameld Meads
Thou go'st; and as thy foot there treads,
Thou seest a present God-like Power
Imprinted in each Herbe and Flower:
And smell'st the breath of great-ey'd Kine,
Sweet as the blossomes of the Vine.
Here thou behold'st thy large sleek Neat
Unto the Dew-laps up in meat:

And, as thou look'st, the wanton Steere,
The Heifer, Cow, and Oxe draw neere
To make a pleasing pastime there.
These seen, thou go'st to view thy flocks
Of sheep, (safe from the Wolfe and Fox)
And find'st their bellies there as full
Of short sweet grasse, as backs with wool.
And leav'st them (as they feed and fill)
A Shepherd piping on a hill.
For Sports, for Pagentrie, and Playes,
Thou hast thy Eves, and Holydayes:
On which the young men and maids meet,
To exercise their dancing feet:
Tripping the comely country round,
With Daffadils and Daisies crown'd.
Thy Wakes, thy Quintels, here thou hast,
Thy May-poles too with Garlands grac't:
Thy Morris-dance; thy Whitsun-ale;
Thy Sheering-feast, which never faile.
Thy Harvest home; thy Wassaile bowle,
That's tost up after Fox i'th' Hole.
Thy Mummeries; thy Twelfe-tide Kings
And Queenes; thy Christmas revellings:
Thy Nut-browne mirth; thy Russet wit;
And no man payes too deare for it.
To these, thou hast thy times to goe
And trace the Hare i'th' trecherous Snow:
Thy witty wiles to draw, and get
The Larke into the Trammell net:
Thou hast thy Cockrood, and thy Glade
To take the precious Phesant made:
Thy Lime-twigs, Snares, and Pit-falls then
To catch the pilfring Birds, not Men.
O happy life! if that their good
The Husbandmen but understood!
Who all the day themselves doe please,
And Younglings, with such sports as these.
And, lying down, have nought t'affright
Sweet sleep, that makes more short the night.
Cetera desunt —

What kind of Mistresse he would have.

Be the Mistresse of my choice,
Cleane in manners, cleere in voice:
Be she witty, more then wise;
Pure enough, though not Precise:
Be she shewing in her dresse,
Like a civill Wilderness;
That the curious may detect
Order in a sweet neglect:
Be she rowling in her eye,
Tempting all the passers by:
And each Ringlet of her haire,
An Enchantment, or a Snare,
For to catch the Lookers on;
But her self held fast by none.
Let her Lucrece all day be,
Thais in the night, to me.
Be she such, as neither will
Famish me, nor over-fill.

Upon Zelot.

Is Zelot pure? he is: ye see he weares
The signe of Circumcision in his eares.

The Rosemarie branch.

Grow for two ends, it matters not at all,
Be't for my Bridall, or my Buriall.

Upon Crab, Epigr.

Crab faces gownes with sundry Furres; 'tis known,
He keeps the Fox-furre for to face his own.

Upon Madam Ursly, Epigram.

For ropes of pearle, first Madam Ursly showes
A chaine of Cornes, pickt from her eares and toes:
Then, next, to match Tradescant's curious shels,
Nailes from her fingers mew'd, she shewes: what els?
Why then (forsooth) a Carcanet is shown
Of teeth, as deaf as nuts, and all her own.

Once seen, and no more.

Thousands each day passe by, which wee,
Once past and gone, no more shall see.

Love.

This Axiom I have often heard,
Kings ought to be more lov'd, then fear'd.

A Paraneticall, or Advisive Verse, to his
friend, M. John Wicks.

Is this a life, to break thy sleep?
To rise as soon as day doth peep?
To tire thy patient Oxe or Asse
By noone, and let thy good dayes passe,
Not knowing This, that Jove decrees
Some mirth, t'adulce mans miseries?
No; 'tis a life, to have thine oyle,
Without extortion, from thy soyle:
Thy faithfull fields to yeeld thee Graine,
Although with some, yet little paine:
To have thy mind, and nuptiall bed,
With feares, and cares uncumbered:
A Pleasing Wife, that by thy side
Lies softly panting like a Bride.
This is to live, and to endeere
Those minutes, Time has lent us here.
Then, while Fates suffer, live thou free,
(As is that ayre that circles thee)
And crown thy temples too, and let
Thy servant, not thy own self, sweat,
To strut thy barnes with sheafs of Wheat.
Time steals away like to a stream,
And we glide hence away with them.
No sound recalls the houres once fled,
Or Roses, being withered:
Nor us (my Friend) when we are lost,
Like to a Deaw, or melted Frost.
Then live we mirthfull, while we should,
And turn the iron Age to Gold.
Let's feast, and frolick, sing, and play,
And thus lesse last, then live our Day.
Whose life with care is overcast,
That man's not said to live, but last:
Nor is't a life, seven yeares to tell,
But for to live that half seven well:

And that wee'l do; as men, who know,
Some few sands spent, we hence must go,
Both to be blended in the Urn,
From whence there's never a return.

Deniall in women no disheartning to men.

Women, although they ne're so goodly make it,
Their fashion is, but to say no, to take it.

Adversity.

Love is maintain'd by wealth; when all is spent,
Adversity then breeds the discontent.

To M. Denham, on his Prospective Poem.

Or lookt I back unto the Times hence flown,
To praise those Muses, and dislike our own?
Or did I walk those Pean-Gardens through,
To kick the Flow'rs, and scorn their odours too?
I might (and justly) be reputed (here)
One nicely mad, or peevishly severe.
But by Apollo! as I worship wit,
(Where I have cause to burn perfumes to it:)
So, I confesse, 'tis somwhat to do well
In our high art, although we can't excell,
Like thee; or dare the Buskins to unloose
Of thy brave, bold, and sweet Maronian Muse.
But since I'm cal'd (rare Denham) to be gone,
Take from thy Herrick this conclusion:
'Tis dignity in others, if they be
Crown'd Poets; yet live Princes under thee:
The while their wreaths and Purple Robes do shine,
Lesse by their own jemms, then those beams of thine.

A Hymne, to the Lares.

It was, and still my care is,
To worship ye, the Lares,
With crowns of greenest Parsley,
And Garlick chives not scarcely:
For favours here to warme me,
And not by fire to harme me.
For gladding so my hearth here,
With inoffensive mirth here;
That while the Wassaile Bowle here
With North-down Ale doth troule here,
No sillable doth fall here,
To marre the mirth at all here.
For which, Ù Chimney-keepers!
(I dare not call ye Sweepers)
So long as I am able
To keep a countrey-table,
Great be my fare, or small cheere,
I'll eat and drink up all here.

To Fortune.

Tumble me down, and I will sit
Upon my ruines (smiling yet:)
Teare me to tatters; yet I'll be
Patient in my necessitie.
Laugh at my scraps of cloaths, and shun
Me, as a fear'd infection:
Yet scarre-crow-like I'll walk, as one,
Neglecting thy derision.

To Anthea.

Come Anthea, know thou this,
Love at no time idle is:
Let's be doing, though we play
But at push-pin (half the day:)
Chains of sweet bents let us make,
Captive one, or both, to take:
In which bondage we will lie,
Soules transfusing thus, and die.

Cruelties.

Nero commanded; but withdrew his eyes
From the beholding Death, and cruelties.

Perseverance.

Hast thou begun an act? ne're then give o're:
No man despaires to do what's done before.

Distance betters Dignities.

Kings must not oft be seen by publike eyes;
State at a distance adds to dignities.

Health.

Health is no other (as the learned hold)
But a just measure both of Heat and Cold.

Upon his Verses.

What off-spring other men have got,
The how, where, when, I question not.
These are the Children I have left;
Adopted some; none got by theft.
But all are toucht (like lawfull plate)
And no Verse illegitimate.

To Dianeme. A Ceremonie in Glocester.

I'll to thee a Simnell bring,
'Gainst thou go'st a mothering,
So that, when she blesseth thee,
Half that blessing thou'lt give me.

To the King.

Give way, give way, now, now my Charles shines here,
A Publike Light (in this immensive Sphere.)
Some starres were fixt before; but these are dim,
Compar'd (in this my ample Orbe) to Him.
Draw in your feeble fiers, while that He
Appeares but in His Meaner Majestie.
Where, if such glory flashes from His Name,
Which is His Shade, who can abide His Flame!
Princes, and such like Publike Lights as these,
Must not be lookt on, but at distances:
For, if we gaze on These brave Lamps too neer,
Our eyes they'l blind, or if not blind, they'l bleer.

The Funerall Rites of the Rose.

The Rose was sick, and smiling di'd;
And (being to be sanctifi'd)
About the Bed, there sighing stood
The sweet, and flowrie Sisterhood.
Some hung the head, while some did bring
(To wash her) water from the Spring.
Some laid her forth, while other wept,
But all a solemne Fast there kept.
The holy Sisters some among
The sacred Dirge and Trentall sung.
But ah! what sweets smelt every where,
As Heaven had spent all perfumes there.
At last, when prayers for the dead,
And Rites were all accomplished;
They, weeping, spread a Lawnie Loome,
And clos'd her up, as in a Tombe.

The Rainbow: or curious Covenant.

Mine eyes, like clouds, were drizling raine,
And as they thus did entertaine
The gentle Beams from Julia's sight
To mine eyes level'd opposite:
O Thing admir'd! there did appeare
A curious Rainbow smiling there;
Which was the Covenant, that she
No more wo'd drown mine eyes, or me.

The last stroke strike sure.

Though by well-warding many blowes w'ave past,
That stroke most fear'd is, which is struck the last.

Fortune.

Fortune's a blind profuser of her own,
Too much she gives to some, enough to none.

Stool-ball.

At Stool-ball, Lucia, let us play,
    For Sugar-cakes and Wine;
Or for a Tansie let us pay,
    The losse or thine, or mine.

If thou, my Deere, a winner be
    At trundling of the Ball,
The wager thou shalt have, and me,
    And my misfortunes all.

But if (my Sweetest) I shall get,
    Then I desire but this;
That likewise I may pay the Bet,
    And have for all a kisse.

To Sappho.

Let us now take time, and play,
Love, and live here while we may;
Drink rich wine; and make good cheere,
While we have our being here:
For, once dead, and laid i'th grave,
No return from thence we have.

On Poet Prat, Epigr.

Prat He writes Satyres; but herein's the fault,
In no one Satyre there's a mite of salt.

Upon Tuck, Epigr.

At Post and Paire, or Slam, Tom Tuck would play
This Christmas, but his want wherwith, sayes Nay.

Biting of Beggars.

Who, railing, drives the Lazar from his door,
Instead of almes, sets dogs upon the poor.

The May-pole.

The May-pole is up,
Now give me the cup;
I'll drink to the Garlands a-round it:
But first unto those
Whose hands did compose
The glory of flowers that crown'd it.

A health to my Girles,
Whose husbands may Earles
Or Lords be, (granting my wishes)
And when that ye wed
To the Bridall Bed,
Then multiply all, like to Fishes.

Men mind no state in sicknesse.

That flow of Gallants which approach
To kisse thy hand from out the coach;
That fleet of Lackeyes, which do run
Before thy swift Postilion;
Those strong-hoof'd Mules, which we behold,
Rein'd in with Purple, Pearl, and gold,
And shod with silver, prove to be
The drawers of the axeltree.
Thy Wife, thy Children, and the state
Of Persian Loomes, and antique Plate:
All these, and more, shall then afford
No joy to thee their sickly Lord.

Adversity.

Adversity hurts none, but onely such
Whom whitest Fortune dandled has too much.

Want.

Need is no vice at all; though here it be,
With men, a loathed inconveniencie.

Griefe.

Sorrowes divided amongst many, lesse
Discruciate a man in deep distresse.

Love palpable.

I prest my Julia's lips, and in the kisse
Her Soule and Love were palpable in this.

No action hard to affection.

Nothing hard, or harsh can prove
Unto those that truly love.

Meane things overcome mighty.

By the weak'st means things mighty are o'rethrown,
He's Lord of thy life, who contemnes his own.

Upon Trigg, Epigram.

Trigg having turn'd his sute, he struts in state,
And tells the world, he's now regenerate.

Upon Smeaton.

How co'd Luke Smeaton weare a shoe, or boot,
Who two and thirty cornes had on a foot.

The Bracelet of Pearle: to Silvia.

I brake thy Bracelet 'gainst my will;
    And, wretched, I did see
Thee discomposed then, and still
    Art discontent with me.

One jemme was lost; and I will get
    A richer pearle for thee,
Then ever, dearest Silvia, yet
    Was drunk to Antonie.

Or, for revenge, I'll tell thee what
    Thou for the breach shalt do;
First, crack the strings, and after that,
    Cleave thou my heart in two.

How Roses came red.

'Tis said, as Cupid danc't among
The Gods, he down the Nectar flung;
Which, on the white Rose being shed,
Made it for ever after red.

Kings.

Men are not born Kings, but are men renown'd;
Chose first, confirm'd next, & at last are crown'd.

First work, and then wages.

Prepost'rous is that order, when we run
To ask our wages, e're our work be done.

Teares, and Laughter.

Knew'st thou, one moneth wo'd take thy life away,
Thou'dst weep; but laugh, sho'd it not last a day.

Glory.

Glory no other thing is (Tullie sayes)
Then a mans frequent Fame, spoke out with praise.

Possessions.

Those possessions short-liv'd are,
Into the which we come by warre.

Laxare fibulam.

To loose the button, is no lesse,
Then to cast off all bashfulnesse

Poverty the greatest pack.

To mortall men great loads allotted be,
But of all packs, no pack like poverty.

His returne to London.

From the dull confines of the drooping West,
To see the day spring from the pregnant East,
Ravisht in spirit, I come, nay more, I flie
To thee, blest place of my Nativitie!
Thus, thus with hallowed foot I touch the ground,
With thousand blessings by thy Fortune crown'd.
O fruitfull Genius! that bestowest here
An everlasting plenty, yeere by yeere.
O Place! O People! Manners! fram'd to please
All Nations, Customes, Kindreds, Languages!
I am a free-born Roman; suffer then,
That I amongst you live a Citizen.
London my home is: though by hard fate sent
Into a long and irksome banishment;
Yet since cal'd back; henceforward let me be,
O native countrey, repossest by thee!
For, rather then I'll to the West return,
I'll beg of thee first here to have mine Urn.
Weak I am grown, and must in short time fall;
Give thou my sacred Reliques Buriall.

A Prognostick.

As many Lawes and Lawyers do expresse
Nought but a Kingdoms ill-affectednesse:
Ev'n so, those streets and houses do but show
Store of diseases, where Physitians flow.

Not every day fit for Verse.

'Tis not ev'ry day, that I
Fitted am to prophesie:
No, but when the Spirit fils
The fantastick Pannicles:
Full of fier; then I write
As the Godhead doth indite.
Thus inrag'd, my lines are hurl'd,
Like the Sybells, through the world.
Look how next the holy fier
Either slakes, or doth retire;
So the Fancie cooles, till when
That brave Spirit comes agen.

Upon Julia's sweat.

Wo'd ye oyle of Blossomes get?
Take it from my Julia's sweat:
Oyl of Lillies, and of Spike,
From her moysture take the like:
Let her breath, or let her blow,
All rich spices thence will flow.

A Beucolick, or discourse of Neatherds.

Come blithefull Neatherds, let us lay
A wager, who the best shall play,
Of thee, or I, the Roundelay,
That fits the businesse of the Day.

Chor. And Lallage the Judge shall be,
To give the prize to thee, or me.

Content, begin, and I will bet
A Heifer smooth, and black as jet,
In every part alike compleat,
And wanton as a Kid as yet.

Chor. And Lallage (with cow-like eyes)
Shall be Disposeresse of the prize.

Against thy Heifer, I will here
Lay to thy stake a lustie Steere,
With gilded hornes, and burnisht cleere.

Chor. Why then begin, and let us heare
The soft, the sweet, the mellow note
That gently purles from eithers Oat.

The stakes are laid: let's now apply
Each one to make his melody:
Lal. The equall Umpire shall be I,
Who'l hear, and so judge righteously.

Chor. Much time is spent in prate; begin,
And sooner play, the sooner win.
                                        (He playes)

That's sweetly touch't, I must confesse:
Thou art a man of worthinesse:
But hark how I can now expresse
My love unto my Neatherdesse.

(He sings)

Chor. A suger'd note! and sound as sweet
As Kine, when they at milking meet.

Now for to win thy Heifer faire,
I'll strike thee such a nimble Ayre,
That thou shalt say (thy selfe) 'tis rare;
And title me without compare.

Chor. Lay by a while your Pipes, and rest,
Since both have here deserved best.

To get thy Steerling, once again,
I'll play thee such another strain;
That thou shalt swear, my Pipe do's raigne
Over thine Oat, as Soveraigne.

(He sings)

Chor. And Lallage shall tell by this,
Whose now the prize and wager is.

Give me the prize: The day is mine:
Not so; my Pipe has silenc't thine:
And hadst thou wager'd twenty Kine,
They were mine own. Lal. In love combine.

Chor. And lay we down our Pipes together,
As wearie, not o'recome by either.

True safety.

'Tis not the Walls, or purple, that defends
A Prince from Foes; but 'tis his Fort of Friends.

Proof to no purpose.

You see this gentle streame, that glides,
Shov'd on, by quick succeeding Tides:
Trie if this sober streame you can
Follow to th'wilder Ocean:
And see, if there it keeps unspent
In that congesting element.
Next, from that world of waters, then
By poares and cavernes back agen
Induc't that inadultrate same
Streame to the Spring from whence it came.
This with a wonder when ye do,
As easie, and els easier too:
Then may ye recollect the graines
Of my particular Remaines;
After a thousand Lusters hurld,
By ruffling winds, about the world.

Fame.

'Tis still observ'd, that Fame ne're sings
The order, but the Sum of things.

By use comes easinesse

Oft bend the Bow, and thou with ease shalt do,
What others can't with all their strength put to.

To the Genius of his house.

Command the Roofe great Genius, and from thence
Into this house powre downe thy influence,
That through each room a golden pipe may run
Of living water by thy Benizon.
Fulfill the Larders, and with strengthning bread
Be evermore these Bynns replenished.
Next, like a Bishop consecrate my ground,
That luckie Fairies here may dance their Round:
And after that, lay downe some silver pence,
The Masters charge and care to recompence.
Charme then the chambers; make the beds for ease,
More then for peevish pining sicknesses.
Fix the foundation fast, and let the Roofe
Grow old with time, but yet keep weather-proofe.

His Grange, or private wealth.

                Though Clock,
To tell how night drawes hence, I've none,
                A Cock,
I have, to sing how day drawes on.
                I have
A maid (my Prew) by good luck sent,
                To save
That little, Fates me gave or lent.
                A Hen
I keep, which creeking day by day,
                Tells when
She goes her long white egg to lay.
                A Goose
I have, which, with a jealous eare,
                Lets loose
Her tongue, to tell what danger's neare.
                A Lamb
I keep (tame) with my morsells fed,
                Whose Dam
An Orphan left him (lately dead.)
                A Cat
I keep, that playes about my House,
                Grown fat,
With eating many a miching Mouse.
                To these
A Trasy I do keep, whereby His Spaniel
                I please
The more my rurall privacie:
                Which are
But toyes, to give my heart some ease:
                Where care
None is, slight things do lightly please.

Good precepts, or counsell.

In all thy need, be thou possest
Still with a well-prepared brest:
Nor let the shackles make thee sad;
Thou canst but have, what others had.
And this for comfort thou must know,
Times that are ill wo'nt still be so.
Clouds will not ever powre down raine;
A sullen day will cleere againe.
First, peales of Thunder we must heare,
Then Lutes and Harpes shall stroke the eare.

Money makes the mirth.

When all Birds els do of their musick faile,
Money's the still-sweet-singing Nightingale.

Upon Franck.

Franck wo'd go scoure her teeth; and setting to't,
Twice two fell out, all rotten at the root.

Up tailes all.

Begin with a kisse,
Go on too with this:
And thus, thus, thus let us smother
Our lips for a while,
But let's not beguile
Our hope of one for the other.

This play, be assur'd,
Long enough has endur'd,
Since more and more is exacted;
For love he doth call
For his Uptailes all;
And that's the part to be acted.

Upon Lucia dabled in the deaw.

My Lucia in the deaw did go,
And prettily bedabled so,
Her cloaths held up, she shew'd withall
Her decent legs, cleane, long and small.
I follow'd after to descrie
Part of the nak't sincerity;
But still the envious Scene between
Deni'd the Mask I wo'd have seen.

Charon and Phylomel, a Dialogue sung.

Ph.Charon! O gentle Charon! let me wooe thee,
By tears and pitie now to come unto mee.
Ch. What voice so sweet and charming do I heare?
Say what thou art. Ph. I prithee first draw neare.
Ch. A sound I heare, but nothing yet can see,
Speak where thou art. Ph. O Charon pittie me!
I am a bird, and though no name I tell,
My warbling note will say I'm Phylomel.
Ch. What's that to me, I waft nor fish or fowles,
Nor Beasts (fond thing) but only humane soules.
Ph. Alas for me! Ch. Shame on thy witching note,
That made me thus hoist saile, and bring my Boat:
But I'll returne; what mischief brought thee hither?
Ph. A deale of Love, and much, much Griefe together.
Ch. What's thy request? Ph. That since she's now beneath
Who fed my life, I'll follow her in death.
Ch. And is that all? I'm gone. Ph. By love I pray thee,
Ch. Talk not of love, all pray, but few soules pay me.
Ph. I'll give thee vows & tears. Ch. can tears pay skores
For mending sails, for patching Boat and Oares?
Ph. I'll beg a penny, or I'll sing so long,
Till thou shalt say, I've paid thee with a song.
Ch. Why then begin, and all the while we make
Our slothfull passage o're the Stygian Lake,
Thou & I'll sing to make these dull Shades merry,
Who els with tears wo'd doubtles drown my ferry.

Upon Paul. Epigr.

Pauls hands do give, what give they bread or meat,
Or money? no, but onely deaw and sweat.
As stones and salt gloves use to give, even so
Pauls hands do give, nought else for ought we know.

Upon Sibb. Epigr.

Sibb when she saw her face how hard it was,
For anger spat on thee her Looking-glasse:
But weep not, Christall; for the shame was meant
Not unto thee, but That thou didst present.

Upon the Roses in Julia's bosome.

Thrice happie Roses, so much grac't, to have
Within the Bosome of my Love your grave.
Die when ye will, your sepulchre is knowne,
Your Grave her Bosome is, the Lawne the Stone.

A Ternarie of littles, upon a pipkin of
Jellie sent to a Lady.

A little Saint best fits a little Shrine,
A little prop best fits a little Vine,
As my small Cruse best fits my little Wine.

A little Seed best fits a little Soyle,
A little Trade best fits a little Toyle:
As my small Jarre best fits my little Oyle.

A little Bin best fits a little Bread,
A little Garland fits a little Head:
As my small stuffe best fits my little Shed.

A little Hearth best fits a little Fire,
A little Chappell fits a little Quire,
As my small Bell best fits my little Spire.

A little streame best fits a little Boat;
A little lead best fits a little Float;
As my small Pipe best fits my little note.

A little meat best fits a little bellie,
As sweetly Lady, give me leave to tell ye,
This little Pipkin fits this little Jellie.

Maids nay's are nothing.

Maids nay's are nothing, they are shie
But to desire what they denie.

The smell of the Sacrifice.

The Gods require the thighes
Of Beeves for sacrifice;
Which rosted, we the steam
Must sacrifice to them:
Who though they do not eat,
Yet love the smell of meat.

Lovers how they come and part.

A Gyges Ring they beare about them still,
To be, and not seen when and where they will.
They tread on clouds, and though they sometimes fall,
They fall like dew, but make no noise at all.
So silently they one to th'other come,
As colours steale into the Peare or Plum,
And Aire-like, leave no pression to be seen
Where e're they met, or parting place has been.

To women, to hide their teeth, if they be
rotten or rusty.

Close keep your lips, if that you meane
To be accounted inside cleane:
For if you cleave them, we shall see
There in your teeth much Leprosie.

In praise of women.

O Jupiter, sho'd I speake ill
Of woman-kind, first die I will;
Since that I know, 'mong all the rest
Of creatures, woman is the best.

The Candor of Julia's teeth.

White as Zenobias teeth, the which the Girles
Of Rome did weare for their most precious Pearles.

The Apron of Flowers.

To gather Flowers Sappha went,
    And homeward she did bring
Within her Lawnie Continent,
    The treasure of the Spring.

She smiling blusht, and blushing smil'd,
    And sweetly blushing thus,
She lookt as she'd been got with child
    By young Favonius.

Her Apron gave (as she did passe)
    An Odor more divine,
More pleasing too, then ever was
    The lap of Proserpine.

Upon her weeping.

She wept upon her cheeks, and weeping so,
She seem'd to quench loves fires that there did glow.

Another upon her weeping.

She by the River sate, and sitting there,
She wept, and made it deeper by a teare.

Delay.

Break off Delay, since we but read of one
That ever prosper'd by Cunctation.

To Sir John Berkley, Governour of Exeter.

Stand forth brave man, since Fate has made thee here
The Hector over Aged Exeter;
Who for a long sad time has weeping stood,
Like a poore Lady lost in Widdowhood:
But feares not now to see her safety sold
(As other Townes and Cities were) for gold,
By those ignoble Births, which shame the stem
That gave Progermination unto them:
Whose restlesse Ghosts shall heare their children sing,
Our Sires betraid their Countrey and their King.
True, if this Citie seven times rounded was
With rock, and seven times circumflankt with brasse,
Yet if thou wert not, Berkley, loyall proofe,
The Senators down tumbling with the Roofe,
Would into prais'd (but pitied) ruines fall,
Leaving no shew, where stood the Capitoll.
But thou art just and itchlesse, and dost please
Thy Genius with two strength'ning Buttresses,
Faith, and Affection: which will never slip
To weaken this thy great Dictator-ship.

To Electra. Love looks for Love.

Love love begets, then never be
Unsoft to him who's smooth to thee.
Tygers and Beares (I've heard some say)
For profer'd love will love repay:
None are so harsh, but if they find
Softnesse in others, will be kind;
Affection will affection move,
Then you must like, because I love.

Regression spoiles Resolution.

Hast thou attempted greatnesse? then go on,
Back-turning slackens Resolution.

Contention.

Discreet and prudent we that Discord call,
That either profits, or not hurts at all.

Consultation.

Consult ere thou begin'st, that done, go on
With all wise speed for execution.

Love dislikes nothing.

Whatsoever thing I see,
Rich or poore although it be;
'Tis a Mistresse unto mee.

Be my Girle, or faire or browne,
Do's she smile, or do's she frowne:
Still I write a Sweet-heart downe.

Be she rough, or smooth of skin;
When I touch, I then begin
For to let Affection in.

Be she bald, or do's she weare
Locks incurl'd of other haire;
I shall find enchantment there.

Be she whole, or be she rent,
So my fancie be content,
She's to me most excellent.

Be she fat, or be she leane,
Be she sluttish, be she cleane,
I'm a man for ev'ry Sceane.

Our own sinnes unseen.

Other mens sins wee ever beare in mind;
None sees the fardell of his faults behind.

No Paines, no Gaines.

If little labour, little are our gaines:
Mans fortunes are according to his paines.

Upon Slouch.

Slouch he packs up, and goes to sev'rall Faires,
And weekly Markets for to sell his wares:
Meane time that he from place to place do's rome,
His wife her owne ware sells as fast at home.

Vertue best united.

By so much, vertue is the lesse,
By how much, neere to singlenesse.

The eye.

A wanton and lascivious eye
Betrayes the Hearts Adulterie.

To Prince Charles upon his coming to Exeter.

What Fate decreed, Time now ha's made us see
A Renovation of the West by Thee.
That Preternaturall Fever, which did threat
Death to our Countrey, now hath lost his heat:
And calmes succeeding, we perceive no more
Th'unequall Pulse to beat, as heretofore.
Something there yet remaines for Thee to do;
Then reach those ends that thou wast destin'd to.
Go on with Sylla's Fortune; let thy Fate
Make Thee like Him, this, that way fortunate,
Apollos Image side with Thee to blesse
Thy Warre (discreetly made) with white successe.
Meane time thy Prophets Watch by Watch shall pray;
While young Charles fights, and fighting wins the day.
That done, our smooth-pac't Poems all shall be
Sung in the high Doxologie of Thee.
Then maids shall strew Thee, and thy Curles from them
Receive (with Songs) a flowrie Diadem.

A Song.

Burne, or drowne me, choose ye whether,
So I may but die together:
Thus to slay me by degrees,
Is the height of Cruelties.
What needs twenty stabs, when one
Strikes me dead as any stone?
O shew mercy then, and be
Kind at once to murder mee.

Princes and Favourites.

Princes and Fav'rites are most deere, while they
By giving and receiving hold the play:
But the Relation then of both growes poor,
When These can aske, and Kings can give no more.

Examples, or like Prince, like People.

Examples lead us, and wee likely see,
Such as the Prince is, will his People be.

Potentates.

Love and the Graces evermore do wait
Upon the man that is a Potentate.

The Wake.

Come Anthea let us two
Go to Feast, as others do.
Tarts and Custards, Creams and Cakes,
Are the Junketts still at Wakes:
Unto which the Tribes resort,
Where the businesse is the sport:
Morris-dancers thou shalt see,
Marian too in Pagentrie:
And a Mimick to devise
Many grinning properties.
Players there will be, and those
Base in action as in clothes:
Yet with strutting they will please
The incurious Villages.
Neer the dying of the day,
There will be a Cudgell-Play,
Where a Coxcomb will be broke,
Ere a good word can be spoke:
But the anger ends all here,
Drencht in Ale, or drown'd in Beere.
Happy Rusticks, best content
With the cheapest Merriment:
And possesse no other feare,
Then to want the Wake next Yeare.

The Peter-penny.

Fresh strowings allow
To my Sepulcher now,
To make my lodging the sweeter;
A staffe or a wand
Put then in my hand,
With a pennie to pay S. Peter.

Who has not a Crosse,
Must sit with the losse,
And no whit further must venture;
Since the Porter he
Will paid have his fee,
Or els not one there must enter.

Who at a dead lift,
Can't send for a gift
A Pig to the Priest for a Roster,
Shall heare his Clarke say,
By yea and by nay,
No pennie, no Pater Noster.

To Doctor Alablaster.

Nor art thou lesse esteem'd, that I have plac'd
(Amongst mine honour'd) Thee (almost) the last:
In great Processions many lead the way
To him, who is the triumph of the day,
As these have done to Thee, who art the one,
One onely glory of a million,
In whom the spirit of the Gods do's dwell,
Firing thy soule, by which thou dost foretell
When this or that vast Dinastie must fall
Downe to a Fillit more Imperiall.
When this or that Horne shall be broke, and when
Others shall spring up in their place agen:
When times and seasons and all yeares must lie
Drown'd in the Sea of wild Eternitie:
When the Black Dooms-day Bookes (as yet unseal'd)
Shall by the mighty Angell be reveal'd:
And when the Trumpet which thou late hast found
Shall call to Judgment; tell us when the sound
Of this or that great Aprill day shall be,
And next the Gospell wee will credit thee.
Meane time like Earth-wormes we will craule below,
And wonder at Those Things that thou dost know.

Upon his Kinswoman Mrs. M. S.

Here lies a Virgin, and as sweet
As ere was wrapt in winding sheet.
Her name if next you wo'd have knowne,
The Marble speaks it Mary Stone:
Who dying in her blooming yeares,
This Stone, for names sake, melts to teares.
If fragrant Virgins you'l but keep
A Fast, while Jets and Marbles weep,
And praying, strew some Roses on her,
You'l do my Neice abundant honour.

Felicitie knowes no Fence.

Of both our Fortunes good and bad we find
Prosperitie more searching of the mind:
Felicitie flies o're the Wall and Fence,
While misery keeps in with patience.

Death ends all woe.

Time is the Bound of things, where e're we go,
Fate gives a meeting. Death's the end of woe.

A Conjuration, to Electra.

By those soft Tods of wooll
With which the aire is full:
By all those Tinctures there,
That paint the Hemisphere:
By Dewes and drisling Raine,
That swell the Golden Graine:
By all those sweets that be
I'th flowrie Nunnerie:
By silent Nights, and the
Three Formes of Heccate:
By all Aspects that blesse
The sober Sorceresse,
While juice she straines, and pith
To make her Philters with:
By Time, that hastens on
Things to perfection:
And by your self, the best
Conjurement of the rest:
O my Electra! be
In love with none, but me.

Courage cool'd.

I cannot love, as I have lov'd before:
For, I'm grown old; &, with mine age, grown poore:
Love must be fed by wealth: this blood of mine
Must needs wax cold, if wanting bread and wine.

The Spell.

Holy Water come and bring;
Cast in Salt, for seasoning:
Set the Brush for sprinkling:
Sacred Spittle bring ye hither;
Meale and it now mix together;
And a little Oyle to either:
Give the Tapers here their light,
Ring the Saints-Bell, to affright
Far from hence the evill Sp'rite.

His wish to privacie.

Give me a Cell
    To dwell,
Where no foot hath
    A path:
There will I spend,
    And end
My wearied yeares
    In teares.

A good Husband.

A master of a house (as I have read)
Must be the first man up, and last in bed:
With the Sun rising he must walk his grounds;
See this, View that, and all the other bounds:
Shut every gate; mend every hedge that's torne,
Either with old, or plant therein new thorne:
Tread ore his gleab, but with such care, that where
He sets his foot, he leaves rich compost there.

Upon Pusse and her Prentice. Epigram.

Pusse and her Prentice both at Draw-gloves play;
That done, they kisse, and so draw out the day:
At night they draw to Supper; then well fed,
They draw their clothes off both, so draw to bed.

Blame the reward of Princes.

Among disasters that discention brings,
This not the least is, which belongs to Kings.
If Wars goe well; each for a part layes claime:
If ill, then Kings, not Souldiers beare the blame.

A Hymne to Bacchus.

I sing thy praise Iacchus,
Who with thy Thyrse dost thwack us:
And yet thou so dost back us
With boldness that we feare
No Brutus entring here;
Nor Cato the severe.
What though the Lictors threat us,
We know they dare not beate us;
So long as thou dost heat us.
When we thy Orgies sing,
Each Cobler is a King;
Nor dreads he any thing:
And though he doe not rave,
Yet he'l the courage have
To call my Lord Maior knave;
Besides too, in a brave,
Although he has no riches,
But walks with dangling breeches,
And skirts that want their stiches,
And shewes his naked flitches;
Yet he'le be thought or seen,
So good as George-a-Green;
And calls his Blouze, his Queene;
And speaks in language keene:
O Bacchus! let us be
From cares and troubles free;
And thou shalt heare how we
Will chant new Hymnes to thee.

Clemency in Kings.

Kings must not only cherish up the good,
But must be niggards of the meanest bloud.

Anger.

Wrongs, if neglected, vanish in short time;
But heard with anger, we confesse the crime.

A Psalme or Hymne to the Graces.

Glory be to the Graces!
That doe in publike places,
Drive thence what ere encumbers,
The listning to my numbers.

Honour be to the Graces!
Who doe with sweet embraces,
Shew they are well contented
With what I have invented.

Worship be to the Graces!
Who do from sowre faces,
And lungs that wo'd infect me,
For evermore protect me.

An Hymne to the Muses.

Honour to you who sit!
Neere to the well of wit;
And drink your fill of it.

Glory and worship be!
To you sweet Maids (thrice three)
Who still inspire me.

And teach me how to sing
Unto the Lyrick string
My measures ravishing.

Then while I sing your praise,
My Priest-hood crown with bayes
Green, to the end of dayes.

Upon Julia's Clothes.

When as in silks my Julia goes, (flowes
Then, then (me thinks) how sweetly
That liquefaction of her clothes.

Next, when I cast mine eyes and see
That brave Vibration each way free;
O how that glittering taketh me!

Moderation.

In things a moderation keepe,
Kings ought to sheare, not skin their sheepe.

To Anthea.

Lets call for Hymen if agreed thou art;
Delays in love but crucifie the heart.
Loves thornie Tapers yet neglected lye:
Speak thou the word, they'l kindle by and by.
The nimble howers wooe us on to wed,
And Genius waits to have us both to bed.
Behold, for us the Naked Graces stay
With maunds of roses for to strew the way:
Besides, the most religious Prophet stands
Ready to joyne, as well our hearts as hands.
Juno yet smiles; but if she chance to chide,
Ill luck 'twill bode to th'Bridegroome and the Bride.
Tell me Anthea, dost thou fondly dread
The loss of that we call a Maydenhead?
Come, I'll instruct thee. Know, the vestall fier
Is not by mariage quencht, but flames the higher.

Upon Prew his Maid.

In this little Urne is laid
Prewdence Baldwin (once my maid)
From whose happy spark here let
Spring the purple Violet.

The Invitation.

To sup with thee thou didst me home invite;
And mad'st a promise that mine appetite
Sho'd meet and tire, on such lautitious meat,
The like not Heliogabalus did eat:
And richer Wine wo'dst give to me (thy guest)
Then Roman Sylla powr'd out at his feast.
I came; (tis true) and lookt for Fowle of price,
The bastard Phenix; bird of Paradice;
And for no less then Aromatick Wine
Of Maydens-blush, commixt with Jessimine.
Cleane was the herth, the mantle larded jet;
Which wanting Lar, and smoke, hung weeping wet;
At last, i'th' noone of winter, did appeare
A ragd-soust-neats-foot with sick vineger:
And in a burnisht Flagonet stood by
Beere small as Comfort, dead as Charity.
At which amaz'd, and pondring on the food,
How cold it was, and how it child my blood;
I curst the master; and I damn'd the souce;
And swore I'de got the ague of the house.
Well, when to eat thou dost me next desire,
I'll bring a Fever; since thou keep'st no fire.

Ceremonies for Christmasse.

Come, bring with a noise,
My merrie merrie boyes,
The Christmas Log to the firing;
While my good Dame, she
Bids ye all be free;
And drink to your hearts desiring.

With the last yeeres brand
Light the new block, And
For good successe in his spending,
On your Psaltries play,
That sweet luck may
Come while the Log is a teending.

Drink now the strong Beere,
Cut the white loafe here,
The while the meat is a shredding;
For the rare Mince-Pie
And the Plums stand by
To fill the Paste that's a kneading.

Christmasse-Eve, another Ceremonie.

Come guard this night the Christmas-Pie,
That the Thiefe, though ne'r so slie,
With his Flesh-hooks, don't come nie
                    To catch it.

From him, who all alone sits there,
Having his eyes still in his eare,
And a deale of nightly feare
                    To watch it.

Another to the Maids.

Wash your hands, or else the fire
Will not teend to your desire;
Unwasht hands, ye Maidens, know,
Dead the Fire, though ye blow.

Another.

Wassaile the Trees, that they may beare
You many a Plum, and many a Peare:
For more or lesse fruits they will bring,
As you doe give them Wassailing.

Power and Peace.

'Tis never, or but seldome knowne,
Power and Peace to keep one Throne.

To his deare Valentine, Mistresse
Margaret Falconbrige.

Now is your turne (my Dearest) to be set
A Jem in this eternall Coronet:
'Twas rich before; but since your Name is downe,
It sparkles now like Ariadne's Crowne.
Blaze by this Sphere for ever: Or this doe,
Let Me and It shine evermore by you.

To Oenone.

Sweet Oenone, doe but say
Love thou dost, though Love sayes Nay.
Speak me faire; for Lovers be
Gently kill'd by Flatterie.

Verses.

Who will not honour Noble Numbers, when
Verses out-live the bravest deeds of men?

Happinesse.

That Happines do's still the longest thrive,
Where Joyes and Griefs have Turns Alternative.

Things of choice, long a comming.

We pray 'gainst Warre, yet we enjoy no Peace
Desire deferr'd is, that it may encrease.

Poetry perpetuates the Poet.

Here I my selfe might likewise die,
And utterly forgotten lye,
But that eternall Poetrie
Repullulation gives me here
Unto the thirtieth thousand yeere,
When all now dead shall re-appeare.

Upon Bice.

Bice laughs, when no man speaks; and doth protest
It is his own breech there that breaks the jest.

Upon Trencherman.

Tom shifts the Trenchers; yet he never can
Endure that luke-warme name of Serving-man:
Serve or not serve, let Tom doe what he can,
He is a serving, who's a Trencher-man.

Kisses.

Give me the food that satisfies a Guest:
Kisses are but dry banquets to a Feast.

Orpheus.

Orpheus he went (as Poets tell)
To fetch Euridice from Hell;
And had her; but it was upon
This short but strict condition:
Backward he should not looke while he
Led her through Hells obscuritie:
But ah! it hapned as he made
His passage through that dreadfull shade:
Revolve he did his loving eye;
(For gentle feare, or jelousie)
And looking back, that look did sever
Him and Euridice for ever.

Upon Comely a good speaker
but an ill singer, Epigram.

Comely Acts well; and when he speaks his part,
He doth it with the sweetest tones of Art:
But when he sings a Psalme, ther's none can be
More curst for singing out of tune then he.

Any way for wealth.

E'ene all Religious courses to be rich
Had been reherst, by Joell Michelditch:
But now perceiving that it still do's please
The sterner Fates, to cross his purposes;
He tacks about, and now he doth profess
Rich he will be by all unrighteousness:
Thus if our ship fails of her Anchor hold,
We'l love the Divell, so he lands the gold.

Upon an old Woman.

Old Widdow Prouse to do her neighbours evill
Wo'd give (some say) her soule unto the Devill.
Well, when sh'as kild, that Pig, Goose, Cock or Hen,
What wo'd she give to get that soule agen?

Upon Pearch. Epigram.

Thou writes in Prose, how sweet all Virgins be;
But ther's not one, doth praise the smell of thee.

To Sappho.

Sappho, I will chuse to go
Where the Northern Winds do blow
Endlesse Ice, and endlesse Snow:
Rather then I once wo'd see,
But a Winters face in thee,
To benumme my hopes and me.

The Bride-Cake.

This day my Julia thou must make
For Mistresse Bride, the wedding Cake:
Knead but the Dow and it will be
To paste of Almonds turn'd by thee:
Or kisse it thou, but once, or twice,
And for the Bride-Cake ther'l be Spice.

To his faithfull friend, Master John Crofts,
Cup-bearer to the King.

For all thy many courtesies to me,
Nothing I have (my Crofts) to send to Thee
For the requitall; save this only one
Halfe of my just remuneration.
For since I've travail'd all this Realm throughout
To seeke, and find some few Immortals out
To circumspangle this my spacious Sphere,
(As Lamps for everlasting shining here:)
And having fixt Thee in mine Orbe a Starre,
(Amongst the rest) both bright and singular;
The present Age will tell the world thou art
If not to th'whole, yet satisfy'd in part.
As for the rest, being too great a summe
Here to be paid; I'll pay't i'th'world to come.

To be merry.

Let's now take our time;
    While w'are in our Prime;
And old, old Age is a farre off:
    For the evill evill dayes
    Will come on apace;
Before we can be aware of.

Buriall.

Man may want Land to live in; but for all,
Nature finds out some place for buriall.

Lenitie.

Tis the Chyrurgions praise, and height of Art,
Not to cut off, but cure the vicious part.

Penitence.

Who after his transgression doth repent,
Is halfe, or altogether innocent.

Griefe.

Consider sorrowes, how they are aright:
Griefe, if't be great, 'tis short; if long, 'tis light.

The Meane.

Imparitie doth ever discord bring:
The Mean the Musique makes in every thing.

The Maiden-blush.

So look the mornings when the Sun
Paints them with fresh Vermilion:
So Cherries blush, and Kathern Peares,
And Apricocks, in youthfull yeares:
So Corrolls looke more lovely Red,
And Rubies lately polished:
So purest Diaper doth shine,
Stain'd by the Beames of Clarret wine:
As Julia looks when she doth dress
Her either cheeke with bashfullness.

Haste hurtfull.

Haste is unhappy: What we Rashly do
Is both unluckie; I, and foolish too.
Where War with rashnesse is attempted, there
The Soldiers leave the Field with equall feare.

Purgatory.

Readers wee entreat ye pray
For the soule of Lucia;
That in little time she be
From her Purgatory free:
In th'intrim she desires
That your teares may coole her fires.

The Cloud.

Seest thou that Cloud that rides in State
Part Ruby-like, part Candidate?
It is no other then the Bed
Where Venus sleeps (halfe smothered.)

Upon Loach.

Seeal'd up with Night-gum, Loach each morning lyes,
Till his Wife licking, so unglews his eyes.
No question then, but such a lick is sweet,
When a warm tongue do's with such Ambers meet.

The Amber Bead.

I saw a Flie within a Beade
Of Amber cleanly buried:
The Urne was little, but the room
More rich then Cleopatra's Tombe.

To my dearest Sister M. Mercie Herrick.

When ere I go, or what so ere befalls
Me in mine Age, or forraign Funerals,
This Blessing I will leave thee, ere I go,
Prosper thy Basket, and therein thy Dow.
Feed on the paste of Filberts, or else knead
And Bake the floure of Amber for thy bread.
Balm may thy Trees drop, and thy Springs runne
And everlasting Harvest crown thy Soile! (oyle
These I but wish for; but thy selfe shall see,
The Blessing fall in mellow times on Thee.

The Transfiguration.

Immortall clothing I put on,
So soone as Julia I am gon
To mine eternall Mansion.

Thou, thou art here, to humane sight
Cloth'd all with incorrupted light;
But yet how more admir'dly bright

Wilt thou appear, when thou art set
In thy refulgent Thronelet,
That shin'st thus in thy counterfeit?

Suffer that thou canst not shift.

Do's Fortune rend thee? Beare with thy hard Fate:
Vertuous instructions ne'r are delicate.
Say, do's she frown? still countermand her threats:
Vertue best loves those children that she beates.

To the Passenger.

If I lye unburied Sir,
These my Reliques, (pray) interre.
'Tis religious part to see
Stones, or turfes to cover me.
One word more I had to say;
But it skills not; go your way;
He that wants a buriall roome
For a Stone, ha's Heaven his Tombe.

Upon Nodes.

Where ever Nodes do's in the Summer come,
He prayes his Harvest may be well brought home.
What store of Corn has carefull Nodes, thinke you,
Whose Field his foot is, and whose Barn his shooe?

To the King,
Upon his taking of Leicester.

This Day is Yours, Great CHARLES! and in this War
Your Fate, and Ours, alike Victorious are.
In her white Stole; now Victory do's rest
Enspher'd with Palm on Your Triumphant Crest.
Fortune is now Your Captive; other Kings
Hold but her hands; You hold both hands and wings.

To Julia, *in Her Dawn, or Daybreak*

By the next kindling of the day
    My *Julia* thou shalt see,
Ere *Ave-Mary* thou canst say
    I'll come and visit thee.

Yet ere thou counsl'st with thy Glasse,
    Appeare thou to mine eyes
As smooth, and nak't, as she that was
    The prime of *Paradise.*

If blush thou must, then blush thou through
    A Lawn, that thou mayst looke
As purest Pearles, or Pebbles do
    When peeping through a Brooke.

As Lilies shrin'd in Christall, so
    Do thou to me appeare;
Or Damask Roses, when they grow
    To sweet acquaintance there.

Counsell.

Twas Cesars saying: Kings no lesse Conquerors are
By their wise Counsell, then they be by Warre.

Bad Princes pill their People.

Like those infernall Deities which eate
The best of all the sacrificed meate;
And leave their servants, but the smoak & sweat:
So many Kings, and Primates too there are,
Who claim the Fat, and Fleshie for their share,
And leave their Subjects but the starved ware.

Most Words, lesse Workes.

In desp'rate cases, all, or most are known
Commanders, few for execution.

To Dianeme.

I co'd but see thee yesterday
    Stung by a fretfull Bee;
And I the Javelin suckt away,
    And heal'd the wound in thee.

A thousand thorns, and Bryars & Stings,
    I have in my poore Brest;
Yet ne'r can see that salve which brings
    My Passions any rest.

As Love shall helpe me, I admire
    How thou canst sit and smile,
To see me bleed, and not desire
    To stench the blood the while.

If thou compos'd of gentle mould
    Art so unkind to me;
What dismall Stories will be told
    Of those that cruell be?

Upon Tap.

Tap (better known then trusted) as we heare
Sold his old Mothers Spectacles for Beere:
And not unlikely; rather too then fail,
He'l sell her Eyes, and Nose, for Beere and Ale.

His Losse.

All has been plundered from me, but my wit;
Fortune her selfe can lay no claim to it.

Draw, and Drinke.

Milk stil your Fountains, and your Springs, for why?
The more th'are drawn, the lesse they wil grow dry.

Upon Punchin. Epigram.

Give me a reason why men call
Punchin a dry plant-animall.
Because as Plants by water grow,
Punchin by Beere and Ale, spreads so.

To Oenone.

Thou sayest Loves Dart
Hath prickt thy heart;
And thou do'st languish too:
If one poore prick,
Can make thee sick,
Say, what wo'd many do ?

Upon Blinks. Epigram.

Tom Blinks his Nose is full of wheales, and these
Tom calls not pimples, but Pimpleides:
Sometimes (in mirth) he sayes each whelk's a sparke
(When drunke with Beere) to light him home, i'th' dark.

Upon Adam Peapes. Epigram.

Peapes he do's strut, and pick his Teeth, as if
His jawes had tir'd on some large Chine of Beefe.
But nothing so; The Dinner Adam had,
Was cheese full ripe with Teares, with Bread as sad.

To Electra.

Shall I go to Love and tell,
Thou art all turn'd isicle?
Shall I say her Altars be
Disadorn'd, and scorn'd by thee?
O beware! in time submit;
Love has yet no wrathfull fit:
If her patience turns to ire,
Love is then consuming fire.

To Mistresse Amie Potter.

Ai me! I love, give him your hand to kisse
Who both your wooer, and your Poet is.
Nature has pre-compos'd us both to Love;
Your part's to grant; my Scean must be to move.
Deare, can you like, and liking love your Poet?
If you say (I) Blush-guiltinesse will shew it.
Mine eyes must wooe you; (though I sigh the while)
True Love is tonguelesse as a Crocodile.
And you may find in Love these differing Parts;
Wooers have Tongues of Ice, but burning hearts.

Upon a Maide.

Here she lyes (in Bed of Spice)
Faire as Eve in Paradice:
For her beauty it was such
Poets co'd not praise too much.
Virgins Come, and in a Ring
Her supreamest Requiem sing;
Then depart, but see ye tread
Lightly, lightly ore the dead.

Upon Love.

Love is a Circle, and an Endlesse Sphere;
From good to good, revolving here, & there.

Beauty.

Beauti's no other but a lovely Grace
Of lively colours, flowing from the face.

Upon Love.

Some salve to every sore, we may apply;
Only for my wound there's no remedy.
Yet if my Julia kisse me, there will be
A soveraign balme found out to cure me.

Upon Hanch a Schoolmaster. Epigram.

Hanch, since he (lately) did interre his wife,
He weepes and sighs (as weary of his life.)
Say, is't for reall griefe he mourns? not so;
Teares have their springs from joy, as well as woe.

Upon Peason. Epigram.

Long Locks of late our Zelot Peason weares,
Not for to hide his high and mighty eares;
No, but because he wo'd not have it seen, (been.
That Stubble stands, where once large eares have

To his Booke.

Make haste away, and let one be
A friendly Patron unto thee:
Lest rapt from hence, I see thee lye
Torn for the use of Pasterie:
Or see thy injur'd Leaves serve well,
To make loose Gownes for Mackarell:
Or see the Grocers in a trice,
Make hoods of thee to serve out Spice.

Readinesse.

The readinesse of doing, doth expresse
No other, but the doers willingnesse.

Writing.

When words we want, Love teacheth to endite;
And what we blush to speake, she bids us write.

Society.

Two things do make society to stand;
The first Commerce is, & the next Command.

Satisfaction for sufferings.

For all our workes, a recompence is sure:
'Tis sweet to thinke on what was hard t'endure.

Upon a Maid.

Gone she is a long, long way,
But she has decreed a day
Back to come, (and make no stay.)
So we keepe till her returne
Here, her ashes, or her Urne.

To M. Henry Lawes, the excellent
Composer of his Lyricks.

Touch but thy Lire (my Harrie) and I heare
From thee some raptures of the rare Gotire.
Then if thy voice commingle with the String
I heare in thee rare Laniere to sing;
Or curious Wilson: Tell me, canst thou be
Less then Apollo, that ursurp'st such Three?
Three, unto whom the whole world give applause;
Yet their Three praises, praise but One; that's Lawes.

The delaying Bride.

Why so slowly do you move
To the centre of your love?
On your niceness though we wait,
Yet the houres say 'tis late:
Coynesse takes us to a measure;
But o'racted deads the pleasure.
Go to Bed, and care not when
Cheerfull day shall spring agen.
One Brave Captain did command,
(By his word) the Sun to stand:
One short charme if you but say
Will enforce the Moon to stay,
Till you warn her hence (away)
T'ave your blushes seen by day.

Age unfit for Love.

Maidens tell me I am old;
Let me in my Glasse behold
Whether smooth or not I be,
Or if haire remaines to me.
Well, or be't or be't not so,
This for certainty I know;
Ill it fits old men to play,
When that Death bids come away.

The Bed-man, or Grave-maker.

Thou hast made many Houses for the Dead;
When my Lot calls me to be buried,
For Love or Pittie, prethee let there be
I'th' Church-yard, made, one Tenement for me.

To Anthea.

Anthea I am going hence
With some small stock of innocence:
But yet those blessed gates I see
Withstanding entrance unto me.
To pray for me doe thou begin,
The Porter then will let me in.

Need.

Who begs to die for feare of humane need,
Wisheth his body, not his soule, good speed.

On Julia's lips.

Sweet are my Julia's lips and cleane,
As if or'e washt in Hippocrene.

Twilight.

Twilight, no other thing is, Poets say,
Then the last part of night, and first of day.

Kings and Tyrants.

'Twixt Kings & Tyrants there's this difference known;
Kings seek their Subjects good: Tyrants their owne.

To Julia.

I am zeallesse, prethee pray
For my well-fare (Julia)
For I thinke the gods require
Male perfumes, but Female fire.
To his Friend, Master J. Jincks.

Love, love me now, because I place
Thee here among my righteous race:
The bastard Slips may droop and die
Wanting both Root, and Earth; but thy
Immortall selfe, shall boldly trust
To live for ever, with my Just.

On himselfe.

If that my Fate has now fulfill'd my yeere,
And so soone stopt my longer living here;
What was't (ye Gods!) a dying man to save,
But while he met with his Paternall grave;
Though while we living 'bout the world do roame,
We love to rest in peacefull Urnes at home,
Where we may snug, and close together lye
By the dead bones of our deare Ancestrie.

Crosses.

Our Crosses are no other then the rods,
And our Diseases, Vultures of the Gods:
Each griefe we feele, that likewise is a Kite
Sent forth by them, our flesh to eate, or bite.

Upon Love.

Love brought me to a silent Grove,
 And shew'd me there a Tree,
Where some had hang'd themselves for love,
 And gave a Twist to me.

The Halter was of silk, and gold,
 That he reacht forth unto me:
No otherwise, then if he would
 By dainty things undo me.

He bade me then that Neck-lace use;
 And told me too, he maketh
A glorious end by such a Noose,
 His Death for Love that taketh.

'Twas but a dream; but had I been
 There really alone;
My desp'rate feares, in love, had seen
 Mine Execution.

The Body.

The Body is the Soules poore house, or home,
Whose Ribs the Laths are, & whose Flesh the Loame.

No difference i'th' dark.

Night makes no difference 'twixt the Priest and Clark;
Jone as my Lady is as good i'th' dark.

On Love.

Love is a kind of warre; Hence those who feare,
No cowards must his royall Ensignes beare.

Another.

Where love begins, there dead thy first desire:
A sparke neglected makes a mighty fire.

To Sappho.

Thou saist thou lov'st me Sappho; I say no;
But would to Love I could beleeve 'twas so!
Pardon my feares (sweet Sappho,) I desire
That thou be righteous found; and I the Lyer.

Out of Time, out of Tune.

We blame, nay we despise her paines
That wets her Garden when it raines:
But when the drought has dri'd the knot;
Then let her use the watring pot.
We pray for showers (at our need)
To drench, but not to drown our seed.

To his Booke.

Take mine advise, and go not neere
Those faces (sower as Vineger.)
For these, and Nobler numbers can
Ne'r please the supercillious man.

To his Honour'd friend, Sir Thomas Heale.

Stand by the Magick of my powerfull Rhymes
'Gainst all the indignation of the Times.
Age shall not wrong thee; or one jot abate
Of thy both Great, and everlasting fate.
While others perish, here's thy life decreed
Because begot of my Immortall seed.

To Apollo.

Thou mighty Lord and master of the Lyre,
Unshorn Apollo, come, and re-inspire
My fingers so, the Lyrick-strings to move,
That I may play, and sing a Hymne to Love.

The Sacrifice, by way of Discourse betwixt himselfe and Julia.

Herr. Come and let's in solemn wise
Both addresse to sacrifice:
Old Religion first commands
That we wash our hearts, and hands.
Is the beast exempt from staine,
Altar cleane, no fire prophane?
Are the Garlands, Is the Nard

Jul. Ready here? All well prepar'd,
With the Wine that must be shed
(Twixt the hornes) upon the head
Of the holy Beast we bring
(For our Trespasse-offering.

Herr. All is well; now next to these
Put we on pure Surplices;
And with Chaplets crown'd, we'l rost
With perfumes the Holocaust:
And (while we the gods invoke)
Reade acceptance by the smoake.

To Electra.

Let not thy Tomb-stone er'e be laid by me:
Nor let my Herse, be wept upon by thee:
But let that instant when thou dy'st be known,
The minute of mine expiration.
One knell be rung for both; and let one grave
To hold us two, an endlesse honour have.

An Hymne to Cupid.

Thou, thou that bear'st the sway
With whom the Sea-Nimphs play;
And Venus, every way:
When I embrace thy knee;
And make short pray'rs to thee:
In love, then prosper me.
This day I goe to wooe;
Instruct me how to doe
This worke thou put'st me too.
From shame my face keepe free,
From scorne I begge of thee,
Love to deliver me:
So shall I sing thy praise;
And to thee Altars raise,
Unto the end of daies.

How his soule came ensnared.

My soule would one day goe and seeke
For Roses, and in Julia's cheeke,
A richess of those sweets she found,
(As in an other Rosamond.)
But gathering Roses as she was;
(Not knowing what would come to passe)
It chanst a ringlet of her haire,
Caught my poore soule, as in a snare:
Which ever since has been in thrall,
Yet freedome, shee enjoyes withall.

Factions.

The factions of the great ones call,
To side with them, the Commons all.

Kisses Loathsome.

I abhor the slimie kisse,
(Which to me most loathsome is.)
Those lips please me which are plac't
Close, but not too strictly lac't:
Yeilding I wo'd have them; yet
Not a wimbling Tongue admit:
What sho'd poking-sticks make there,
When the ruffe is set elsewhere?

Upon Reape.

Reapes eyes so rawe are, that (it seemes) the flyes
Mistake the flesh, and flye-blow both his eyes;
So that an Angler, for a daies expence,
May baite his hooke, with maggots taken thence.

Upon Julia's haire, bundled up in a golden net.

Tell me, what needs those rich deceits,
These golden Toyles, and Trammel-nets,
To take thine haires when they are knowne
Already tame, and all thine owne?
'Tis I am wild, and more then haires
Deserve these Mashes and those snares.
Set free thy Tresses, let them flow
As aires doe breathe, or winds doe blow:
And let such curious Net-works be
Lesse set for them, then spred for me.

Upon Teage.

Teage has told lyes so long, that when Teage tells
Truth, yet Teages truths are untruths, (nothing else.)

Upon Truggin.

Truggin a Footman was; but now, growne lame,
Truggin now lives but to belye his name.

Upon Spenke.

Spenke has a strong breath, yet short Prayers saith:
Not out of want of breath, but want of faith.

The showre of Blossomes.

Love in a showre of Blossomes came
Down, and halfe drown'd me with the same:
The Blooms that fell were white and red;
But with such sweets commingled,
As whether (this) I cannot tell
My sight was pleas'd more, or my smell:
But true it was, as I rowl'd there,
Without a thought of hurt, or feare;
Love turn'd himselfe into a Bee,
And with his Javelin wounded me:
From which mishap this use I make,
Where most sweets are, there lyes a Snake.
Kisses and Favours are sweet things;
But Those have thorns, and These have stings.

A defence for Women.

Naught are all Women: I say no,
Since for one Bad, one Good I know:
For Clytemnestra most unkind,
Loving Alcestis there we find:
For one Medea that was bad,
A good Penelope was had:
For wanton Lais, then we have
Chaste Lucrece, or a wife as grave:
And thus through Woman-kind we see
A Good and Bad. Sirs credit me.

Slavery.

'Tis liberty to serve one Lord; but he
Who many serves, serves base servility.

Upon Lulls.

Lulls swears he is all heart; but you'l suppose
By his Probossis that he is all nose.

Charmes.

Bring the holy crust of Bread,
Lay it underneath the head;
'Tis a certain Charm to keep
Hags away, while Children sleep.

Another.

Let the superstitious wife
Neer the childs heart lay a knife:
Point be up, and Haft be downe;
(While she gossips in the towne)
This 'mongst other mystick charms
Keeps the sleeping child from harms.

Another to bring in the Witch.

To house the Hag, you must doe this;
Commix with Meale a little Pisse
Of him bewitcht: then forthwith make
A little Wafer or a Cake;
And this rawly bak't will bring
The old Hag in. No surer thing.

Another Charme for Stables.

Hang up Hooks, and Sheers to scare
Hence the Hag, that rides the Mare,
Till they be all over wet,
With the mire, and the sweat:
This observ'd, the Manes shall be
Of your horses, all knot-free.

The Ceremonies for Candlemasse day.

Kindle the Christmas Brand, and then
    Till Sunne-set, let it burne;
Which quencht, then lay it up agen,
    Till Christmas next returne.

Part must be kept wherewith to teend
    The Christmas Log next yeare;
And where 'tis safely kept, the Fiend,
    Can do no mischiefe (there.)

Ceremonies for Candlemasse Eve.

Down with the Rosemary and Bayes,
     Down with the Misleto;
In stead of Holly, now up-raise
     The greener Box (for show.)

The Holly hitherto did sway;
     Let Box now domineere;
Untill the dancing Easter-day,
     Or Easters Eve appeare.

Then youthfull Box which now hath grace,
     Your houses to renew;
Grown old, surrender must his place,
     Unto the crisped Yew.

When Yew is out, then Birch comes in,
     And many Flowers beside;
Both of a fresh, and fragrant kinne
     To honour Whitsontide.

Green Rushes then, and sweetest Bents,
     With cooler Oken boughs;
Come in for comely ornaments,
     To re-adorn the house.
Thus times do shift; each thing his turne do's hold;
New things succeed, as former things grow old.

Upon Candlemasse day.

End now the White-loafe, & the Pye,
And let all sports with Christmas dye.

Surfeits.

Bad are all surfeits: but Physitians call
That surfeit tooke by bread, the worst of all.`

Upon Nis.

Nis, he makes Verses; but the Lines he writes,
Serve but for matter to make Paper-kites.

Teares.

Teares most prevaile; with teares too thou mayst move
Rocks to relent, and coyest maids to love.

To Biancha, to blesse him.

Wo'd I wooe, and wo'd I winne,
Wo'd I well my worke begin?
Wo'd I evermore be crown'd
With the end that I propound?
Wo'd I frustrate, or prevent
All Aspects malevolent?
Thwart all Wizzards, and with these
Dead all black contingencies:
Place my words, and all works else
In most happy Parallels?
All will prosper, if so be
I be kist, or blest by thee.

To his Book.

Before the Press scarce one co'd see
A little-peeping-part of thee:
But since th'art Printed, thou dost call
To shew thy nakedness to all.
My care for thee is now the less;
(Having resign'd thy shamefac'tness:)
Go with thy Faults and Fates; yet stay
And take this sentence, then away;
Whom one belov'd will not suffice,
She'l runne to all adulteries.

Julia's Churching, or Purification.

Put on thy Holy Fillitings, and so
To th'Temple with the sober Midwife go.
Attended thus (in a most solemn wise)
By those who serve the Child-bed misteries.
Burn first thine incense; next, when as thou see'st
The candid Stole thrown ore the Pious Priest;
With reverend Curtsies come, and to him bring
Thy free (and not decurted) offering.
All Rites well ended, with faire Auspice come
(As to the breaking of a Bride-Cake) home:
Where ceremonious Hymen shall for thee
Provide a second Epithalamie.
She who keeps chastly to her husbands side
Is not for one, but every night his Bride:
And stealing still with love, and feare to Bed,
Brings him not one, but many a Maiden-head.

To his friend to avoid contention of words.

Words beget Anger: Anger brings forth blowes:
Blowes make of dearest friends immortall Foes.
For which prevention (Sociate) let there be
Betwixt us two no more Logomachie.
Farre better 'twere for either to be mute,
Then for to murder friendship, by dispute.

Upon Prickles. Epigram.

Prickles is waspish, and puts forth his sting,
For Bread, Drinke, Butter, Cheese; for every thing
That Prickles buyes, puts Prickles out of frame;
How well his nature's fitted to his name!

Truth.

Truth is best found out by the time, and eyes;
Falsehood winnes credit by uncertainties.

The Eyes before the Eares.

We credit most our sight; one eye doth please
Our trust farre more then ten eare-witnesses.

Want.

Want is a softer Wax, that takes thereon,
This, that, and every base impression.

Blame.

In Battailes what disasters fall,
The King he beares the blame of all.

To a Friend.

Looke in my Book, and herein see,
Life endlesse sign'd to thee and me.
We o're the tombes, and Fates shall flye;
While other generations dye.

Upon M. William Lawes, the rare Musitian.

Sho'd I not put on Blacks, when each one here
Comes with his Cypresse, and devotes a teare?
Sho'd I not grieve (my Lawes) when every Lute,
Violl, and Voice, is (by thy losse) struck mute?
Thy loss brave man! whose Numbers have been hurl'd,
And no less prais'd, then spread throughout the world.
Some have Thee call'd Amphion; some of us,
Nam'd thee Terpander, or sweet Orpheus:
Some this, some that, but all in this agree,
Musique had both her birth, and death with Thee.

A song upon Silvia.

From me my Silvia ranne away,
And running therewithall;
A Primrose Banke did cross her way,
And gave my Love a fall.

But trust me now I dare not say,
What I by chance did see;
But such the Drap'ry did betray
That fully ravisht me.

The Hony-combe.

If thou hast found an honie-combe,
Eate thou not all, but taste on some:
For if thou eat'st it to excess;
That sweetness turnes to Loathsomness.
Taste it to Temper; then 'twill be
Marrow, and Manna unto thee.

Upon Ben. Johnson.

Here lyes Johnson with the rest
Of the Poets; but the Best.
Reader, wo'dst thou more have known?
Aske his Story, not this Stone.
That will speake what this can't tell
Of his glory. So farewell.

An Ode for him.

Ah Ben!
Say how, or when
Shall we thy Guests
Meet at those Lyrick Feasts,
Made at the Sun,
The Dog, the triple Tunne?
Where we such clusters had,
As made us nobly wild, not mad;
And yet each Verse of thine
Out-did the meate, out-did the frolick wine.

My Ben!
Or come agen:
Or send to us,
Thy wits great over-plus;
But teach us yet
Wisely to husband it;
Lest we that Tallent spend:
And having once brought to an end
That precious stock; the store
Of such a wit the world sho'd have no more.

Upon a Virgin.

Spend Harmless shade thy nightly Houres,
Selecting here, both Herbs, and Flowers;
Of which make Garlands here, and there,
To dress thy silent sepulchre.
Nor do thou feare the want of these,
In everlasting Properties.
Since we fresh strewings will bring hither,
Farre faster then the first can wither.

A request to the Graces.

Ponder my words, if so that any be
Known guilty here of incivility:
Let what is graceless, discompos'd, and rude,
With sweetness, smoothness, softness, be endu'd.
Teach it to blush, to curtsie, lisp, and shew
Demure, but yet, full of temptation too.
Numbers ne'r tickle, or but lightly please,
Unlesse they have some wanton carriages.
This if ye do, each Piece will here be good,
And gracefull made, by your neate Sisterhood.

Upon himselfe.

I lately fri'd, but now behold
I freeze as fast, and shake for cold.
And in good faith I'd thought it strange
T'ave found in me this sudden change;
But that I understood by dreames,
These only were but Loves extreames;
Who fires with hope the Lovers heart,
And starves with cold the self-same part.

Multitude.

We Trust not to the multitude in Warre,
But to the stout; and those that skilfull are.

Feare.

Man must do well out of a good intent,
Not for the servile feare of punishment.

Present Government grievous.

Men are suspicious; prone to discontent:
Subjects still loath the present Government.

Cloathes, are conspirators.

Though from without no foes at all we feare;
We shall be wounded by the cloathes we weare.

To M. Kellam.

What can my Kellam drink his Sack
    In Goblets to the brim,
And see his Robin Herrick lack,
    Yet send no Boules to him?

For love or pitie to his Muse,
    (That she may flow in Verse)
Contemne to recommend a Cruse,
    But send to her a Tearce.

Happinesse to hospitalitie, or a hearty wish to good house-
keeping.

First, may the hand of bounty bring
Into the daily offering
Of full provision; such a store,
Till that the Cooke cries, Bring no more.
Upon your hogsheads never fall
A drought of wine, ale, beere (at all)
But, like full clouds, may they from thence
Diffuse their mighty influence.
Next, let the Lord, and Ladie here
Enjoy a Christning yeare by yeare;
And this good blessing back them still,
T'ave Boyes, and Gyrles too, as they will.
Then from the porch may many a Bride
Unto the Holy Temple ride:
And thence return, (short prayers seyd)
A wife most richly married.
Last, may the Bride and Bridegroome be
Untoucht by cold sterility;
But in their springing blood so play,
As that in Lusters few they may,
By laughing too, and lying downe,
People a City or a Towne.

Cunctation in Correction.

The Lictors bundl'd up their rods: beside,
Knit them with knots (with much adoe unty'd)
That if (unknitting) men wo'd yet repent,
They might escape the lash of punishment.

Rest Refreshes.

Lay by the good a while; a resting field
Will, after ease, a richer harvest yeild:
Trees this year beare; next, they their wealth with-hold:
Continuall reaping makes a land wax old.

Revenge.

Mans disposition is for to requite
An injurie, before a benefite:
Thanksgiving is a burden, and a paine;
Revenge is pleasing to us, as our gaine.

The first marrs or makes.

In all our high designments, 'twill appeare,
The first event breeds confidence or feare.

Beginning, difficult.

Hard are the two first staires unto a Crowne;
Which got, the third, bids him a King come downe.

Faith four-square.

Faith is a thing that's four-square; let it fall
This way or that, it not declines at all.

The present time best pleaseth.

Praise they that will Times past, I joy to see
My selfe now live: this age best pleaseth mee.

Cruelty.

Tis but a dog-like madnesse in bad Kings,
For to delight in wounds and murderings.
As some plants prosper best by cuts and blowes;
So Kings by killing doe encrease their foes.

Faire after foule.

Teares quickly drie: griefes will in time decay:
A cleare will come after a cloudy day.

Hunger.

Aske me what hunger is, and I'll reply,
'Tis but a fierce desire of hot and drie.

Bad wages for good service.

In this misfortune Kings doe most excell,
To heare the worst from men, when they doe well.

The End.

Conquer we shall, but we must first contend;
'Tis not the Fight that crowns us, but the end.

His wish.

Fat be my Hinde; unlearned be my wife;
Peacefull by night; my day devoid of strife:
To these a comely off-spring I desire,
Singing about my everlasting fire.

The Bondman.

Bind me but to thee with thine haire,
    And quickly I shall be
Made by that fetter or that snare
    A bondman unto thee.

Or if thou tak'st that bond away,
    Then bore me through the eare;
And by the Law I ought to stay
    For ever with thee here.

To Silvia.

Pardon my trespasse (Silvia) I confesse,
My kisse out-went the bounds of shamfastnesse:
None is discreet at all times; no, not Jove
Himselfe, at one time, can be wise, and Love.

Faire shewes deceive.

Smooth was the Sea, and seem'd to call
To prettie girles to play withall:
Who padling there, the Sea soone frown'd,
And on a sudden both were drown'd.
What credit can we give to seas,
Who, kissing, kill such Saints as these?

Upon Julia's washing her self in the river.

How fierce was I, when I did see
My Julia wash her self in thee!
So Lillies thorough Christall look:
So purest pebbles in the brook:
As in the River Julia did,
Halfe with a Lawne of water hid,
Into thy streames my self I threw,
And strugling there, I kist thee too;
And more had done (it is confest)
Had not thy waves forbad the rest.

A Meane in our Meanes.

Though Frankinsense the Deities require,
We must not give all to the hallowed fire.
Such be our gifts, and such be our expence,
As for our selves to leave some frankinsence.

Upon Clunn.

A rowle of Parchment Clunn about him beares,
Charg'd with the Armes of all his Ancestors:
And seems halfe ravisht, when he looks upon
That Bar, this Bend; that Fess, this Cheveron;
This Manch, that Moone; this Martlet, and that Mound;
This counterchange of Perle and Diamond.
What joy can Clun have in that Coat, or this,
When as his owne still out at elboes is?

Upon Cupid.

Love, like a Beggar, came to me
     With Hose and Doublet torne:
His Shirt bedangling from his knee,
     With Hat and Shooes out-worne.

He askt an almes; I gave him bread,
     And meat too, for his need:
Of which, when he had fully fed,
     He wished me all Good speed.

Away he went, but as he turn'd
     (In faith I know not how)
He toucht me so, as that I burn,
     And am tormented now.

Love's silent flames, and fires obscure
     Then crept into my heart;
And though I saw no Bow, I'm sure,
     His finger was the dart.

Choose for the best.

Give house-roome to the best; 'Tis never known
Vertue and pleasure, both to dwell in one.

Upon Blisse.

Blisse (last night drunk) did kisse his mothers knee:
Where he will kisse (next drunk) conjecture ye.

Upon Burr.

Burr is a smell-feast, and a man alone,
That (where meat is) will be a hanger on.

Upon Megg.

Megg yesterday was troubled with a Pose,
Which, this night hardned, sodders up her nose.

An Hymne to Love.

I will confesse
With Cheerfulnesse,
Love is a thing so likes me,
That let her lay
On me all day,
I'll kiss the hand that strikes me.

I will not, I,
Now blubb'ring, cry,
.It (Ah!) too late repents me
That I did fall
To love at all,
Since love so much contents me.

No, no, I'll be
In fetters free;
While others they sit wringing
Their hands for paine;
I'll entertaine
The wounds of love with singing

With Flowers and Wine,
And Cakes Divine,
To strike me I will tempt thee:
Which done; no more
I'll come before
Thee and thine Altars emptie.

To his honoured and most Ingenious friend
Mr. Charles Cotton.

For brave comportment, wit without offence,
Words fully flowing, yet of influence:
Thou art that man of men, the man alone,
Worthy the Publique Admiration:
Who with thine owne eyes read'st what we doe write,
And giv'st our Numbers Euphonie, and weight.
Tel'st when a Verse springs high, how understood
To be, or not borne of the Royall-blood.
What State above, what Symmetrie below,
Lines have, or sho'd have, thou the best canst show.
For which (my Charles) it is my pride to be,
Not so much knowne, as to be lov'd of thee.
Long may I live so, and my wreath of Bayes,
Be lesse anothers Laurell, then thy praise.

Women uselesse.

What need we marry Women, when
Without their use we may have men?
And such as will in short time be,
For murder fit, or mutinie;
As Cadmus once a new way found,
By throwing teeth into the ground:
(From which poore seed, and rudely sown)
Sprung up a War-like Nation.
So let us Yron, Silver, Gold,
Brasse, Leade, or Tinne, throw into th' mould;
And we shall see in little space
Rise up of men, a fighting race.
If this can be, say then, what need
Have we of Women or their seed?

Love is a sirrup.

Love is a sirrup; and who er'e we see
Sick and surcharg'd with this sacietie:
Shall by this pleasing trespasse quickly prove,
Ther's loathsomnesse e'en in the sweets of love.

Leven.

Love is a Leven, and a loving kisse
The Leven of a loving sweet-heart is.

Repletion.

Physitians say Repletion springs
More from the sweet then sower things.

No man without Money.

No man such rare parts hath, that he can swim,
If favour or occasion helpe not him.

On Himselfe.

Weepe for the dead, for they have lost this light:
And weepe for me, lost in an endlesse night.
Or mourne, or make a Marble Verse for me,
Who writ for many. Benedicite.

On Himselfe.

Lost to the world; lost to my selfe; alone
Here now I rest under this Marble stone:
In depth of silence, heard, and seene of none.

To M. Leonard Willan his peculiar friend.

I will be short, and having quickly hurl'd
This line about, live Thou throughout the world;
Who art a man for all Sceanes; unto whom
(What's hard to others) nothing's troublesome.
Can'st write the Comick, Tragick straine, and fall
From these to penne the pleasing Pastorall:
Who fli'st at all heights: Prose and Verse run'st through;
Find'st here a fault, and mend'st the trespasse too:
For which I might extoll thee, but speake lesse,
Because thy selfe art comming to the Presse:
And then sho'd I in praising thee be slow,
Posterity will pay thee what I owe.

To his worthy friend M. John Hall,
Student of Grayes-Inne.

Tell me young man, or did the Muses bring
Thee lesse to taste, then to drink up their spring;
That none hereafter sho'd be thought, or be
A Poet, or a Poet-like but Thee.
What was thy Birth, thy starre that makes thee knowne,
At twice ten yeares, a prime and publike one?
Tell us thy Nation, kindred, or the whence
Thou had'st, and hast thy mighty influence,
That makes thee lov'd, and of the men desir'd,
And no lesse prais'd, then of the maides admir'd.
Put on thy Laurell then; and in that trimme
Be thou Apollo, or the type of him:
Or let the Unshorne God lend thee his Lyre,
And next to him, be Master of the Quire.

To Julia.

Offer thy gift; but first the Law commands
Thee Julia, first, to sanctifie thy hands:
Doe that my Julia which the rites require,
Then boldly give thine incense to the fire.

To the most comely and proper M. Elizabeth Finch.

Hansome you are, and Proper you will be
Despight of all your infortunitie:
Live long and lovely, but yet grow no lesse
In that your owne prefixed comelinesse:
Spend on that stock: and when your life must fall,
Leave others Beauty, to set up withall.

Upon Ralph.

Ralph pares his nayles, his warts, his cornes, and Ralph
In sev'rall tills, and boxes keepes 'em safe;
Instead of Harts-horne (if he speakes the troth)
To make a lustie-gellie for his broth.

To his Booke.

If hap it must, that I must see thee lye
Absyrtus-like all torne confusedly:
With solemne tears, and with much grief of heart,
I'll recollect thee (weeping) part by part;
And having washt thee, close thee in a chest
With spice; that done, I'll leave thee to thy rest.

To the King,
Upon his welcome to Hampton-Court.
Set and Sung.

Welcome, Great Cesar, welcome now you are,
As dearest Peace, after destructive Warre:
Welcome as slumbers; or as beds of ease
After our long, and peevish sicknesses.
O Pompe of Glory! Welcome now, and come
To re-possess once more your long'd-for home.
A thousand Altars smoake; a thousand thighes
Of Beeves here ready stand for Sacrifice.
Enter and prosper; while our eyes doe waite
For an Ascendent throughly Auspicate:
Under which signe we may the former stone
Lay of our safeties new foundation:
That done; O Cesar, live, and be to us,
Our Fate, our Fortune, and our Genius;
To whose free knees we may our temples tye
As to a still protecting Deitie.
That sho'd you stirre, we and our Altars too
May (Great Augustus) goe along with You.
Chor. Long live the King; and to accomplish this,
  We'l from our owne, adde far more years to his.

To his Muse, another to the same.

Tell that Brave Man, fain thou wo'dst have access
To kiss his hands, but that for fearfullness;
Or else because th'art like a modest Bride,
Ready to blush to death, sho'd he but chide.

Ultimus Heroum: OR, To the most learned, and to the right
Honourable, Henry, Marquesse of Dorchester.

And as time past when Cato the Severe
Entred the circumspacious Theater; `
In reverence of his person, every one
Stood as he had been turn'd from flesh to stone:
E'ne so my numbers will astonisht be
If but lookt on; struck dead, if scan'd by Thee.

Upon Vineger.

Vineger is no other I define,
Then the dead Corps, or carkase of the Wine.

Upon Mudge.

Mudge every morning to the Postern comes,
(His teeth all out) to rince and wash his gummes.

To his learned friend M. Jo. Harmar, Phisitian
to the Colledge of Westminster.

When first I find those Numbers thou do'st write;
To be most soft, terce, sweet, and perpolite:
Next, when I see Thee towring in the skie,
In an expansion no less large, then high;
Then, in that compass, sayling here and there,
And with Circumgyration every where;
Following with love and active heate thy game,
And then at last to truss the Epigram;
I must confess, distinction none I see
Between Domitians Martiall then, and Thee.
But this I know, should Jupiter agen
Descend from heaven, to re-converse with men;
The Romane Language full, and superfine,
If Jove wo'd speake, he wo'd accept of thine.

Upon his Spaniell Tracie.

Now thou art dead, no eye shall ever see,
For shape and service, Spaniell like to thee.
This shall my love doe, give thy sad death one
Teare, that deserves of me a million.

The Deluge.

Drowning, drowning, I espie
Coming from my Julia's eye:
'Tis some solace in our smart,
To have friends to beare a part:
I have none; but must be sure
Th'inundation to endure.
Shall not times hereafter tell
This for no meane miracle;
When the waters by their fall
Threatn'd ruine unto all?
Yet the deluge here was known,
Of a world to drowne but One.

Upon Lupes.

Lupes for the outside of his suite has paide;
But for his heart, he cannot have it made:
The reason is, his credit cannot get
The inward carbage for his cloathes as yet.

Raggs.

What are our patches, tatters, raggs, and rents,
But the base dregs and lees of vestiments?

Strength to support Soveraignty.

Let Kings and Rulers, learne this line from me;
Where power is weake, unsafe is Majestie.

Upon Tubbs.

For thirty yeares, Tubbs has been proud and poor;
'Tis now his habit, which he can't give ore.

On Tomasin Parsons.

Grow up in Beauty, as thou do'st begin,
And be of all admired, Tomasin.

Crutches.

Thou seest me Lucia this year droope,
Three Zodiaks fill'd more I shall stoope;
Let Crutches then provided be
To shore up my debilitie.
Then while thou laugh'st; Ile, sighing, crie,
A Ruine underpropt am I:
Do'n will I then my Beadsmans gown,
And when so feeble I am grown,
As my weake shoulders cannot beare
The burden of a Grashopper:
Yet with the bench of aged sires,
When I and they keep tearmly fires;
With my weake voice I'll sing, or say
Some Odes I made of Lucia:
Then will I heave my wither'd hand
To Jove the Mighty for to stand
Thy faithfull friend, and to poure downe
Upon thee many a Benizon.

To Julia.

Holy waters hither bring
For the sacred sprinkling:
Baptize me and thee, and so
Let us to the Altar go.
And (ere we our rites commence)
Wash our hands in innocence.
Then I'll be the Rex Sacrorum,
Thou the Queen of Peace and Quorum.

Upon Case.

Case is a Lawyer, that near pleads alone,
But when he hears the like confusion,
As when the disagreeing Commons throw
About their House, their clamorous I, or No:
Then Case, as loud as any Serjant there,
Cries out, (my lord, my Lord) the Case is clear:
But when all's hush't, Case then a fish more mute,
Bestirs his Hand, but starves in hand the Suite.

To Perenna.

I a Dirge will pen for thee;
Thou a Trentall make for me:
That the Monks and Fryers together,
Here may sing the rest of either:
Next, I'm sure, the Nuns will have
Candlemas to grace the Grave.

To his Sister in Law, M. Susanna Herrick.

The Person crowns the Place; your lot doth fall
Last, yet to be with These a Principall.
How ere it fortuned; know for Truth, I meant
You a fore-leader in this Testament.

Upon the Lady Crew.

This Stone can tell the storie of my life,
What was my Birth, to whom I was a Wife:
In teeming years, how soon my Sun was set,
Where now I rest, these may be known by Jet.
For other things, my many Children be
The best and truest Chronicles of me.

Ceremony upon Candlemas Eve.

Down with the Rosemary, and so
Down with the Baies, & misletoe:
Down with the Holly, Ivie, all,
Wherewith ye drest the Christmas Hall:
That so the superstitious find
No one least Branch there left behind:
For look how many leaves there be
Neglected there (maids trust to me)
So many Goblins you shall see.

Upon Spokes.

Spokes when he sees a rosted Pig, he swears
Nothing he loves on't but the chaps and ears:
But carve to him the fat flanks; and he shall
Rid these, and those, and part by part eat all.

To his kinsman M. Tho: Herrick, who
desired to be in his Book.

Welcome to this my Colledge, and though late
Tha'st got a place here (standing candidate)
It matters not, since thou art chosen one
Here of my great and good foundation

A Bucolick betwixt Two: Lacon and Thyrsis.

Lacon.
For a kiss or two, confesse,
What doth cause this pensiveness?
Thou most lovely Neat-heardesse:
Why so lonely on the hill?
Why thy pipe by thee so still,
That ere while was heard so shrill?
Tell me, do thy kine now fail
To fulfill the milkin-paile?
Say, what is't that thou do'st aile?

Thyr.
None of these; but out, alas!
A mischance is come to pass,
And I'll tell thee what it was:
See mine eyes are weeping ripe.
Lacon. Tell, and I'll lay down my Pipe.

Thyr.
I have lost my lovely steere,
That to me was far more deer
Then these kine, which I milke here.
Broad of fore-head, large of eye,
Party colour'd like a Pie;
Smooth in each limb as a die;
Clear of hoof, and clear of horn;
Sharply pointed as a thorn:
With a neck by yoke unworn.
From the which hung down by strings,
Balls of Cowslips, Daisie rings,
Enterplac't with ribbanings.
Faultless every way for shape;
Not a straw co'd him escape;
Ever gamesome as an ape:
But yet harmless as a sheep.
(Pardon, Lacon if I weep)
Tears will spring, where woes are deep.

Now (ai me) (ai me.) Last night
Came a mad dog, and did bite,
I, and kil'd my dear delight.

Lacon.
Alack for grief!

Thyr.
But I'll be brief,
Hence I must, for time doth call
Me, and my sad Play-mates all,
To his Ev'ning Funerall.
Live long, Lacon, so adew.
Lacon. Mournfull maid farewell to you;
Earth afford ye flowers to strew.

Upon Sappho.

Look upon Sappho's lip, and you will swear,
There is a love-like-leven rising there.

Suspicion makes secure.

He that will live of all cares dispossest,
Must shun the bad, I, and suspect the best.

Care a good keeper.

Care keepes the Conquest; 'tis no lesse renowne,
To keepe a Citie, then to winne a Towne.

Rules for our reach.

Men must have Bounds how farre to walke; for we
Are made farre worse, by lawless liberty.

Upon Faunus.

We read how Faunus, he the shepheards God,
His wife to death whipt with a Mirtle Rod.
The Rod (perhaps) was better'd by the name;
But had it been of Birch, the death's the same.

The Quintell.

Up with the Quintill, that the Rout,
May fart for joy, as well as shout:
Either's welcome, Stinke or Civit,
If we take it, as they give it.

A Bachanalian Verse.

Drinke up
Your Cup,
But not spill Wine;
For if you
Do,
'Tis an ill signe;

That we
Foresee,
You are cloy'd here,
If so, no
Hoe,
But avoid here.

To Biancha.

Ah Biancha! now I see,
It is Noone and past with me:
In a while it will strike one;
Then Biancha, I am gone.
Some effusions let me have,
Offer'd on my holy Grave;
Then, Biancha, let me rest
With my face towards the East.

To the handsome Mistresse Grace Potter.

As is your name, so is your comely face,
Toucht every where with such diffused grace,
As that in all that admirable round,
There is not one least solecisme found;
And as that part, so every portion else,
Keepes line for line with Beauties Parallels.

Anacreontike.

I must
Not trust
Here to any;
Bereav'd,
Deceiv'd
By so many:
As one
Undone
By my losses;
Comply
Will I
With my crosses.
Yet still
I will
Not be grieving;
Since thence
And hence
Comes relieving.
But this
Sweet is
In our mourning;
Times bad
And sad
Are a turning:
And he
Whom we
See dejected;
Next day
Wee may
See erected.

More modest, more manly.

'Tis still observ'd, those men most valiant are,
That are most modest ere they come to warre.

Not to covet much where little is the charge.

Why sho'd we covet much, when as we know,
W'ave more to beare our charge, then way to go?

Upon Pennie.

Brown bread Tom Pennie eates, and must of right,
Because his stock will not hold out for white.

Patience in Princes.

Kings must not use the Axe for each offence:
Princes cure some faults by their patience.

Anacrontick Verse.

Brisk methinks I am, and fine,
When I drinke my capring wine:
Then to love I do encline;
When I drinke my wanton wine:
And I wish all maidens mine,
When I drinke my sprightly wine:
Well I sup, and well I dine,
When I drinke my frolick wine:
But I languish, lowre, and Pine,
When I want my fragrant wine.

Feare gets force.

Despaire takes heart, when ther's no hope to speed:
The Coward then takes Armes, and do's the deed.

Parcell-gil't-Poetry.

Let's strive to be the best; the Gods, we know it,
Pillars and men, hate an indifferent Poet.

Upon Love, by way of question and answer.

I bring ye Love, *Quest.* What will love do?
    Ans. Like, and dislike ye:
I bring ye love: *Quest.* What will Love do?
    Ans. Stroake ye to strike ye.
I bring ye love: *Quest.* What will Love do?
    Ans. Love will be-foole ye:
I bring ye love: *Quest.* What will love do?
    Ans. Heate ye to coole ye:
I bring ye love: *Quest.* What will love do?
    Ans. Love gifts will send ye:
I bring ye love: *Quest.* What will love do?
    Ans. Stock ye to spend ye:
I bring ye love: *Quest.* What will love do?
    Ans. Love will fulfill ye:
I bring ye love: *Quest.* What will love do?
    Ans. Kisse ye, to kill ye.

To the Lord Hopton, on his fight in Cornwall.

Go on brave Hopton, to effectuate that
Which wee, and times to come, shall wonder at.
Lift up thy Sword; next, suffer it to fall,
And by that One blow set an end to all.

His Grange.

How well contented in this private Grange
Spend I my life (that's subject unto change:)
Under whose Roofe with Mosse-worke wrought, there I
Kisse my Brown wife, and black Posterity.

Good manners at meat.

This rule of manners I will teach my guests,
To come with their own bellies unto feasts:
Not to eat equall portions; but to rise
Farc't with the food, that may themselves suffice.

Leprosie in houses.

When to a House I come, and see
The Genius wastefull, more then free:
The servants thumblesse, yet to eat,
With lawlesse tooth the floure of wheate:
The Sonnes to suck the milke of Kine,
More then the teats of Discipline:
The Daughters wild and loose in dresse;
Their cheekes unstain'd with shamefac'tnesse:
The Husband drunke, the Wife to be
A Baud to incivility:
I must confesse, I there descrie,
A House spred through with Leprosie.

Anthea's Retractation.

Anthea laught, and fearing lest excesse
Might stretch the cords of civill comelinesse:
She with a dainty blush rebuk't her face;
And cal'd each line back to his rule and space.

Comforts in Crosses.

Be not dismaide, though crosses cast thee downe;
Thy fall is but the rising to a Crowne.

Seeke and finde.

Attempt the end, and never stand to doubt;
Nothing's so hard, but search will find it out.

Rest.

On with thy worke, though thou beest hardly prest;
Labour is held up, by the hope of rest.

Bastards.

Our Bastard-children are but like to Plate,
Made by the Coyners illegitimate.

Leprosie in Cloathes.

When flowing garments I behold
Enspir'd with Purple, Pearle, and Gold;
I think no other but I see
In them a glorious leprosie
That do's infect, and make the rent
More mortall in the vestiment.
As flowrie vestures doe descrie
The wearers rich immodestie;
So plaine and simple cloathes doe show
Where vertue walkes, not those that flow.

Upon Buggins.

Buggins is Drunke all night, all day he sleepes;
This is the Levell-coyle that Buggins keeps.

Great Maladies, long Medicines.

To an old soare a long cure must goe on;
Great faults require great satisfaction.

His Answer to a friend.

You aske me what I doe, and how I live?
And (Noble friend) this answer I must give:
Drooping, I draw on to the vaults of death,
Or'e which you'l walk, when I am laid beneath.

The Begger.

Shall I a daily Begger be,
For loves sake asking almes of thee?
Still shall I crave, and never get
A hope of my desired bit?
Ah cruell maides! I'll goe my way,
Whereas (perchance) my fortunes may
Finde out a Threshold or a doore,
That may far sooner speed the poore:
Where thrice we knock, and none will heare,
Cold comfort still I'm sure lives there.

His change.

My many cares and much distress,
Has made me like a wilderness:
Or (discompos'd) I'm like a rude,
And all confused multitude:
Out of my comely manners worne;
And as in meanes, in minde all torne.

The Vision.

Me thought I saw (as I did dreame in bed)
A crawling Vine about Anacreon's head:
Flusht was his face; his haires with oyle did shine;
And as he spake, his mouth ranne ore with wine.
Tipled he was; and tipling lispt withall;
And lisping reeld, and reeling like to fall.
A young Enchantresse close by him did stand
Tapping his plump thighes with a mirtle wand:
She smil'd; he kist; and kissing, cull'd her too;
And being cup-shot, more he co'd not doe.
For which (me thought) in prittie anger she
Snatcht off his Crown, and gave the wreath to me:
Since when (me thinks) my braines about doe swim,
And I am wilde and wanton like to him.

A vow to Venus.

Happily I had a sight
Of my dearest deare last night;
Make her this day smile on me,
And I'll Roses give to thee.

On his Booke.

The bound (almost) now of my book I see
But yet no end of those therein or me:
Here we begin new life; while thousands quite
Are lost, and theirs, in everlasting night.

A sonnet of Perilla.

Then did I live when I did see
Perilla smile on none but me.
But (ah!) by starres malignant crost,
The life I got I quickly lost:
But yet a way there doth remaine,
For me embalm'd to live againe;
And that's to love me; in which state
I'll live as one Regenerate.

Bad may be better.

Man may at first transgress, but next do well:
Vice doth in some but lodge awhile, not dwell.

Posting to Printing.

Let others to the Printing Presse run fast,
Since after death comes glory, I'll not haste.

Rapine brings Ruine.

What's got by Justice is establisht sure;
No Kingdomes got by Rapine long endure.

Comfort to a youth that had lost his Love.

What needs complaints,
When she a place
Has with the race
    Of Saints?
In endlesse mirth,
She thinks not on
What's said or done
    In earth:
She sees no teares,
Or any tone
Of thy deep grone
    She heares:
Nor do's she minde,
Or think on't now,
That ever thou
    Wast kind.
But chang'd above,
She likes not there,
As she did here,
    Thy Love.
Forbeare therefore,
And Lull asleepe
Thy woes and weep
    No more.

Saint Distaffs day, or the morrow after Twelfth day.

Partly worke and partly play
Ye must on S. Distaffs day:
From the Plough soone free your teame;
Then come home and fother them.
If the Maides a spinning goe,
Burne the flax, and fire the tow:
Scorch their plackets, but beware
That ye singe no maiden-haire.
Bring in pailes of water then,
Let the Maides bewash the men.
Give S. Distaffe all the right,
Then bid Christmas sport good-night;
And next morrow, every one
To his owne vocation.

His teares to Thamasis.

I send, I send here my supremest kiss
To thee my silver-footed Thamasis.
No more shall I reiterate thy Strand,
Whereon so many Stately Structures stand:
Nor in the summers sweeter evenings go,
To bath in thee (as thousand others doe.)
No more shall I a long thy christall glide,
In Barge (with boughes and rushes beautifi'd)
With soft-smooth Virgins (for our chast disport)
To Richmond, Kingstone, and to Hampton-Court:
Never againe shall I with Finnie-Ore
Put from, or draw unto the faithfull shore:
And Landing here, or safely Landing there,
Make way to my Beloved Westminster:
Or to the Golden-cheap-side, where the earth
Of Julia Herrick gave to me my Birth.
May all clean Nimphs and curious water Dames,
With Swan-like-state, flote up & down thy streams:
No drought upon thy wanton waters fall
To make them Leane, and languishing at all.
No ruffling winds come hither to discease
Thy pure, and Silver-wristed Naides.
Keep up your state ye streams; and as ye spring,
Never make sick your Banks by surfeiting.
Grow young with Tydes, and though I see ye never,
Receive this vow, so fare-ye-well for ever.

Pardons.

Those ends in War the best contentment bring,
Whose Peace is made up with a Pardoning.

Peace not Permanent.

Great Cities seldome rest: If there be none
T'invade from far: They'l finde worse foes at home.

Truth and Errour.

Twixt Truth and Errour, there's this difference known,
Errour is fruitfull, Truth is onely one.

Things mortall still mutable.

Things are uncertain, and the more we get,
The more on ycie pavements we are set.

Sufferance.

In the hope of ease to come,
Let's endure one Martyrdome.

Upon Boreman. Epigram.

Boreman takes tole, cheats, flatters, lyes, yet Boreman,
For all the Divell helps, will be a poore man.

Studies to be supported.

Studies themselves will languish and decay,
When either price, or praise is ta'ne away.

Wit punisht, prospers most.

Dread not the shackles: on with thine intent;
Good wits get more fame by their punishment.

Twelfe night, or King and Queene.

    Now, now the mirth comes
    With the cake full of plums,
Where Beane's the King of the sport here;
    Beside we must know,
    The Pea also
Must revell, as Queene, in the Court here.

    Begin then to chuse,
    (This night as ye use)
Who shall for the present delight here,
    Be a King by the lot,
    And who shall not
Be Twelfe-day Queene for the night here.

    Which knowne, let us make
    Joy-sops with the cake;
And let not a man then be seen here,
    Who unurg'd will not drinke
    To the base from the brink
A health to the King and the Queene here.

    Next crowne the bowle full
    With gentle lambs-wooll;
Adde sugar, nutmeg and ginger,
    With store of ale too;
    And thus ye must doe
To make the wassaile a swinger.

    Give then to the King
    And Queene wassailing;
And though with ale ye be whet here;
    Yet part ye from hence,
    As free from offence,
As when ye innocent met here.

His desire.

Give me a man that is not dull,
When all the world with rifts is full:
But unamaz'd dares clearely sing,
When as the roof's a tottering:
And, though it falls, continues still
Tickling the Citterne with his quill.

Caution in Councell.

Know when to speake; for many times it brings
Danger to give the best advice to Kings.

Moderation.

Let moderation on thy passions waite
Who loves too much, too much the lov'd will hate.

Advice the best actor.

*Still take advice; though counsels when they flye
At randome, sometimes hit most happily.*

Conformity is Comely.

Conformity gives comelinesse to things.
And equall shares exclude all murmerings.

Lawes.

Who violates the Customes, hurts the Health,
Not of one man, but all the Common-wealth.

The meane.

Tis much among the filthy to be clean;
Our heat of youth can hardly keep the mean.

Like loves his like.

Like will to like, each Creature loves his kinde;
Chaste words proceed still from a bashfull minde.

His hope or sheat-Anchor.

Among these Tempests great and manifold
My Ship has here one only Anchor-hold;
That is my hope; which if that slip, I'm one
Wildred in this vast watry Region.

Comfort in Calamity.

Tis no discomfort in the world to fall,
When the great Crack not Crushes one, but all.

Twilight.

The Twi-light is no other thing (we say)
Then Night now gone, and yet not sprung the Day.

False Mourning.

He who wears Blacks, and mournes not for the Dead,
Do's but deride the Party buried.

The will makes the work, or consent makes the Cure.

No grief is grown so desperate, but the ill
Is halfe way cured, if the party will.

Diet.

If wholsome Diet can re-cure a man,
What need of Physick, or Physitian?

Smart.

Stripes justly given yerk us (with their fall)
But causelesse whipping smarts the most of all.

Sincerity.

Wash clean the Vessell, lest ye soure
What ever Liquor in ye powre.

The Tinker's Song.

Along, come along,
Let's meet in a throng
    Here of Tinkers;
And quaffe up a Bowle
As big as a Cowle
    To Beer Drinkers.
The Pole of the Hop
Place in the Ale-shop
    To Bethwack us;
If ever we think
So much as to drink
    Unto Bacchus.
Who frolick will be,
For little cost he
    Must not vary,
From Beer-broth at all,
So much as to call
    For Canary.

His Comfort.

The only comfort of my life
Is, that I never yet had wife;
Nor will hereafter; since I know
Who Weds, ore-buyes his weal with woe.

To Anthea.

Sick is Anthea, sickly is the spring,
The Primrose sick, and sickly every thing:
The while my deer Anthea do's but droop,
The Tulips, Lillies, Daffadills do stoop;
But when again sh'as got her healthfull houre,
Each bending then, will rise a proper flower.

Nor buying or selling.

Now, if you love me, tell me,
For as I will not sell ye,
So not one cross to buy thee
I'll give, if thou deny me.

To his peculiar friend M. Jo: Wicks.

Since shed or Cottage I have none,
I sing the more, that thou hast one;
To whose glad threshold, and free door
I may a Poet come, though poor;
And eat with thee a savory bit,
Paying but common thanks for it.
Yet sho'd I chance, (my Wicks) to see
An over-leven-looks in thee,
To soure the Bread, and turn the Beer
To an exalted vineger;
Or sho'dst thou prize me as a Dish
Of thrice-boyl'd-worts, or third dayes fish;
I'de rather hungry go and come,
Then to thy house be Burdensome;
Yet, in my depth of grief, I'de be
One that sho'd drop his Beads for thee.

The more mighty, the more mercifull.

Who may do most, do's least: The bravest will
Shew mercy there, where they have power to kill.

After Autumne, Winter.

Die ere long I'm sure, I shall;
After leaves, the tree must fall.

A good death.

For truth I may this sentence tell,
No man dies ill, that liveth well.

Recompence.

Who plants an Olive, but to eate the Oile?
Reward, we know, is the chiefe end of toile.

To Sir George Parrie, Doctor of the Civill Law.

I have my Laurel Chaplet on my head,
If 'mongst these many Numbers to be read,
But one by you be hug'd and cherished.

Peruse my Measures thoroughly, and where
Your judgement finds a guilty Poem, there
Be you a Judge; but not a Judge severe.

The meane passe by, or over, none contemne;
The good applaud: the peccant lesse condemne,
Since Absolution you can give to them.

Stand forth Brave Man, here to the publique sight;
And in my Booke now claim a two-fold right:
The first as Doctor, and the last as Knight.

Charmes.

This I'll tell ye by the way,
Maidens when ye Leavens lay,
Crosse your Dow, and your dispatch,
Will be better for your Batch.

Another.

In the morning when ye rise
Wash your hands, and cleanse your eyes.
Next be sure ye have a care,
To disperse the water farre.
For as farre as that doth light,
So farre keepes the evill Spright.

Another.

If ye feare to be affrighted
When ye are (by chance) benighted:
In your Pocket for a trust,
Carrie nothing but a Crust:
For that holy piece of Bread,
Charmes the danger, and the dread.

Upon Gorgonius.

Unto Pastillus ranke Gorgonius came,
To have a tooth twitcht out of's native frame.
Drawn was his tooth; but stanke so, that some say,
The Barber stopt his Nose, and ranne away.

Gentlenesse.

That Prince must govern with a gentle hand,
Who will have love comply with his command.

On Fortune.

This is my comfort, when she's most unkind,
She can but spoile me of my Meanes, not Mind.

Speake in season.

When times are troubled, then forbeare; but speak,
When a cleare day, out of a Cloud do's break.

Another on the same.

No man so well a Kingdome Rules, as He,
Who hath himselfe obaid the Soveraignty.

A Dialogue betwixt himselfe and Mistresse Eliza: Wheeler, under
the name of Amarillis.

My dearest Love, since thou wilt go,
 And leave me here behind thee;
For love or pitie let me know
 The place where I may find thee.

Amaril. In country Meadowes pearl'd with Dew,
 And set about with Lillies;
There filling Maunds with Cowslips, you
 May find your Amarillis.

Her. What have the Meades to do with thee,
 Or with thy youthfull houres ?
Live thou at Court, where thou mayst be
 The Queen of men, not flowers.

Let Country wenches make 'em fine
 With Poesies, since 'tis fitter
For thee with richest Jemmes to shine,
 And like the Starres to glitter.

Amaril. You set too high a rate upon
 A Shepheardess so homely;
Her. Believe it (dearest) ther's not one
 I'th' Court that's halfe so comly.

I prithee stay. (Am.) I must away,
 Lets kiss first, then we'l sever.
Ambo. And though we bid adieu to day,
 Wee shall not part for ever.

To Julia.

Help me, Julia, for to pray,
Mattens sing, or Mattens say:
This I know, the Fiend will fly
Far away, if thou beest by.
Bring the Holy-water hither;
Let us wash, and pray together:
When our Beads are thus united,
Then the Foe will fly affrighted.

To Roses in Julia's Bosome.

Roses, you can never die,
Since the place wherein ye lye,
Heat and moisture mixt are so,
As to make ye ever grow.

To the Honoured, Master Endimion Porter.

When to thy Porch I come, and (ravisht) see
The State of Poets there attending Thee:
Those Bardes, and I, all in a Chorus sing,
We are Thy Prophets Porter; Thou our King.

Obedience.

The Power of Princes rests in the Consent
Of onely those, who are obedient:
Which if away, proud Scepters then will lye
Low, and of Thrones the Ancient Majesty.

Of Love.

Instruct me now, what love will do;
'Twill make a tongless man to wooe.
Inform me next, what love will do;
'Twill strangely make a one of too.
Teach me besides, what love wil do;
'Twill quickly mar, & make ye too.
Tell me, now last, what love will do;
'Twill hurt and heal a heart pierc'd through.

Upon Trap.

Trap, of a Player turn'd a Priest now is;
Behold a suddaine Metamorphosis.
If Tythe-pigs faile, then will he shift the scean,
And, from a Priest, turne Player once again

Upon Grubs.

Grubs loves his Wife and Children, while that they
Can live by love, or else grow fat by Play:
But when they call or cry on Grubs for meat;
Instead of Bread, Grubs gives them stones to eat.
He raves, he rends, and while he thus doth tear,
His Wife and Chilren fast to death for fear.

Upon Dol.

No question but Dols cheeks wo'd soon rost dry,
Were they not basted by her either eye.

Upon Hog.

Hog has a place i'th' Kitchen, and his share
The flimsie Livers, and blew Gizzards are.

To Perenna.

Thou say'st I'm dull; if edge-lesse so I be,
I'll whet my lips, and sharpen Love on thee.

The School or Perl of Putney, the Mistress of all singular manners, Mistresse Portman.

Whether I was my selfe, or else did see
Out of my self that Glorious Hierarchie!
Or whether those (in orders rare) or these
Made up One State of Sixtie Venuses;
Or whether Fairies, Syrens, Nymphes they were,
Or Muses, on their mountaine sitting there;
Or some enchanted Place, I do not know
(Or Sharon, where eternall Roses grow.)
This I am sure; I Ravisht stood, as one
Confus'd in utter Admiration.
Me thought I saw them stir, and gently move,
And look as all were capable of Love:
And in their motion smelt much like to flowers
Enspir'd by th'Sun-beams after dews & showers.
There did I see the Reverend Rectresse stand,
Who with her eyes-gleam, or a glance of hand,
Those spirits rais'd; and with like precepts then
(As with a Magick) laid them all agen:
(A happy Realme! When no compulsive Law,
Or fear of it, but Love keeps all in awe.)
Live you, great Mistresse of your Arts, and be
A nursing Mother so to Majesty;
As those your Ladies may in time be seene,
For Grace and Carriage, every one a Queene.
One Birth their Parents gave them; but their new,
And better Being, they receive from You.
Mans former Birth is grace-lesse; but the state
Of life comes in, when he's Regenerate.

On himselfe.

Let me not live, if I not love,
Since I as yet did never prove,
Where Pleasures met; at last, doe find,
All Pleasures meet in Woman-kind.

On Love.

That love 'twixt men do's ever longest last
Where War and Peace the Dice by turns doe cast.

Another on Love.

Love's of it self, too sweet; the best of all
Is, when loves hony has a dash of gall.

Upon Gut.

Science puffs up, sayes Gut, when either Pease
Make him thus swell, or windy Cabbages,

Pleasures Pernicious.

Where Pleasures rule a Kingdome, never there
Is sober virtue, seen to move her sphere.

Upon Chub.

When Chub brings in his harvest, still he cries,
Aha my boyes! heres wheat for Christmas Pies!
Soone after, he for beere so scores his wheat,
That at the tide, he has not bread to eate.

To M. Laurence Swetnaham.

Read thou my Lines, my Swetnaham, if there be
A fault, tis hid, if it be voic't by thee.
Thy mouth will make the sourest numbers please;
How will it drop pure hony, speaking these?

On himself.

A wearied Pilgrim, I have wandred here
Twice five and twenty (bate me but one yeer)
Long I have lasted in this world; (tis true)
But yet those yeers that I have liv'd, but few.
Who by his gray Haires, doth his lusters tell,
Lives not those yeers, but he that lives them well.
One man has reatch't his sixty yeers, but he
Of all those three-score, has not liv'd halfe three:
He lives, who lives to virtue: men who cast
Their ends for Pleasure, do not live, but last.

His Covenant or Protestation to Julia.

Why do'st thou wound, & break my heart?
As if we sho'd for ever part?
Hast thou not heard an Oath from me,
After a day, or two, or three,
I wo'd come back and live with thee?
Take, if thou do'st distrust, that Vowe;
This second Protestation now.
Upon thy cheeke that spangel'd Teare,
Which sits as Dew of Roses there:
That Teare shall scarce be dri'd before
I'll kisse the Threshold of thy dore.
Then weepe not sweet; but thus much know,
I'm halfe return'd before I go.

On himselfe.

I will no longer kiss,
    I can no longer stay;
The way of all Flesh is,
    That I must go this day:
Since longer I can't live,
    My frolick Youths adieu;
My Lamp to you I'll give,
    And all my troubles too.

To the most accomplisht Gentleman Master Michael Oulsworth.

Nor thinke that Thou in this my Booke art worst,
Because not plac't here with the midst, or first.
Since Fame that sides with these, or goes before
Those, that must live with Thee for evermore.
That Fame, and Fames rear'd Pillar, thou shalt see
In the next sheet Brave Man to follow Thee.
Fix on That Columne then, and never fall;
Held up by Fames eternall Pedestall.

To his Girles who would have him sportfull.

Alas I can't, for tell me how
Can I be gamesome (aged now)
Besides ye see me daily grow
Here Winter-like, to Frost and Snow.
And I ere long, my Girles shall see,
Ye quake for cold to looke on me.

His last request to Julia.

I have been wanton, and too bold I feare,
To chafe o're much the Virgins cheek or eare:
Beg for my Pardon Julia; He doth winne
Grace with the Gods, who's sorry for his sinne.
That done, my Julia, dearest Julia, come,
And go with me to chuse my Buriall roome:
My Fates are ended; when thy Herrick dyes,
Claspe thou his Book, then close thou up his Eyes.

On himselfe.

One Eare tingles; some there be,
That are snarling now at me:
Be they those that Homer bit,
I will give them thanks for it.

Upon Kings.

Kings must be dauntlesse: Subjects will contemne
Those, who want Hearts, and weare a Diadem.

Truth and Falsehood.

Truth by her own simplicity is known,
Falsehood by Varnish and Vermillion.

To his Girles.

Wanton Wenches doe not bring
For my haires black colouring:
For my Locks (Girles) let 'em be
Gray or white, all's one to me.

Upon Spur.

Spur jingles now, and sweares by no meane oathes,
He's double honour'd, since h'as got gay cloathes:
Most like his Suite, and all commend the Trim;
And thus they praise the Sumpter; but not him:
As to the Goddesse, people did conferre
Worship, and not to' th' Asse that carried her.

To his Brother Nicolas Herrick.

What others have with cheapnesse seene, and ease,
In Varnisht maps; by'th' helpe of Compasses:
Or reade in Volumes, and those Bookes (with all
Their large Narrations, Incanonicall)
Thou hast beheld those seas, and Countries farre;
And tel'st to us, what once they were, and are.
So that with bold truth, thou canst now relate
This Kingdomes fortune, and that Empires fate:
Canst talke to us of Sharon; where a spring
Of Roses have an endlesse flourishing.
Of Sion, Sinai, Nebo, and with them,
Make knowne to us the now Jerusalem.
The Mount of Olives; Calverie, and where
Is (and hast seene) thy Saviours Sepulcher.
So that the man that will but lay his eares,
As Inapostate, to the thing he heares,
Shall by his hearing quickly come to see
The truth of Travails lesse in bookes then Thee.

The Voice and Violl.

Rare is the voice it selfe; but when we sing
To'th Lute or Violl, then 'tis ravishing.

Warre.

If Kings and kingdomes, once distracted be,
The sword of war must trie the Soveraignty.

A King and no King.

That Prince, who may doe nothing but what's just,
Rules but by leave, and takes his Crowne on trust.

Plots not still prosperous.

All are not ill Plots, that doe sometimes faile;
Nor those false vows, which oft times don't prevaile.

Flatterie.

What is't that wasts a Prince? example showes,
'Tis flatterie spends a King, more then his foes.

Upon Rumpe.

Rumpe is a Turne-broach, yet he seldome can
Steale a swolne sop out of the Dripping pan.

Upon Shopter.

Old Widow Shopter, when so ere she cryes,
Lets drip a certain Gravie from her eyes.

Upon Deb.

If felt and heard, (unseen) thou dost me please;
If seen, thou lik'st me, Deb, in none of these.

Excesse.

Excesse is sluttish: keepe the meane; for why?
Vertue's clean Conclave is sobriety.

Upon Croot.

One silver spoon shines in the house of Croot;
Who cannot buie, or steale a second to't.

The soul is the salt.

The body's salt, the soule is; which when gon,
The flesh soone sucks in putrifaction.

Upon Pimpe.

When Pimpes feat sweat (as they doe often use)
There springs a sope-like-lather in his shoos.

Upon Flood, or a thankfull man.

Flood, if he has for him and his a bit,
He sayes his fore and after Grace for it:
If meate he wants, then Grace he sayes to see
His hungry belly borne by Legs Jaile-free.
Thus have, or have not, all alike is good,
To this our poore, yet ever patient Flood.

Upon Luske.

In Den'-shire Kerzie Lusk (when he was dead)
Wo'd shrouded be, and therewith buried.
When his Assignes askt him the reason why?
He said, because he got his wealth thereby.

Upon Rush.

Rush saves his shooes, in wet and snowie wether;
And feares in summer to weare out the lether:
This is strong thrift that warie Rush doth use
Summer and Winter still to save his shooes.

Foolishnesse.

In's Tusc'lanes, Tullie doth confesse,
No plague ther's like to foolishnesse.

Abstinence.

Against diseases here the strongest fence
Is the defensive vertue, Abstinence.

No danger to men desperate.

When feare admits no hope of safety, then
Necessity makes dastards valiant men.

Sauce for sorrowes.

Although our suffering meet with no reliefe,
An equall mind is the best sauce for griefe.

To Cupid.

I have a leaden, thou a shaft of gold ;
Thou kil'st with heate, and I strike dead with cold.
Let's trie of us who shall the first expire;
Or thou by frost, or I by quenchlesse fire:
Extreames are fatall, where they once doe strike,
And bring to' th' heart destruction both alike.

The Hagg.

The staffe is now greas'd,
And very well pleas'd,
She cocks out her Arse at the parting,
To an old Ram Goat,
That rattles i'th' throat,
Halfe choakt with the stink of her farting.

In a dirtie Haire-lace
She leads on a brace
Of black-bore-cats to attend her;
Who scratch at the Moone,
And threaten at noone
Of night from Heaven for to rend her.

A hunting she goes;
A crackt horne she blowes;
At which the hounds fall a bounding;
While th'Moone in her sphere
Peepes trembling for feare,
And night's afraid of the sounding.

The mount of the Muses.

After thy labour take thine ease,
Here with the sweet Pierides.
But if so be that men will not
Give thee the Laurell Crowne for lot;
Be yet assur'd, thou shalt have one
Not subject to corruption.

On Himselfe.

Il'e write no more of Love; but now repent
Of all those times that I in it have spent.
I'll write no more of life; but wish twas ended,
And that my dust was to the earth commended.

To his Booke.

Goe thou forth my booke, though late ;
Yet be timely fortunate.
It may chance good-luck may send
Thee a kinsman, or a friend,
That may harbour thee, when I,
With my fates neglected lye.
If thou know'st not where to dwell,
See, the fier's by: Farewell.

Distrust.

What ever men for Loyalty pretend,
'Tis Wisdomes part to doubt a faithfull friend.

The end of his worke.

Part of the worke remaines; one part is past:
And here my ship rides having Anchor cast.

To Crowne it.

My wearied Barke, O Let it now be Crown'd!
The Haven reacht to which I first was bound.

On Himselfe.

The worke is done: young men, and maidens set
Upon my curles the Mirtle Coronet,
Washt with sweet ointments; Thus at last I come
To suffer in the Muses Martyrdome:
But with this comfort, if my blood be shed,
The Muses will weare blackes, when I am dead.

The pillar of Fame.

Fames pillar here, at last, we set,
Out-during Marble, Brasse, or Jet,
Charm'd and enchanted so,
As to withstand the blow
Of overthrow:
Nor shall the seas,
Or OUTRAGES
Of storms orebear
What we up-rear,
Tho Kingdoms fal,
This pillar never shall
Decline or waste at all;
But stand for ever by his owne
Firme and well fixt foundation.

To his Book's end this last line he'd have plac't,
Jocond his Muse was; but his Life was chast.

FINIS.

A Note On Robert Herrick

ROBERT HERRICK (1591-1674) was one of the Cavalier poets (other Cavalier poets included Suckling, Carew and Lovelace). He was born in London and lived much of his life in the rough remoteness of a parish in Devonshire. He studied at Cambridge (St John's College and Trinity Hall), graduating in 1617 as a Bachelor of Arts and a Master of Arts in 1620. His law studies were dropped in 1623, and he was ordained as a deacon and priest in 1624. His major work (*Hesperides or The Works both Humane and Divine* of Robert Herrick, Esq.) was published in 1648. There are some 1130 poems in the first, secular part, *Hesperides*, and 272 in *Noble Numbers*, the religious works. F.R. Leavis reckoned that Herrick was 'trivially charming',[1] a view easily refuted by any close perusal of his verse. For T.S. Eliot, Herrick was the paradigmatic 'minor poet'.[2] One can understand how it is that Herrick was for so long viewed in this way. The more one considers his *Hesperides*, though, which one recent critic called 'a seductively sweet, strangely tumultuous exploration of love, art, friendship, festivity, and loss',[3] the greater Robert Herrick becomes.

One of the delights included in this book is Robert Herrick's magnificent 'The Argument of His Book'. This is a truly majestic fourteen-line poem, an invocation to nature, and of humans interacting with nature. It is, essentially, a list-poem, where the poet catalogues the things he will sing about in the rest of his book:

I sing of *Brooks*, of *Blossomes, Birds,* and *Bowers*:
Of *April, May,* of *June,* and *July*-Flowers.
I sing of *May-poles, Hock-carts, Wassails, Wakes,*
Of *Bride-grooms, Brides,* and of their *Bridall-cakes.*
I write of *Youth,* of *Love,* and have Accesse
By these, to sing of cleanly-*Wantonesse.*

Robert Herrick couches his list in simple, dramatic English, a form of direct, powerful English that people since Herrick's time have associated with the (King James) *Bible*. The rest of his poetry (in his *Hesperides*) followed the plan outlined the poem 'The Argument of His Book'. Herrick was particularly well situated, geographically, to write nature poetry. Like Coleridge, Words-worth and Brontë, Herrick lived in the midst of the countryside – in the relative isolation of Dean Prior, on the edge of Dartmoor in Devon (he compared his exile with that of Ovid and Horace). Herrick lived in the vicarage in the village halfway between Exeter and Plymouth from 1630 to 1648, and from 1660 to his death, at 83, in 1674. Though at times he fought against the isolation and roughness of his provincial setting,[4] and hankered after the civilization of London, one can see the deep inspiration that the landscape of Devonshire had for Herrick in his poetry. Exiled from the capital and civilized society and culture, Herrick did have his books (his beloved *Bible* and Latin poets) as well as the friendship of his pets (they appear in his poems, sometimes in heartfelt elegies when they die – such as 'Upon His Spaniel Tracie'), his housekeeper (Prudence Baldwin), his sister, and friends at the nearby Dean Court.

Some of Robert Herrick's most delightful poems are about the wonders of nature, such as blossoms, flowers and fields ('The Shower of Blossoms', 'The Lilly in a Christal', 'To Pansies', 'To Cherry-blossomes', 'To a Bed of Tulips', 'To Laurels', 'Upon Roses', 'The Succession of Four Sweet Months', 'The Rainbow', 'To the Rose: Song', 'To Flowers', 'To Blossoms', 'To Groves', 'To Violets', 'To Carnations', 'To Sycamores', 'To Springs and Fountains', 'To Daffadills', 'To Meddowes', 'To the Willow-tree' and 'To Primroses Fill'd With Morning-dew').

For mediæval, Renaissance and Cavalier poets (like Robert Herrick). Britain would have been a much more 'pastoral' landscape than it is in the modern era. There would have many more trees, far fewer roads, no cars, planes, trains, electric lights, pylons, pipes, road signs, telephones, and so on. The landscape that poets such as Langland, Chaucer, Wyatt, Parnell, Smith, Keats and Brontë lived in was dramatically different from the urbanized world of today. There are, of course, continuities between the mediæval and Elizabethan period and now: the same rivers flow, the same birds sing (minus a few species), the same trees rustle their leaves in Autumn. It is (partly) this continuity that makes the poetry of Herrick so enduring. The relationship with nature is one of those everlasting relationships that humanity is perpetually dealing with (like the relation to the body, to God, to politics). In his poetry Herrick tackles the great themes – love, time, God, nature, the body.

Much of Robert Herrick's poetry concerns the themes and imagery of Elizabethan (and mediæval) poetry: the evocation of a pastoral, Arcadian, pre-Fall landscape, a Paradise, in fact, populated with shepherdesses, nymphs, animals and the abundance of nature. Already in the art of William Shakespeare this pastoral mythology was fading, being supplanted by a worldly knowingness (if not cynicism). Herrick's poetry, though, often harks back to a paradisal earlier age, and rues the passing of time that has changed it all (for the worse, in his opinion). We find the same Greek, Roman, Biblical, mediæval, Christian and Renaissance/ humanist themes in Herrick's work that are the staple of Elizabethan poetry.[5] As well as learned and literary, Herrick's subjects are often seemingly 'ordinary' or 'commonplace'. He writes of bucolic traditions; of old age; of bawdy times; of his mistress's breasts; of cherry blossom; of fashionable clothes (one of his famous poems is 'Delight in Disorder', where 'a careless shoestring' betokens a 'wild civility' which 'bewitches' the poet more than precision).

There are many poems in Robert Herrick's work of love – about love desired, lost and mourned. Herrick is very definitely a 'Muse poet', to use Robert Graves's term. There are many poems to several mistresses, 'my dearest Beauties' he calls them in 'To His Lovely Mistresses' (Anthea, Perilla, Electra, Blanch, Judith, Silvia, and the most beloved of all, Julia). There are many poems to certain 'muses' or 'maidens'. The sheer number (and quality) of Herrick's poems to Julia attests to his deep passion for women, the friendship and strength of women: among the 'Julia' poems are:

'To Julia', 'To Roses in Julia's Bosom', 'To the Fever Not to Trouble Julia', 'Julia's Petticoat', 'The Frozen Zone: or, Julia Disdainful', 'To Julia, in Her Dawn, or Daybreak', 'His Last Request to Julia', 'The Parliament of Roses to Julia', 'Upon Julia's Recovery', 'Upon Julia's Fall', 'His Sailing From Julia', 'His Embalming to Julia', 'Her Legs', 'Her Bed', 'On Julia's Picture', 'The Bracelet to Julia', 'A Ring Presented to Julia', 'To Julia in the Temple' and so on.

Apart from poems entitled 'To His Book', there are probably more poems in Robert Herrick's work addressed 'To Julia' than to anything else. Julia is 'the prime of *Paradise*' ('To Julia, in Her Dawn, or Day-breake'). She is utterly adored, often erotically. There are many poems which eulogize her breasts and nipples, for instance: 'Display thy breasts… / Between whose glories, there my lips I'll lay,/ Ravisht' he writes (in 'Upon Julia's Breasts'); other pæans to Julia's breasts include 'Upon the Roses in Julia's Bosom' and 'Upon the Nipples of Julia's Breast'. Herrick makes the age-old connections between the fertility of nature outside (the rain, the lush vegetation, the rivers of the Paradisal Earth) and the bounty of women inside (Julia's breasts form a valley of abundance, as in William Shakespeare's poem 'Venus and Adonis', in which the poet would like to languish).

Women in Robert Herrick's poetry are seen as the givers of pleasure (expressed as sex), nurturance (breast milk), and all things worthy in the world (love). 'All Pleasures meet in Woman-kind', he writes in 'On Himself'. They are just as important in his poetry as God, the King or Christianity. Much of Herrick's poetry concerns (masculine) public, worldly, and religious themes (such as King Charles and politics, or God and the *Bible*), but just as much (more, probably) celebrates (feminine) erotic pleasure, food, nature, folk rituals, music and women, in that 'cleanly-wanton' way which is Herrick's own (the phrase, which describes much of his work, comes from the opening poem of *Hesperides*).

Robert Herrick happily fuses erotic descriptions of nature or food with lush, sensual evocations of erotic love.[6] To describe how wonderful sensual love can be, Herrick, like so many poets before him, uses the metaphor of abundant nature, expressed in flowers, trees, rivers, hills, and food. In 'To Phillis To love, and Love With Him', for example, Herrick's narrator proclaims:

Live, live with me, and thou shalt see
The pleasures I'll prepare for thee...

And goes into a long list of the bounty of nature: 'sweet soft Moss shall by thy bed', 'Fleeces purest Downe', 'Cream of Cowslips buttered', daisies, violets, daffodils, primroses, roses, the 'blushing Apple, bashful Peare,/ And shame-fac't Plum'. Robert Herrick's poetry is, like Percy Bysshe Shelley's or William Shakespeare's, tremendously sensual. In poem after poem he uses metaphors and images of shiny, ripe fruit, or radiant flowers, or soft grass, or silk, or fresh springwater. Images of natural abundance occur throughout his poetry. Even rain, which he would have known day after day in Dartmoor, is treated spectrally, as in 'A Conjuration to Electra', where he speaks of the 'Dewes and drisling Raine,/ That swell the Golden Graine'. Some of the most erotic poems around concerning perfume and smell are Herrick's: In 'Love Perfumes All Parts', Herrick writes of his mistress Anthea's body in a state of heightened intoxication, claiming that her hands, thighs and legs 'are all/ Richly Aromatical'. So deliciously musky is the beloved for the poet, he says she is sweeter than Juno and muskier than the Goddess Isis, no less.

Some of Robert Herrick's finest landscape poems are not about Dartmoor or Devonshire, but about London, his birthplace and beloved city. 'His Return to London' is perhaps the best of these city-poems, in which his return to the capital is seen as a yearned-for homecoming.

O *Place! O People!* Manners! fram'd to please
All *Nations, Customers, Kindreds, Language!*

There are poems in Robert Herrick's *œuvre* on the pleasures of music, which he calls 'thou *Queen of Heaven*, Care-charming-spell' (in 'To Musick. A Song'). The theme of the music-poems is the enchantment that music can bring. 'Charm me asleep, and melt me so/ With thy Delicious Numbers', he urges music in 'To Musique, To Becalme His Fever'. 'And make me smooth as Balme, and Oile againe', he entreats in 'To Musick'.

There are some hearty and tender pæans to holidays, feasts, festivals and rituals (pagan as well as Christian) in Robert Herrick's poetry: such as 'The Succession of Four Sweet Months', and the best of them all, 'Corinna's Going a Maying'. The celebration of the seasons and annual holidays chimes with Herrick's abiding theme of the passing of time, and the need to seize the moment and enjoy it.

It's typical of Robert Herrick, too, to mention in his nature poems the passing of time. The very first verse of his 'To

Blossoms' asks the question of the blossoms 'Why do ye fall so fast?' As soon as the beauty of the blossoms is invoked, time and death follow on immediately (echoing *sakura* as the embodiment of impermanence in Japanese culture). The line of 'To Blossoms' is 'They glide/ Into the grave.' The same protestations to nature's pleasures being over so swiftly occur in 'To Daisies, Not To Shut So Soone' and 'To Daffadills' ('we weep to see/ You haste away so soone'). In 'All Things Decay and Die' he states quite baldly: '*All things decay with Time*'.

The many poems called 'To His Book' attest to Robert Herrick's deep concern for his art – how long (or if) it will last, who will enshrine it, and soon. The same concerns with the relations between mortality, time and death and the artist and his art are central to William Shakespeare's *œuvre* (it is the guiding theme of the *Sonnets*). The key Herrickian theme is to enjoy life before death takes it away. 'While Fate permits us, let's be merry' as he puts it in 'To Enjoy the Time'. 'Every time seems so short to be' he says in 'Felicity, Quick of Flight'.

It's true that Robert Herrick did not write long poems, like John Keats or William Wordsworth (in the sense that long, 'epic' poems equal seriousness and *gravitas*),[7] but, in his own way, his nature poetry is every bit as valuable as theirs. His love-poetry is sometimes compared unfavourably with that of John Donne: again, in his own way, Herrick is every bit as fruitful a love-poet as John Donne (or Thomas Campion, Kit Marlowe, even William Shakespeare or Edmund Spenser). He was not as showy a poet as S.T. Coleridge or Alexander Pope, not so ambitious, formally, yet he is a superb writer, witty, hedonistic, impassioned, common-sensical.

Notes

1. F.R. Leavis: *Revaluation*, Chatto & Windus 1936, 36
2. T.S. Eliot: "What is Minor Poetry?", *Swanee Review*, 54, 1946
3. Leah S. Marcus: "Robert Herrick", in Coms, 1993, 180
4. In 'Discontents in Devon' Herrick writes:

More discontents I never had
Since I was born, then here;
Where I have been, and still am sad,
In this dull *Devon-shire*...

5. In his poetry Herrick alludes to, among others, Anacreon, Horace, Catullus, Marital and other (Roman) poets, as well as Ben Jonson (whom Herrick admired) and the *Bible*.

6. As Stephen Coote puts it, in Herrick's poetry the 'sensuousness is the more telling for its sophisticated simplicity and, at its best, is returned to nature.' (Coote: *The Penguin Short History of English Literature*, Penguin 1993, 175)

7. There are lengthy poems (such as 'Upon His Kinswoman Mistress Elizabeth Herrick', 'His Age, Dedicated To His Peculiar Friend, M. John Wickes, Under the Name of Posthumus', 'A Nuptial Song, or Epithalamie, on Sir Clipseby Crew and His Lady', 'Corinna's Going a Maying', 'A Country Life: To His Brother, M. Tho: Herrick', 'The Welcome to Sack' and 'An Epithalamie to Sir Thomas Southwell and His Ladie') but nothing as long as *Prometheus Unbound* or *The Replude*.

Bibliography

Cleanth Brooks: *The Well Wrought Urn*, Dennis Dobson 1957

A.B. Coiro: *Robert Herrick's 'Hesperides' and the Epigram Book Tradition*, John Hopkins University Press 1988

—ed: *Robert Herrick*, special no. of *George Herbert Journal* 14, 1-2, Autumn 1990

N. Coms, ed: *The Cambridge Companion to English Poetry: Donne to Marvell*, Cambridge University Press 1993

R.H. Deming: *Ceremony and Art: Robert Herrick's Poetry*, Mouton, Hague 1974

A. Leigh Deneef: *'This Poetick Liturgie': Robert Herrick's Ceremonial Mode*, Duke University Press 1974

E.H. Hageman: *Robert Herrick: A Reference Guide*, G.K. Hall, Boston 1983

G. Hammond: *Fleeting Things: English Poets and Poems 1616-1660*, Harvard University Press 1990

Robert Herrick: *The Poems of Robert Herrick*, ed. L.C. Martin, Oxford University Press 1965

—*Poems*, ed. J. Max Patrick, New York University Press 1963

—*Robert Herrick: The Hesperides and Noble Numbers*, ed. Alfred Pollard, Muse's Library, London 1891

—*The Poetical Works of Robert Herrick*, Oxford English Texts 1915

—*Hesperides: The Poems and Other Remains of Robert Herrick Now First Collected*, ed. W. Carew Hazlitt, London 1869

—*The Complete Works of Robert Herrick*, ed. Alexander B. Grosart, London 1876

—*Selected Poems*, ed. David Jesson-Dibley, Carcanet 1989

M. MacLeod: *Concordance to the Poems of Robert Herrick*, Oxford University Press, New York 1936

Leah S. Marcus: *The Politics of Mirth: Jonson, Herrick, Milton, Marvell and the Defense of Old Holiday Pastimes*, University of Chicago Press 1986

F.W. Moorman: *Robert Herrick: a Biographical and Critical Study*, Russell & Russell, New York 1910

S. Musgrove: "The Universe of Robert Herrick", *Auckland University College Bulletin*, 38, 1950

John Press: *Herrick*, Longmans, Green & Co

Roger Rollin: *Robert Herrick*, Twayne, New York 1966/92

— & J. Max Patrick, eds: *Trust to Good Verses: Herrick Tercentenary Essays*, University of Pittsburgh Press 1977

George W. Scott: *Robert Herrick*, Sidgwick & Jackson 1974

CRESCENT MOON PUBLISHING

web: www.crmoon.com e-mail: cresmopub@yahoo.co.uk

ARTS, PAINTING, SCULPTURE

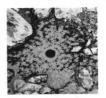

The Art of Andy Goldsworthy
Andy Goldsworthy: Touching Nature
Andy Goldsworthy in Close-Up
Andy Goldsworthy: Pocket Guide
Andy Goldsworthy In America
Land Art: A Complete Guide
The Art of Richard Long
Richard Long: Pocket Guide
Land Art In the UK
Land Art in Close-Up
Land Art In the U.S.A.
Land Art: Pocket Guide
Installation Art in Close-Up
Minimal Art and Artists In the 1960s and After
Colourfield Painting
Land Art DVD, TV documentary
Andy Goldsworthy DVD, TV documentary
The Erotic Object: Sexuality in Sculpture From Prehistory to the Present Day
Sex in Art: Pornography and Pleasure in Painting and Sculpture
Postwar Art
Sacred Gardens: The Garden in Myth, Religion and Art
Glorification: Religious Abstraction in Renaissance and 20th Century Art
Early Netherlandish Painting
Leonardo da Vinci
Piero della Francesca
Giovanni Bellini
Fra Angelico: Art and Religion in the Renaissance
Mark Rothko: The Art of Transcendence
Frank Stella: American Abstract Artist
Jasper Johns
Brice Marden
Alison Wilding: The Embrace of Sculpture
Vincent van Gogh: Visionary Landscapes
Eric Gill: Nuptials of God
Constantin Brancusi: Sculpting the Essence of Things
Max Beckmann
Caravaggio
Gustave Moreau
Egon Schiele: Sex and Death In Purple Stockings
Delizioso Fotografico Fervore: Works In Process 1
Sacro Cuore: Works In Process 2
The Light Eternal: J.M.W. Turner
The Madonna Glorified: Karen Arthurs

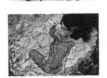

POETRY

Ursula Le Guin: Walking In Cornwall
Peter Redgrove: Here Comes The Flood
Peter Redgrove: Sex-Magic-Poetry-Cornwall
Dante: Selections From the Vita Nuova
Petrarch, Dante and the Troubadours
William Shakespeare: Sonnets
William Shakespeare: Complete Poems
Blinded By Her Light: The Love-Poetry of Robert Graves
Emily Dickinson: Selected Poems
Emily Brontë: Poems
Thomas Hardy: Selected Poems
Percy Bysshe Shelley: Poems
John Keats: Selected Poems
Joh n Keats: Poems of 1820
D.H. Lawrence: Selected Poems
Edmund Spenser: Poems
Edmund Spenser: Amoretti
John Donne: Poems
Henry Vaughan: Poems
Sir Thomas Wyatt: Poems
Robert Herrick: Selected Poems
Rilke: Space, Essence and Angels in the Poetry of Rainer Maria Rilke
Rainer Maria Rilke: Selected Poems
Friedrich Hölderlin: Selected Poems
Arseny Tarkovsky: Selected Poems
Arthur Rimbaud: Selected Poems
Arthur Rimbaud: A Season in Hell
Arthur Rimbaud and the Magic of Poetry
Novalis: Hymns To the Night
German Romantic Poetry
Paul Verlaine: Selected Poems
Elizaethan Sonnet Cycles
D.J. Enright: By-Blows
Jeremy Reed: Brigitte's Blue Heart
Jeremy Reed: Claudia Schiffer's Red Shoes
Gorgeous Little Orpheus
Radiance: New Poems
Crescent Moon Book of Nature Poetry
Crescent Moon Book of Love Poetry
Crescent Moon Book of Mystical Poetry
Crescent Moon Book of Elizabethan Love Poetry
Crescent Moon Book of Metaphysical Poetry
Crescent Moon Book of Romantic Poetry
Pagan America: New American Poetry

MEDIA, CINEMA, FEMINISM and CULTURAL STUDIES

J.R.R. Tolkien: The Books, The Films, The Whole Cultural Phenomenon
J.R.R. Tolkien: Pocket Guide
The *Lord of the Rings* Movies: Pocket Guide
The Cinema of Hayao Miyazaki
Hayao Miyazaki: *Princess Mononoke*: Pocket Movie Guide
Hayao Miyazaki: *Spirited Away*: Pocket Movie Guide
Tim Burton : Hallowe'en For Hollywood
Ken Russell
Ken Russell: *Tommy*: Pocket Movie Guide
The Ghost Dance: The Origins of Religion
The Peyote Cult
Cixous, Irigaray, Kristeva: The *Jouissance* of French Feminism
Julia Kristeva: Art, Love, Melancholy, Philosophy, Semiotics and Psychoanalysis
Luce Irigaray: Lips, Kissing, and the Politics of Sexual Difference
Hélene Cixous I Love You: The *Jouissance* of Writing
Andrea Dworkin
'Cosmo Woman': The World of Women's Magazines
Women in Pop Music
HomeGround: The Kate Bush Anthology
Discovering the Goddess (Geoffrey Ashe)
The Poetry of Cinema
The Sacred Cinema of Andrei Tarkovsky
Andrei Tarkovsky: Pocket Guide
Andrei Tarkovsky: *Mirror*: Pocket Movie Guide
Andrei Tarkovsky: *The Sacrifice*: Pocket Movie Guide
Walerian Borowczyk: Cinema of Erotic Dreams
Jean-Luc Godard: The Passion of Cinema
Jean-Luc Godard: *Hail Mary*: Pocket Movie Guide
Jean-Luc Godard: *Contempt*: Pocket Movie Guide
Jean-Luc Godard: *Pierrot le Fou*: Pocket Movie Guide
John Hughes and Eighties Cinema
Ferris Bueller's Day Off: Pocket Movie Guide
Jean-Luc Godard: Pocket Guide
The Cinema of Richard Linklater
Liv Tyler: Star In Ascendance
Blade Runner and the Films of Philip K. Dick
Paul Bowles and Bernardo Bertolucci
Media Hell: Radio, TV and the Press
An Open Letter to the BBC
Detonation Britain: Nuclear War in the UK
Feminism and Shakespeare
Wild Zones: Pornography, Art and Feminism
Sex in Art: Pornography and Pleasure in Painting and Sculpture
Sexing Hardy: Thomas Hardy and Feminism

The Light Eternal is a model monograph, an exemplary job. The subject matter of the book is beautifully organised and dead on beam. (Lawrence Durrell)
It is amazing for me to see my work treated with such passion and respect. (Andrea Dworkin)

CRESCENT MOON PUBLISHING
P.O. Box 1312, Maidstone, Kent, ME14 5XU, Great Britain. www.crmoon.com

cresmopub@yahoo.co.uk   www.crescentmoon.org.uk

Made in the USA
Middletown, DE
23 August 2021